RAYMOND HAINS

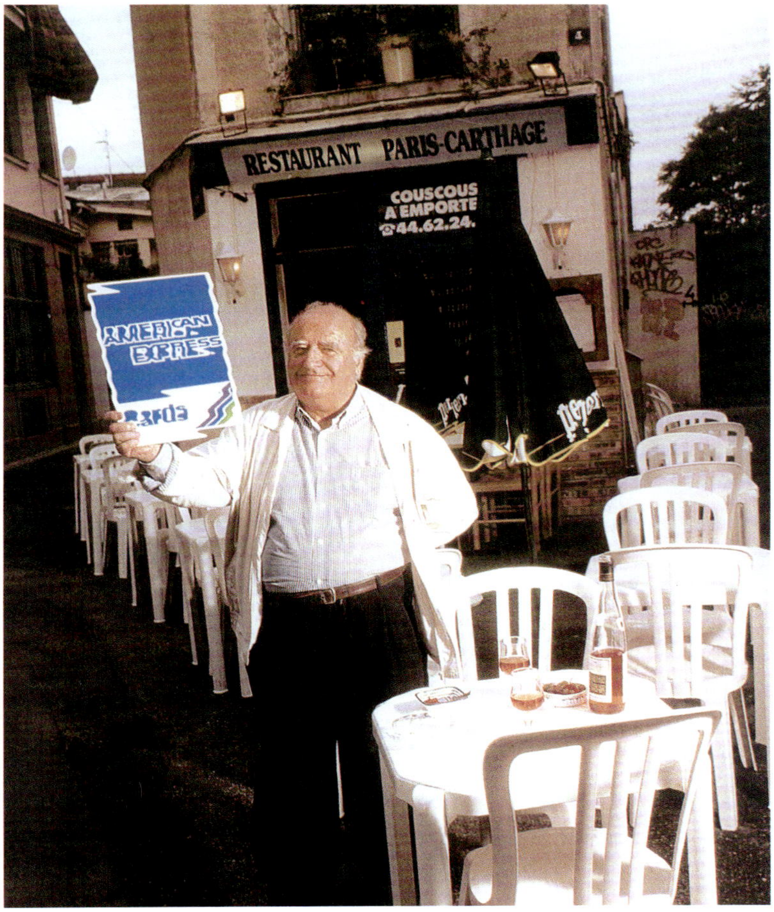

MOORE INTERNATIONAL DISCOVERY SERIES **5**

RAYMOND HAINS: ART SPECULATOR

NOVEMBER 5–DECEMBER 15, 2002

GOLDIE PALEY GALLERY

MOORE COLLEGE OF ART AND DESIGN

PHILADELPHIA, PENNSYLVANIA

CONCEIVED BY THE CENTRE POMPIDOU, MUSÉE NATIONAL D'ART MODERNE—CENTRE DE CRÉATION INDUSTRIELLE, PARIS—AND ORGANIZED BY THE GOLDIE PALEY GALLERY

RAYMOND HAINS: ART SPECULATOR

Conceived by the Centre Pompidou, Musée National d'Art Moderne—
Centre de Création Industrielle, Paris—and organized by the Goldie Paley Gallery.

The exhibition "Raymond Hains, La Tentative" was initiated, conceived,
and realized by the Centre National d'Art et de Culture Georges Pompidou.
The exhibition was presented at the Centre Georges Pompidou, in Paris, from June 27 to September 3, 2001.
First edition in French language for bibliography and catalog of films by Laure Leprince, and
texts by Christine Macel and Christian Schlatter: ©Editions of the Centre Georges Pompidou, Paris, 2001.
First edition in French language for text by Aude Bodet: ©Editions of the Centre Georges Pompidou,
Paris, 2002.
Library of Congress Control Number: 2002112673
ISBN: 1-58442-053-7
Guest curator: Christine Macel
Gallery director: Molly Dougherty
Essayists: Aude Bodet, Raymond Hains, Christine Macel, Tom McDonough, Christian Schlatter
Translating services: Charles Penwarden
Design: Purtill Family Business
Editorial services: Gerald Zeigerman
Printed in Iceland by Oddi Printing
This exhibition was made possible by major funding from the Philadelphia Exhibitions
Initiative (PEI), a grant program funded by The Pew Charitable Trusts and administered by
The University of the Arts, Philadelphia.
Additional support has been provided by Étant donnés: The French-American Fund
for Contemporary Art, New York. A portion of the galleries' general operating funds for
this fiscal year has been provided by grants from the Pennsylvania Council on the Arts,
Philadelphia Cultural Fund, and the Friends of the Galleries at Moore.
The Institute of Museum and Library Services, a federal agency that fosters innovation,
leadership, and a lifetime of learning, supports the operating expenses of the Galleries at Moore.
Special thanks to the Barra Foundation, Teleflex Foundation, Philadelphia Foundation,
and the Louis N. Cassett Foundation for their support of educational programs.

ACKNOWLEDGMENTS

This book was published on the occasion of the exhibition "Raymond Hains: Art Speculator,"
presented at the Goldie Paley Gallery, Moore College of Art and Design, Philadelphia,
from November 5 to December 15, 2002. The first version of this exhibition was presented in the
Galerie Sud of the Centre Georges Pompidou, Paris, from June 27 to September 3, 2001,
and accompanied by two publications: *Raymond Hains, J'ai la mémoire qui planche* and
Raymond Hains, La Tentative (Paris: Editions of the Centre Georges Pompidou, 2001).

IN PARIS

Exhibition curator Christine Macel, curator at the Musée National d'art Moderne, Centre Georges
Pompidou, Paris, assisted by Laure Leprince, researcher, and Sara Renaud, production manager

IN PHILADELPHIA

Molly Dougherty, director of the Paley/Levy Galleries at Moore, assisted by Jeremiah Misfeldt,
associate curator, and Renée Shortell, gallery manager/registrar

ART SPECULATOR

WE WISH TO THANK THE LENDERS WHO, ONCE AGAIN, AGREED TO BE WITHOUT THEIR WORKS

L'Atelier Soardi, Nice, Colette Soardi

Henry Buhl/SOHO Partnership, New York

Christine and Gérard Cohen, Garches

Ginette Dufrêne, Paris

Éric Fabre, Brussels

Fondation Cartier pour l'Art Contemporain, Paris, Hervé Chandès

Fonds National d'Art Contemporain, Paris, Claude Allemand-Cosneau

Fonds Régional d'Art Contemporain Bretagne, Châteaugiron, Catherine Elkar

Fonds Régional d'Art Contemporain Champagne-Ardenne, Reims, François Quintin

Galerie Françoise Paviot, Paris

Galerie Daniel Templon, Paris

Galerie Lara Vincy, Paris, Liliane Vincy

Galleria L'Elefante, Treviso, Cesare Misserotti

Raymond Hains, Paris

Institut National de l'Audiovisuel, Bry-sur-Marne, Géraldine Bonetti

Yves Jammet, Paris

Adrian Maben, Paris

Jean-Louis Milin, Paris

Musée d'art Moderne de la ville de Paris, Suzanne Pagé

Musée de Bretagne, Rennes, Laurence Prod'homme

Musée National d'art Moderne, Centre Georges Pompidou, Paris, Alfred Pacquement

Yehuda Neiman, Paris

Daniel Pérel, London

Alain Prillard, Saint-Cirq-Lapopie

Jean-Pierre Raynaud, La Garenne-Colombes

Christian Schlatter, Paris

René-Jean Ullmann, Paris

Jacques Villeglé, Paris

PLUS

Patrick Alton, Cristina Agostinelli, Carlos Basualdo, Raphaëlle Bianchi, Lynne Cooke, Albane Duvillier, Daniele Thomas Easton, Michele Favali, Robert Fleck, Nathalie Leleu, Jean-Claude Planchet, Nell Platt, Sara Renaud, Pierre Restany, Martine Silie, Joan Stevens, Judith L. Ujobai, Georges-Philippe & Nathalie Vallois

cover: *La foire aux skis* [Ski fair], 1988. Collection National Contemporary Art Fund, Ministry of Culture and Communication, Paris.
title page: Raymond Hains brandishing his *Armorican Express* in front of the Statue of Liberty.
this page: *Saint-Séverin* (detail), 2001. Courtesy Galerie Jousse-Seguin, Paris.

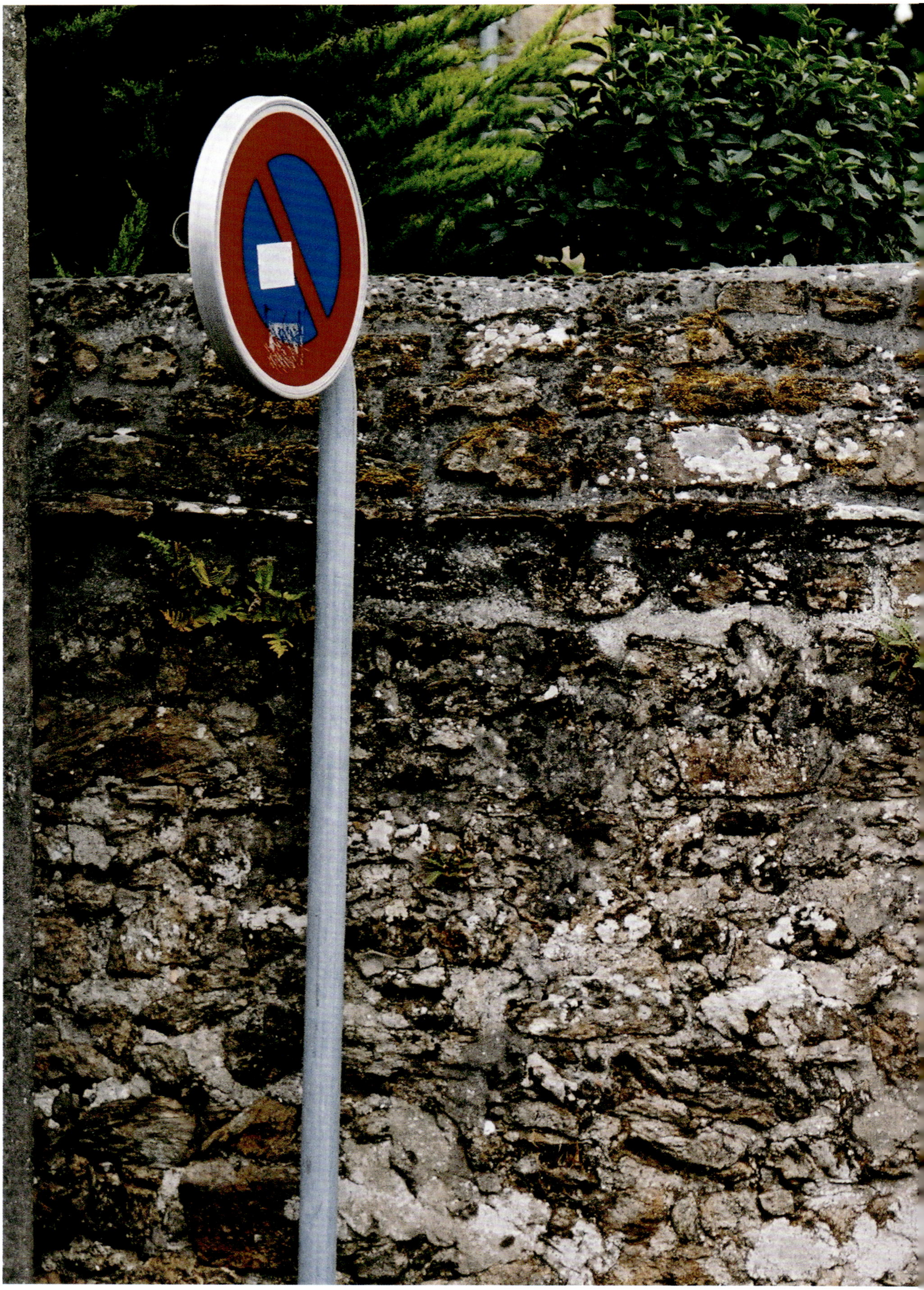

6 Raymond Hains at home, Nice, 2000. Photo: George Dupin, Paris.

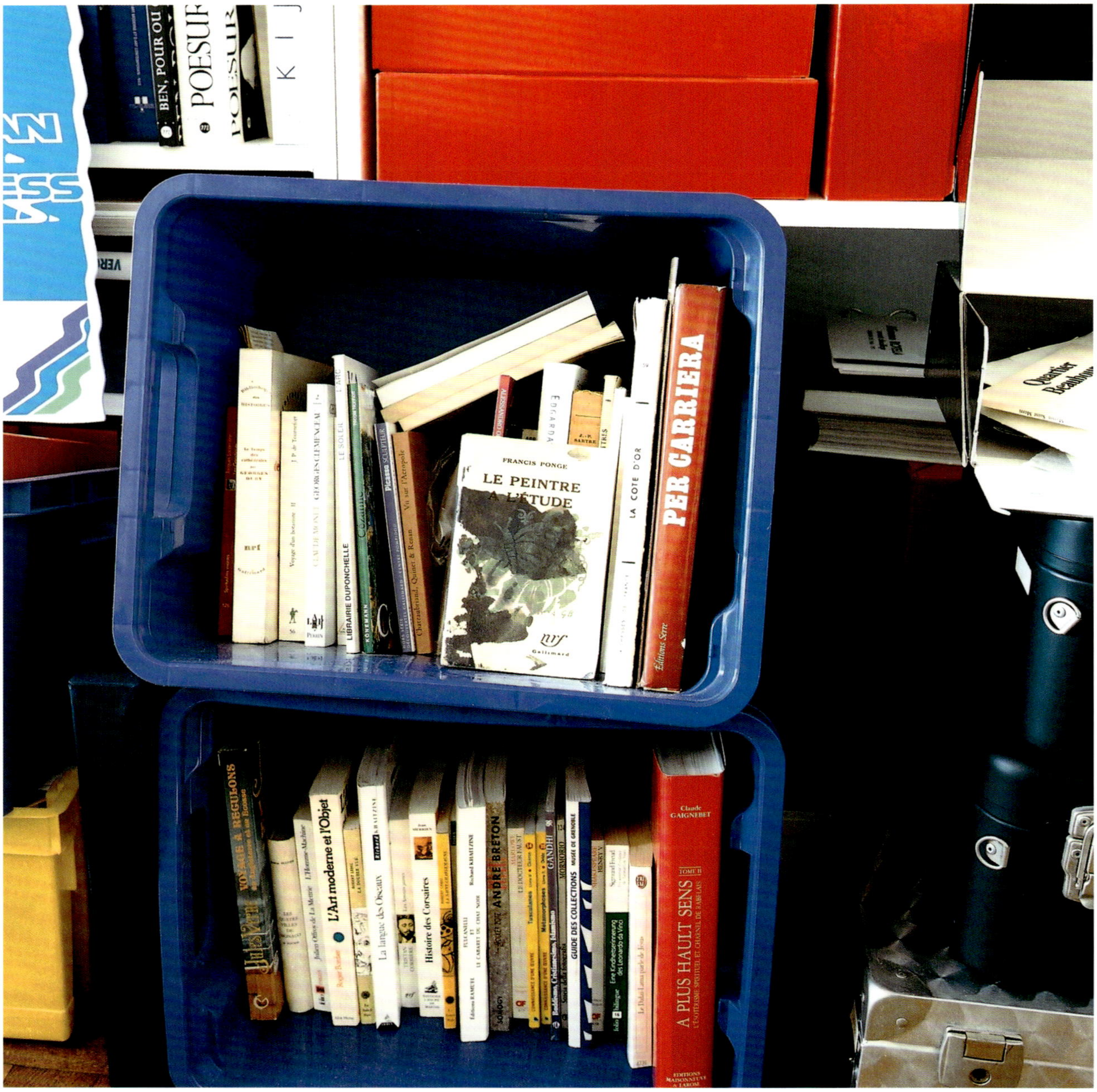

FOREWORD

In January 2000, the Goldie Paley Gallery at Moore College of Art and Design convened a distinguished panel of international curators—Lynne Cooke, curator, Dia Center for the Arts, New York; Robert Fleck, director, École Régionale des Beaux-Arts, Nantes, France; Ulrich Loock, director, Kunstmuseum Lucerne, Switzerland; Marjory Jacobson, author and curatorial consultant, Boston—to choose the fifth artist in the Moore International Discovery Series. Inaugurated in 1992 to introduce important international artists to American audiences, the series has featured Terry Fox, Jean-Frédéric Schnyder, Roman Signer, and VALIE EXPORT.

To our surprise, two of the curators proposed the same artist. Clearly, Raymond Hains's time had arrived. When former gallery director Elsa Longhauser visited Hains in Paris, in June 2000, the artist was two hours late, and in no particular hurry to begin the sensitive discussions necessary for organizing an exhibition in the United States—given that another, larger show was in the offing at the Centre Pompidou. Christine Macel, curator of contemporary art at the Musée national d'art moderne, Centre Pompidou, organized that benchmark exhibition, and, fortuitously, I was able to visit "Raymond Hains, La Tentative" and meet the artist. Referring to our Goldie Paley Gallery exhibition, he assured me there would be "fidelité à Philadelphie." A comforting thought, indeed.

With an exhibition history spanning five decades, Hains's work has been seen in museums and galleries throughout Europe, yet he remains virtually unknown in the United States. For American audiences to appreciate the context from which Hains's work arises, explains catalog essayist Tom McDonough, one must be aware that after the Second World War, in the wake of catastrophic global warfare, language itself appeared traumatized; the occupation of France and widespread collaboration had resulted in the breakdown of linguistic innocence or purity. Artists, writers, and philosophers would reinvent an aesthetic of montage or collage appropriate for the transformed conditions of the postwar world. "From the Lettriste atomization of the word to semantic rubble through the Situationniste aesthetic of literary theft and plagiarism, a sense of language as a field of struggle over meaning emerged" in postwar France—an understanding of the politics of language that was to influence a generation of artists. Hains's wide-ranging oeuvre is simultaneously meticulous and irreverent in its embodiment of this visual, literary, cultural, and political history.

Born in 1926, in Brittany, Hains first displayed his artistic bent in photography. Since that time, alongside the artist's unceasing photographic gaze, the written word has remained at the heart of Hains's complex world, a network of visual and linguistic coincidences. Drawing on a vast erudition enables him to weave together scholarly references with the places, people, and facts of ordinary life. According to Robert Fleck, in an article in *Connaissance des arts*, Hains's playful and seemingly offhand approach reminds us that "while art is founded on intellectual rigor, it must above all be a demonstration of pleasure."

Hains is most often associated with France's Nouveau Réalisme, a loose collaborative formed in 1960. Its declaration was drawn up by Pierre Restany and signed by Hains, Yves Klein, César, Jacques Villeglé, Arman, Jean Tinguely, and Martial Raysse. Often seen as a precursor to American pop art, these new realists embraced the found object and the rapidly developing technologies shaping postwar society. In the midsixties, Hains invented the artists SEITA and SAFFA—named for the French and Italian tobacco monopolies—and attributed a body of work to them, including the giant matchbooks shown in 1965. Fleck writes that "in a way, most of Hains's works are redolent of pop art, too, by virtue of their 'raw' use of everyday objects, of their direct language.... One of the most seductive aspects of his work is its ... relation to the world of advertising and other contemporary modes of image-making."

Known initially for his presentations of torn street posters, begun in 1949, Hains's technique for appropriating and recontextualizing the found object evolved to include sources both written and visual, which placed sophisticated historical referents alongside such banal elements of the urban environment as sidewalk barriers, corrugated metal, and construction scaffolding. Juggling words and images, Hains pairs a giant mannequin of (Paris gallerist) Iris Clert in Kassel with similar figures made in the small French village of Cassel (*Iris Clert, la messagère des arts*, 1997), and, invoking an archaic Roman name for Brittany, transforms the American Express logo (*Armorican Express*, 1987). "It is less a matter of simple wordplay than of disruptive intervention," says Jean-Max Colard in a recent *Artforum* review. The pun, that lowly form of humor, is recast as a secret, fertile catalyst, stimulating viewer's imaginations by way of memory or experience. The play with language, the penchant for punning, and the enormous literary and historical bank from which Hains unceasingly draws have at times obscured the eminently visual character of his work. It is precisely this aesthetic dimension that "Raymond Hains: Art Speculator" seeks to underscore. For younger generations of artists seeking independence from the institutionalized art world, Hains's unconventional methodologies and unpredictable oeuvre continue to challenge and inspire.

I am grateful to the many people who have made this project a reality. First, my thanks to Raymond Hains for his commitment and fidelité. My thanks also to guest curator Christine Macel for her persistence and resolve. The dedication of the gallery staff—Jeremiah Misfeldt, Liz Velardi, Wendy Weber, Jay-Nel Brown, and, in particular, Renée Shortell—ensured success. Our intrepid installation technicians—John Gibbons, Michael Gibbons, Norman Paris, Matthew Pruden, Gary Smith, Sean Stoops, and Tom Vance—exercised their customary diligence. The catalog itself was a labor of love. My thanks to Conny Purtill and Jenelle Porter for their design in the *ésprit de Hains*, Charles Penwarden for his sensitive translation services, and Gerald Zeigerman for his editorial direction. My appreciation to the leadership of Moore College of Art and Design, particularly Happy Fernandez, and the Centre Pompidou, Musée National d'art Moderne, Paris, for their support of this project, in particular current Pompidou president Bruno Racine, former president Jean-Jacques Aillagon, and director Alfred Pacquement. Also essential were the catalog authors and symposium participants whose insights enriched our understanding of the artist's work.

For its generous financial support, we are indebted to the Philadelphia Exhibitions Initiative (PEI), a grant program funded by The Pew Charitable Trusts and administered by The University of the Arts, Philadelphia, established to stimulate artistic development in the regional visual arts community by supporting public exhibitions and accompanying publications of high artistic caliber and cultural significance. Additional support has been provided by Étant donnés: The French-American Fund for Contemporary Art, New York. My special thanks to Paula Marincola, PEI director, and Antoine Vigne, director of visual arts at the French embassy in New York, for their unswerving support and sage counsel.

Molly Dougherty, Director, The Galleries at Moore

Raymond Hains at home, Nice, 2000. Photo: George Dupin, Paris.

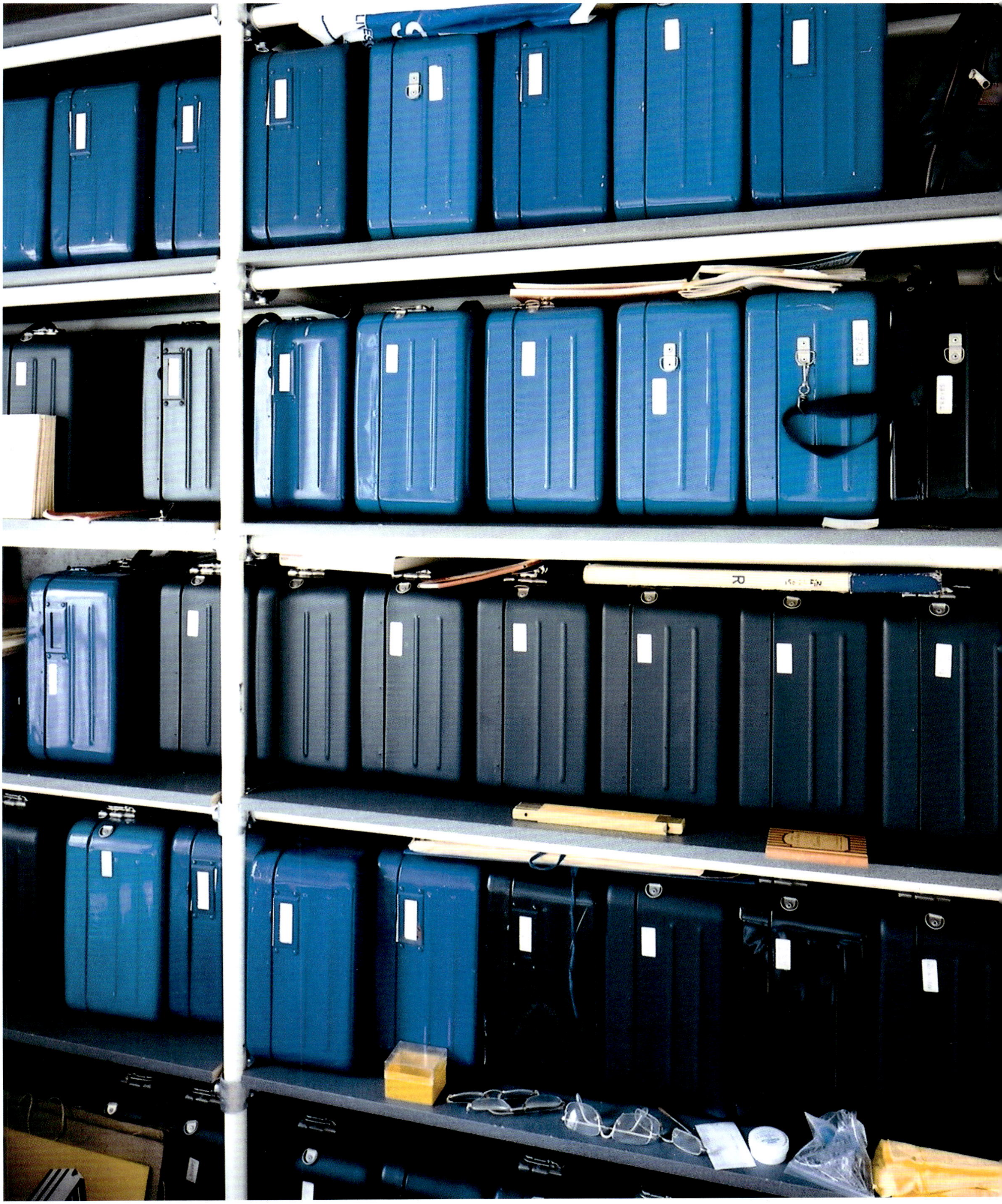

PREFACE

Raymond Hains is one of France's most admired artists. He is recognized both by older artists, such as Daniel Buren and Bertrand Lavier, and by members of the younger generation, who sometimes work with him on his interminable projects (as did Matthieu Laurette, recently, at the Galerie Jousse-Seguin, in Paris). Hains's maverick art and beguiling personality have made him something of a myth here, but the rest of Europe, and, even more, the United States, did not discover Hains until quite recently. Unlike his friends in the Nouveaux Réalistes group (Yves Klein, Martial Raysse, and Arman), Hains has in fact never been to the U.S., although he has always dreamed of the States. It is true, too, that, for Hains, travel is time-consuming: When he visited Italy in 1964, he did not come back until 1971. He also prefers, if possible, to go by train. In the meantime, several of his works have been about America. For instance, after taking part in the 1964 Venice Biennale, the one where American art "stole the idea of modern art from French art," Hains made his famous *Biennale éclatée* (Fragmented biennale [1968]), starting with a deformation of the catalog cover for the American Pavilion. More than two decades later, in 1989, P.S.1, in New York, offered him an exhibition, in which one of his works reminded visitors of the name shared by the artist Frank Stella and the Belgian beer Stella Artois (Untitled photograph, 1989). Hains's wordplay has since become more familiar on the international scene, what with the 1990 exhibition and big 2001 "retroprospective" at the Centre Georges Pompidou, plus shows at the Fondation Cartier in Jouy-en-Josas and Paris, Portikus in Frankfurt, the MACBA in Barcelona, the Fundaçao Serralves in Porto, and Documenta X in Kassel. Now, Hains's imaginary geography is expanding, thanks to the invitation extended by the Goldie Paley Gallery of Moore College of Art and Design, in Philadelphia, where his "attempted exhibition" will reprise some of the ensembles from the 2001 Centre Georges Pompidou show, while also exploring the artist's relation to the United States, in general, and the city of Philadelphia, in particular. Thus, in his recent *Macintoshages* pieces, *Castelli, Castellani* (1998), the great New York gallerist Leo Castelli is endowed with a distant cousin in the suburbs of a French town, Nice, dear to this artist, in the form of the "Castelli" nurseries. Hains shows himself standing next to an ad proclaiming "Castelli, Promotion, 39 francs," or remixes the self-portrait next to that of Leo Castelli. If the latter never represented him, he has nonetheless been an inspiration, just like all those who did support his work. They include Iris Clert, the Italian gallerists Misserotti and Palazzoli, Éric Fabre, who stimulated fresh interest in the artist and enabled the emergence of such major pieces as *Le Socle du Louis XIV* and *Monochrome dans le métro*, and Lara Vincy, Colette Soardi, and Daniel Templon.

Raymond Hains defines himself as an "Armorican painter," as opposed to an American one (he is, like his friend Jacques Villeglé, from Brittany). He has entitled his exhibition in Philadelphia "Raymond Hains: Art Speculator," in reference to his unceasing questioning of the nature and value of art. There is also an allusion here to his *Armorican Express*, a deformation obtained by photographing an American Express card through grooved glass. For a while, too, he toyed with the idea of evoking Benjamin Franklin by titling the show "Declaration of Independence and Incomes." Another source of inspiration is Marcel Duchamp, whose major works are exhibited at the Philadelphia Museum of Art. Hence such linguistic games as "Marcel Duchamp-Marchand de sel-Christine Macel"—the second term a reference to Duchamp's volume of prose, *Salt Seller*. The old French duty on salt was known as "la gabelle," and Hains's grandfather was himself a "gabelou," or customs agent. Last, Hains has discovered that there is another Philadelphia in faraway Cappadocia, Turkey, where we felt we had to go before the American show. Lots of trips to look forward to, then.

As is customary with this artist, we will not know if he is going to turn up at the opening of his exhibition until the very last minute. Aude Bodet points out in her essay that Hains cultivates the art of paradox, in particular, with regard to the question of exhibiting/not exhibiting; however, this man who defines himself as, above all, a freethinker and "citizen of the world" has often thought of boarding the boat to America at Saint-Malo and making his way to what was the first capital of the United States. The first ID papers Hains ever owned were indeed those given to him in 2001 by the association of World Citizens, an organization supported by such luminaries as André Breton, and founded by Garry Davis, an American pilot who tore up his passport, in Paris, in 1948, symbolically

 Raymond Hains, Paris, May 2001. Photo: Christine Macel, Paris.

abolishing frontiers. Hains is now doing the same thing with this show, which, after much too long a wait, builds a bridge between the American and French pop artists.

I wish to thank all those who have supported the artist in preparing this exhibition and its accompanying catalog. In particular, I must acknowledge the key roles played by Molly Dougherty, the director of the Galleries at Moore, and Lynne Cooke, curator of the Dia Center for the Arts in New York. Without them, the show could not have taken place. My gratitude extends to all those who worked closely on this project in Philadelphia and Paris, especially Laure Leprince, who worked unflaggingly on the catalog, and Christian Schlatter, for his loyal collaboration.

Christine Macel, Exhibition Curator
Curator at the Musée National d'art Moderne,
Centre Georges Pompidou

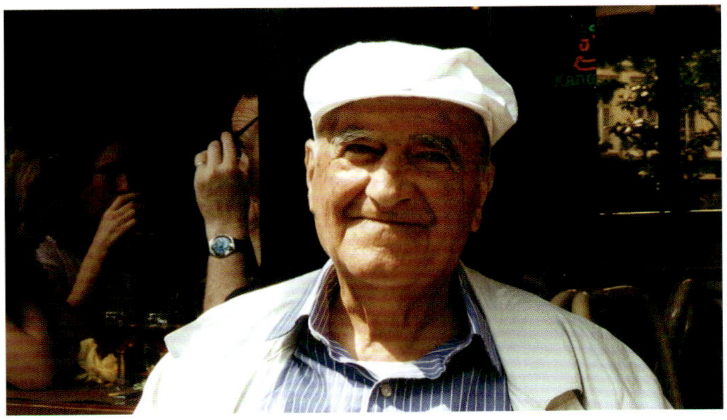

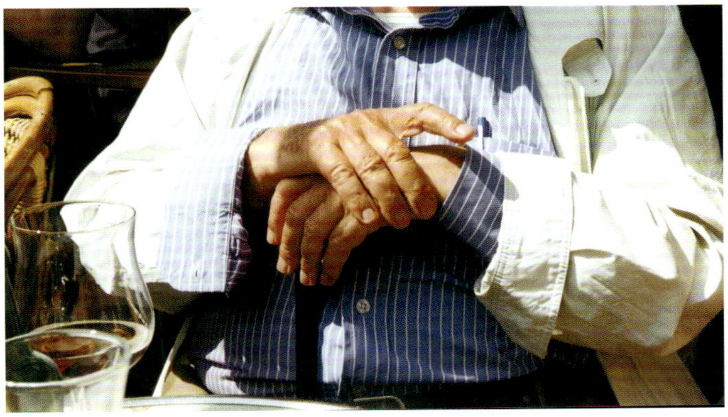

 this page: *Le perroquet de Colette Allendy* [Colette Allendy's parrot], 1957. Collection Paolo Guili, Malgrate-Lecco.
facing page, left: Untitled, 1960. Collection Jean-Pierre Raynaud, La Garenne-Colombes.
facing page, right: Untitled, 1957. Collection Jean-Louis Milin, Paris.

FROM COLLETTE ALLENDY'S PARROT TO MATTHIEU LAURETTE

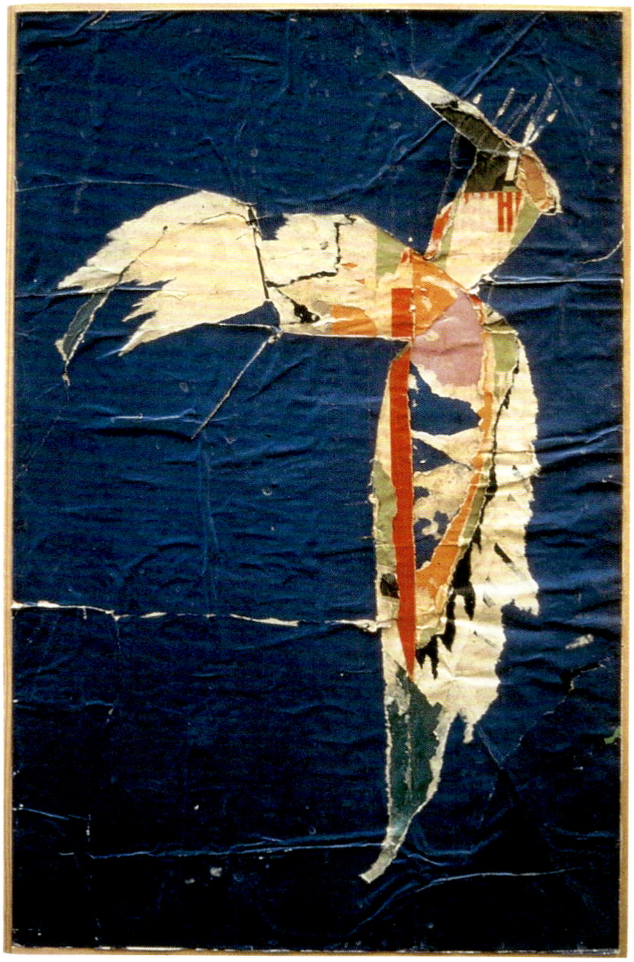

COLETTE ALLENDY : **On Monday, January 13, 1947, at 9 pm, Raymond Hains was at the Vieux Colombier theater for *Histoire vécue d'Artaud-Mômo, Tête-à-Tête*, by Antonin Artaud. That same month, he was present at the fourth lettrist event and at Francis Ponge's *Tentative orale*, where the poet concluded by "kissing the table." For Hains, the proper name Artaud, "the etymological name of nothingness," connects with the proper name Allendy. Doctor René Allendy (1889–1942) and his first wife, Yvonne, were friends of Artaud's.**

In December 1947, Raymond Hains and Jacques Villeglé did the rounds of Parisian galleries. At the end of their tour, they met Colette Allendy, the doctor's widow and second wife, who ran a gallery at 67 rue de l'Assomption, in Auteuil. She offered to introduce Hains to Artaud, and put forward his name to write the catalog preface for an upcoming Artaud exhibition. Her gallery exhibited Hains on three occasions: in June 1948, "Photographies hypnagogiques, Raymond Hains," with, as of early July, "Abstract Tapestries and Embroideries," by Camille Bryen, on the first floor; in 1953, *Hépérile éclaté*, with Jacques Villeglé, after the poem by Bryen; and in 1957, *Loi du 29 juillet 1881 ou le lyrisme à la sauvette* [Law of July 29 or hit and run lyricism], again with Villeglé. Also in 1957, Klein showed visitors to his "monochrome" show, the empty room on the second floor. (CS)

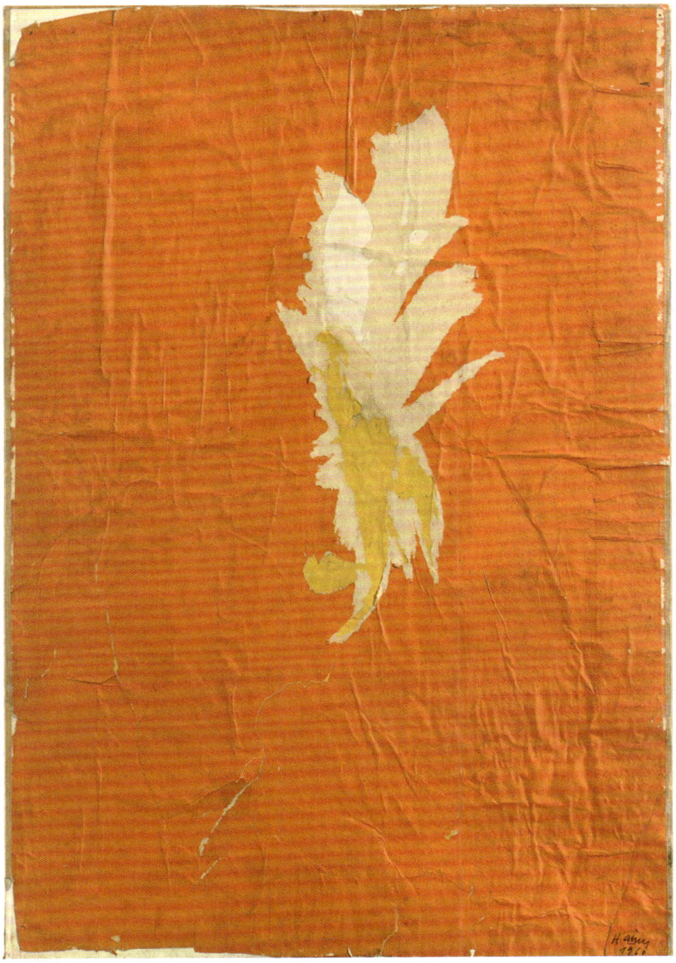

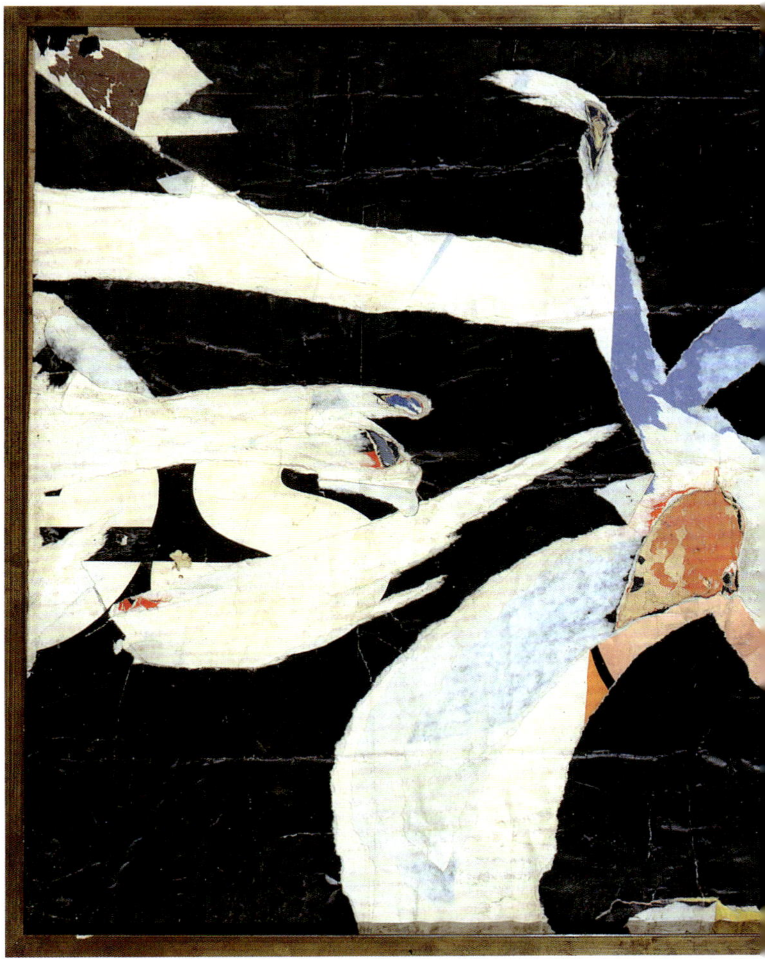

below: Mont Saint-Michel, 2001. The sign for the shop owned by Matthieu Laurette's parents on Mont Saint-Michel.
right: *Saint-Séverin* (detail), 2001. Matthieu Laurette, rue de Revenant. Courtesy Galerie Jousse-Seguin, Paris.

I don't know why, but I'm being followed by parrots. In 1957, I gave Colette Allendy a torn poster, which we called COLETTE ALLENDY'S PARROT. **One day, when I was on my way to photograph a shop sign, I met a man with a red parrot. His name was Père Roquette.* This red parrot was just like the parrot on the menu of the pub at Saint-Germain-des-Prés. Much later, I was given an electronic parrot with a battery. It flapped its wings and repeated everything you said. One evening, I left it behind at a gallery opening. Colette Saordi managed to get it back, in Nice. It's in the gallery where Matthieu Laurette showed his work. They might have run into one another. Parrot, in Italian, is loretto. | Raymond Hains, from Matthieu Laurette,** FREE SAMPLE DEMIX, **Jousse-Seguin Gallery, Paris, 1998 | *The French word for parrot is** PERROQUET. **Thus,** PÈRE ROQUETTE **would resemble a feminization of "Father Parrot." The artist continues his word play in Italian, with** LAURETTE **and** LORETTO.

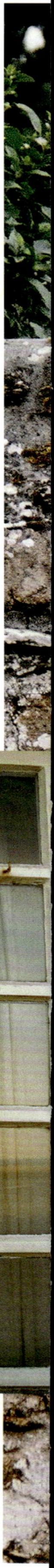

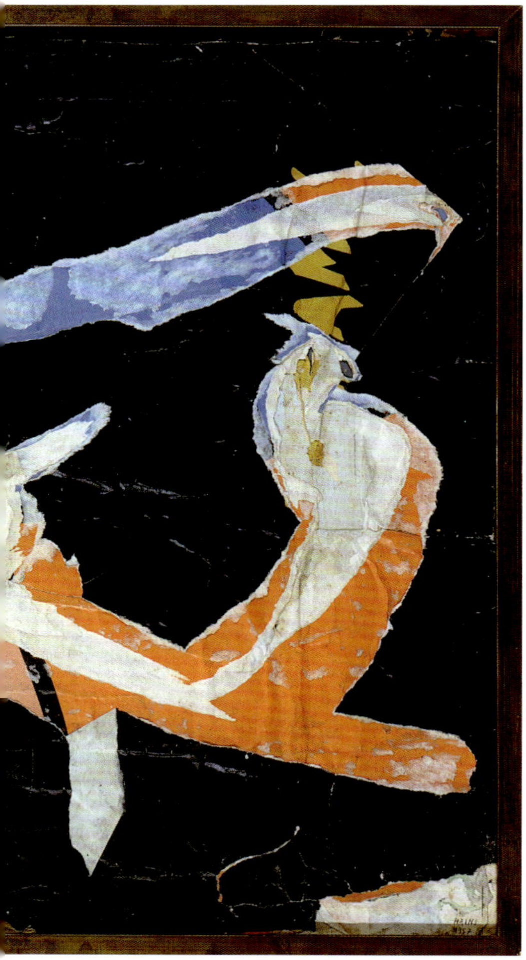

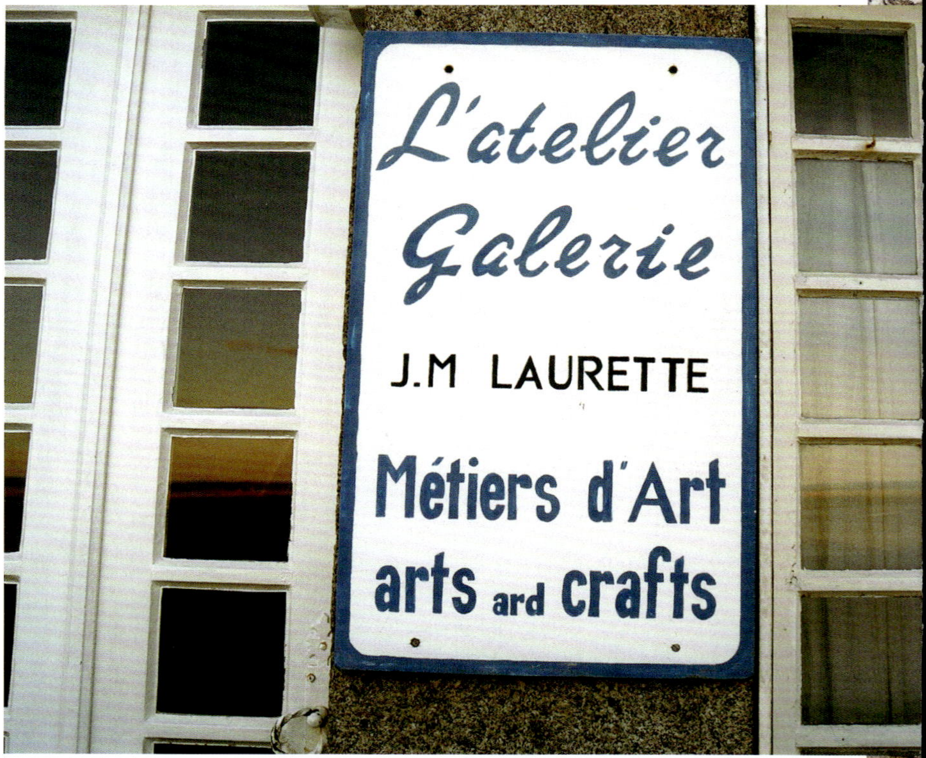

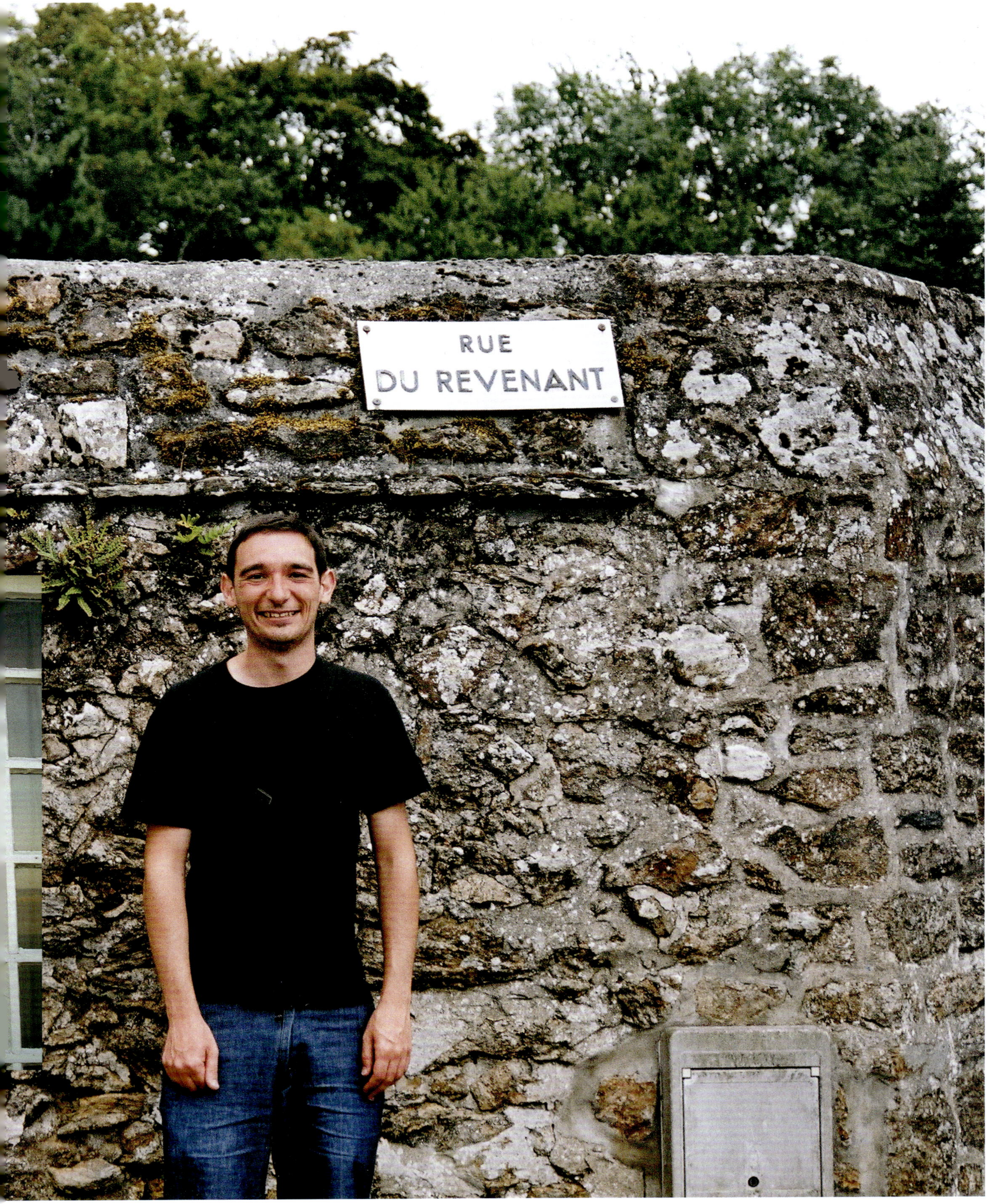
RUE
DU REVENANT

THE AESTHETICS OF COINCIDENC

CHRISTINE MACEL

In 1976, when Raymond Hains had his major retrospective at the CNAC, in the rue Berryer, in Paris, a show that he dubbed "La Chasse au CNAC,"[1] Alain Jouffroy made a comment in a short text he wrote for the Galerie Lanzenberg, Brussels. Although never taken up, it does more than any other to illuminate Hains's aesthetic. "For more than twenty years," he observed, Hains had been "spinning the strangest spider's web in the world: that of a sun which, wherever it shines, falls only on coincidences."[2]

Hains's own exploration of the world of computers in his recent *Macintoshages* has led him to note the implicit connection between "the Web" and the "spider's web," and he has made the metaphor his own: "I am working on a kind of Web," he says.[3] Or: "Life is like a novel, like Brittany lace or a spider's web."[4] And Hains's art can indeed be envisaged as spinning a giant web or piece of lace,[5] linking words and objects, proper names and places, in accordance with a logic that obeys only a deeply subjective form of causality.

In this sense, the connection with the surrealist aesthetic is much more apposite than is now supposed, especially the link with the principles laid down by André Breton's description in *Nadja*, of "sudden parallels, petrifying coincidences ... events whose intrinsic value is difficult to gauge ... and the kind of associations of ideas that they elicit—a way of making you go from the Virgin's thread to the spider's web...."[6] These head-spinning coincidences that punctuate Hains's life allow him to invent a world whose logic may be perverted and, sometimes, inverted, in terms of its principles, notably with regard to time. Two recent events show how Hains's logic reinvents causality by linking proper names and places, at the same time denying the synchronicity of coincidence, thus leading to conclusions that are personal in the extreme. While staying at the Hôtel Athéna, in Lyon, in February 2001, Hains went to the Musée de Grenoble for an exhibition in homage to Emmanuel Sougez. Afterward, he remembered that Freud had stayed at the Athena Hotel when visiting the Acropolis. Hains also recalled the story about Freud feeling faint when he saw the monument, because of the scene's seeming unreality. This coincidence led him to develop ideas about the "uncanny" [*unheimlich*] and to a metaphysical meditation on the nature of the real.[7]

In 2000, as a result of Jean-Jacques Lebel's research for an exhibition of Victor Hugo's drawings, "Du chaos dans le pinceau, Victor Hugo, dessins,"[8] Hains was able to trace connections from his own work, *Brise-lames* (transported from the beach at Saint-Malo to the Fondation Cartier in 1995), to two earlier events. The first was in 1853, when Victor Hugo, struck by the analogy between trees weathered by the sea and human bones, had his son Charles photograph him standing in front of the breakwater [brise-lames] in Jersey, then used the negative to make a wash drawing. The second was in 1926, when the surrealist Georges Hugnet, who may or may not have known about Hugo's work, was photographed in front of the breakwater at Saint-Malo, the very construction beside which Hains had himself photographed and filmed by Hopi Lebel, and that he later transported to Paris for exhibition at the Fondation Cartier and, subsequently, on the Champs-Elysées. This series of coincidences might have ended there had not the exhibition itself revealed two other links in the Hainsian chain of causality: on the way in, visitors were greeted by "a wooden panel painted by Victor Hugo"—a *palissade* [billboard] *avant la lettre*—and the show ended with "the imprints of [Brittany] lace." Hains used these facts to enact a backward rereading of art history and present himself as "champion of criticism."[9]

The whole of Hains's artistic career is full of such unlikely happenstance. For instance, the first poster that he peeled off in the rue de Rennes, Paris, in 1949, offered a formal analogy with the ideogram of the World Citizens organization (the outline of a man in a circle), which the American pilot Garry Davis had initiated one year earlier by tearing up his American passport outside the Palais de Chaillot, in Paris, a gesture that won him the support of Breton, Gide, and Einstein. For Hains, who had attended one of Davis's talks, because of his meeting with the sister-in-law of Romain Rolland, Louise Guieysse, the coincidence was too fine to pass up.

In fact, the torn poster, the idea for which had come to Hains and Jacques de la Villeglé as a result of a prophecy by the surrealist Léo Malet, is, in itself, a form of chance encounter. As Hains has commented, "The torn posters are like falling in love in the street."[10] He has also mentioned this notion of love at first sight in relation to photography. "I kissed a couple in Barcelona," were his words about a recent image.

In 1959, shortly after presenting his first billboard piece, the *Palissade des Emplacements réservés*, at the first Parisian biennial for young artists, Hains looked into the window display of Editions Clartés and saw the publisher's new encyclopedia open to the "Entremets de la Palissade," a dessert consisting of "an avalanche of confectioner's custard held in by a palissade of ladyfinger biscuits."[11] Following which, at a dinner party, he met Geneviève de Chabannes la Palice, the descendent of the Seigneur de la Palice, who gave his name to the pastries known as Les vérités de la Palisse (which Hains would photograph in 1988). In 1963, he came upon a poster advertising a show about the Seigneur de la Palice being put on in Lapalisse, in the department of Allier. He tried to make it there, but was late, and, in the end, happened upon a text about the Marquis de Bièvre, a famous punster, who would be the central figure in his 1986 show at the Fondation Cartier at Jouy-en-Josas—this being in the Bièvre valley.

The coincidences mentioned here all involve rhetorical speculation around proper names, which are central to Hains's elaborations. They are made possible by a practice of the *dérive* [drift], a kind of "psychogeographic exploration," as the situationist Ralph Rumney once described it.[12] Although—unlike François Dufrêne, who, in the end, was brusquely expelled from the Situationist International—Hains's links with Guy Debord were far from close, his approach was certainly germane to the latter's theory of "moments and situations."[13] Travel, be it static or actual, lasting a day or weeks, became a way of coming across places, people, and names in order to reinvent the reasons for their existence. The process is eloquently summed up in this anecdote related to Aude Bodet in 1988: "One day, when Dufrêne was still alive, I met Wolman and his wife on the square at Vence, where there is a great big ash tree [frêne]. When we saw the plaque giving its name, we said, 'Funny, we are on place du Frêne.... This place du Frêne should be place François Dufrêne, with—why not?—a Musée Dufrêne.'"[14]

Hains's art of combinations involves what Pierre Restany described as an appropriation of the real, but one that goes further than the ambit of the readymade. In addition to presenting fragments of the real, whether posters, billboards, sheet metal, photographic records, or sidewalk sculptures,

Hains enacts a total appropriation of the world—of knowledge, of language, of people and things. Regarding which, the artist speaks readily of Claude Lévi-Strauss's *The Savage Mind*, in which the author dwells on the question of classification and proper names.[15]

Hains's art of combinations also brings to mind a tradition that has its roots in antiquity, a mnemonic art founded on places and images that flourished during the Renaissance in the hermetic philosophy expounded by Raymond Lully and Giordano Bruno. Its ambition was to create a true "art of memory" that would be a part of rhetoric and make it possible to master the world in its totality.[16] In the classifying methodology that he developed in the mid-seventies, when he went from "posters to cards," with his reading cards written in blue felt pen and kept in Kiri cheese boxes, then his cardboard boxes and Airbus cases containing notes, books (with reading dates and times), his images and photographs, Hains offers a striking analogy with this hermetic tradition. Here is the description of the Theater of Memory conceived by Giulio Camillo in the sixteenth century, as related by a certain Viglius Zuichemus: "Under the images there were drawers, or boxes and chests, containing masses of papers on which there were discourses...." Hains's mode of thought is, as he says himself, rather like a form of algebra,[17] an obscure language in which memory becomes a major art form. His method of classification is simply the tool of a rhetorical art that invents a new, almost sacred language that, at first glance, is hermetic, but that eventually reveals a kind of coherence, one that objectifies the world in accordance with its own subjectivity.

In this sense, Hains is related not only to the art of memory but also to glossolalia, that invented language that sometimes consists of no more than a few phonemes, and whose most famous exponent (Artaud aside) was none other than Jean-Pierre Brisset, in whom the surrealists took a close interest, and who claimed that linguistic associations could lead to a total understanding of the world.[18] Indeed, one of the unrealized projects that Hains worked on with Camille Bryen and Jacques de la Villeglé concerned an anthology entitled *From Glossolalia to Shattered Letters* ("De la glossolalie aux lettres éclatées"). Hains was also influenced by his reading of Philippe de Félice, whose book *Foules en délire. Extases collectives. Essai sur quelques formes inférieures de la mystique* was all about the kinds of glossolalia that occurred in states of trance.

Hains's aesthetics of coincidence is, therefore, about much more than wordplay. It is grounded in a philosophical tradition whose ambitions are, above all, metaphysical. It makes it possible to ward off reality, the years, and death, and to travel in time. Hains once bought—but never read—a book entitled *The Secret Masters of Time*, whose cover showed an hourglass and a reproduction of Leonardo da Vinci's self-portrait. He must surely have had his reasons for hanging on to this obscure work, published in the J'ai Lu imprint's "Mysterious Adventures" collection. No doubt he himself is one of those masters of time, one of those artists of memory who, like Diogenes, is never fooled. Hains is, in his own terms, a "cynic struggling with a neo-cabalist,"[19] and, more than ever, the "minister of his own culture."[20]

ENDNOTES

1. *Raymond Hains et la photographie*, catalog published for Hains exhibition at the CNAC, 1976, curated by Daniel Abadie. [Hains's title here vaguely echoes Lewis Carroll's *The Hunting of the Snark*.]
2. Alain Jouffroy, *Le Rendez-vous des Amis*, (Brussels: Galerie Lanzenberg, 1976).
3. Interview with RH, 23 January 2001.
4. Interview with RH, 9 November 2000.
5. Note that Hains's aunt, who lived in Montparnasse (26 rue Delambre), had a lace shop.
6. André Breton was the first person to whom Hains showed his hypnagogic photos. They were sitting at a sidewalk café. Apparently, Breton was not very attentive.
7. Interviews with RH, 24 and 26 February 2001.
8. Jean-Jacques Lebel, "Le rhizome Hugo," *Victor Hugo, dessins*, (Paris: Maison de Victor Hugo, 2000).
9. Interview with RH, 24 September 2001.
10. Interview with RH, 12 September 2000.
11. Aude Bodet, *Chronologie Raymond Hains 1926–1988*, unpublished, C24.
12. Ralph Rumney, a friend of François Dufrêne's, admired Hains's torn posters. He published a psychogeographic guide to Venice entitled *The Leaning Tower of Venice*. See Ralph Rumney, *Le Consul*, interviews with Gérard Berréby (Paris: Editions Allia, 1999), 53, 106.
13. "Théorie des moments et construction des situations," *Internationale situationniste*, no. 4 (June 1960).
14. Interview with Aude Bodet, *François Dufrêne*, exhibition catalog, Musée de l'Abbaye Ste-Croix de Poitiers, Château-Musée de Nemours, and Musée d'Art moderne de Villeneuve d'Ascq, 1988.
15. Claude Lévi-Strauss, *The Savage Mind* [*La Pensée sauvage*, 1962], (Chicago: University of Chicago Press, 1962): "Proper names thus form the fringe of a general system of classification; they are both its extension and its limit."
16. See Frances A. Yates, *The Art of Memory*, (Chicago: University of Chicago Press, 1966); one of Hains's bedside books.
17. Interview with RH, 26 February 2001.
18. See his text "La Science de Dieu ou la création de l'homme," reproduced in *André Breton, Anthologie de l'humour noir* (Paris: J.-J. Pauvert, 1970), 244.
19. Interview with RH, 1 December 2000.
20. Raymond Hains in *Le Nouveau Réalisme, conférences et colloques* (Paris: Galerie Nationale du Jeu de Paume), 90. Hains was speaking at a roundtable with Michel Baudson, Pierre Restany, Bertand Lavier, and Olivier Mosset.

AUTHOR

Christine Macel is curator of contemporary art, in charge of the department Création contemporaine et prospective, at the Musée National d'art Moderne, Centre Georges Pompidou. She has curated many thematic shows, among them "Printemps de Cahors," as well as such one-person exhibitions as "Nan Goldin" and "Sophie Calle" (2003). She is an art critic and has served as a teacher at the Ecole du Louvre, Paris, from 1997 to 2002.

19 top: Raymond Hains, c. 1960. Photo: Harry Shunk, New York.
bottom: Untitled, 1962. Collection Lara Vincy, Paris.

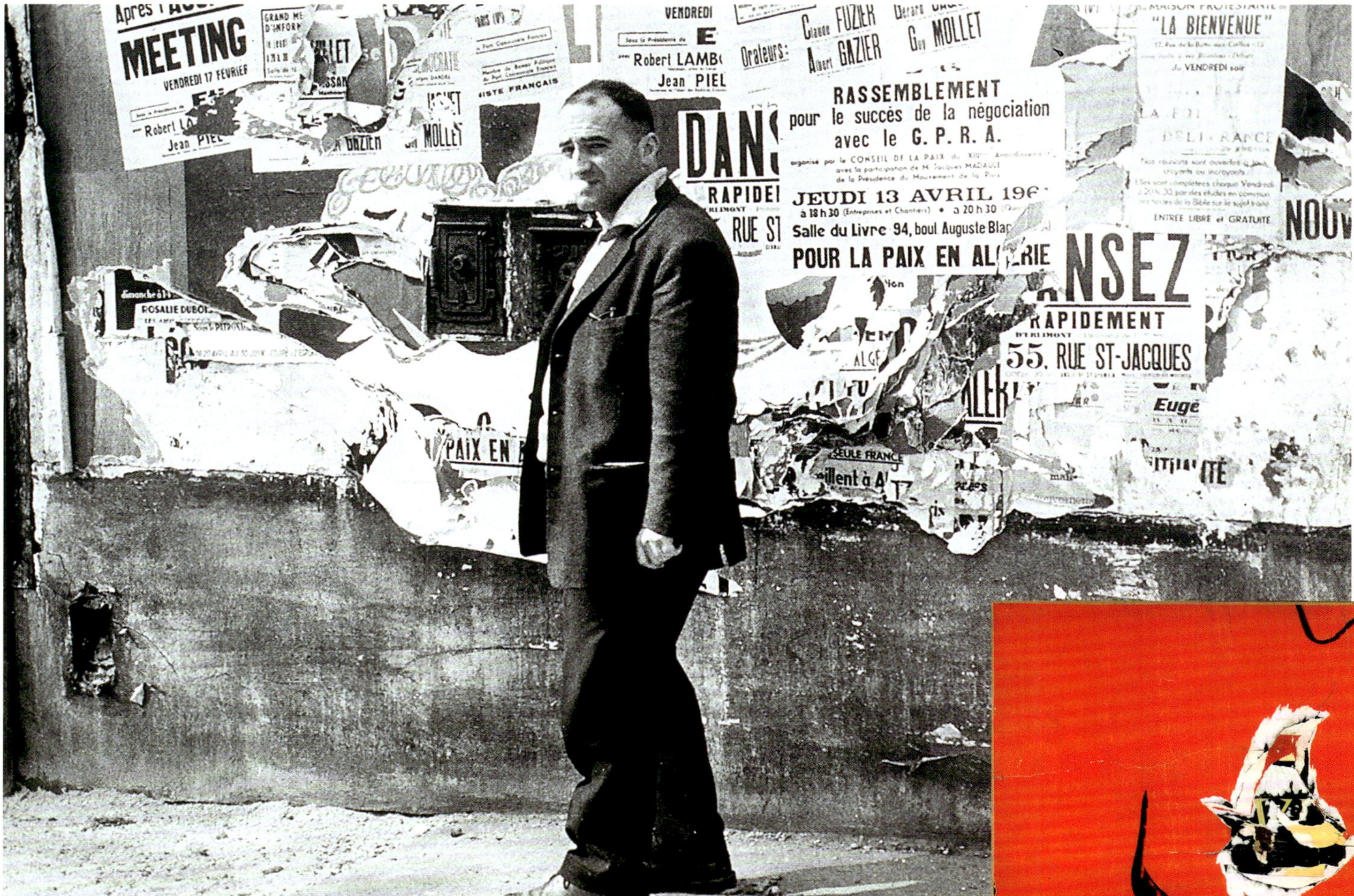

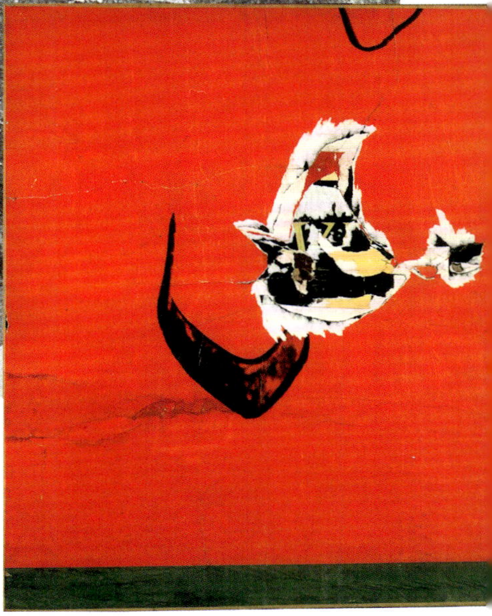

CITIZEN OF THE WORLD: FROM FRANCE DÉCHIRÉE TO *MACINTOSHAGES*

left: *Paix en Algérie* [Peace in Algeria], 1956. Collection Ginette Dufrêne, Paris.
right: Raymond Hains, c. 1960. Photo: Harry Shunk, New York.

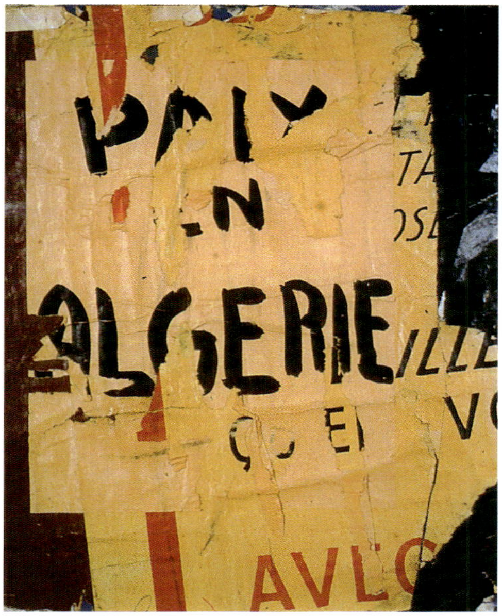

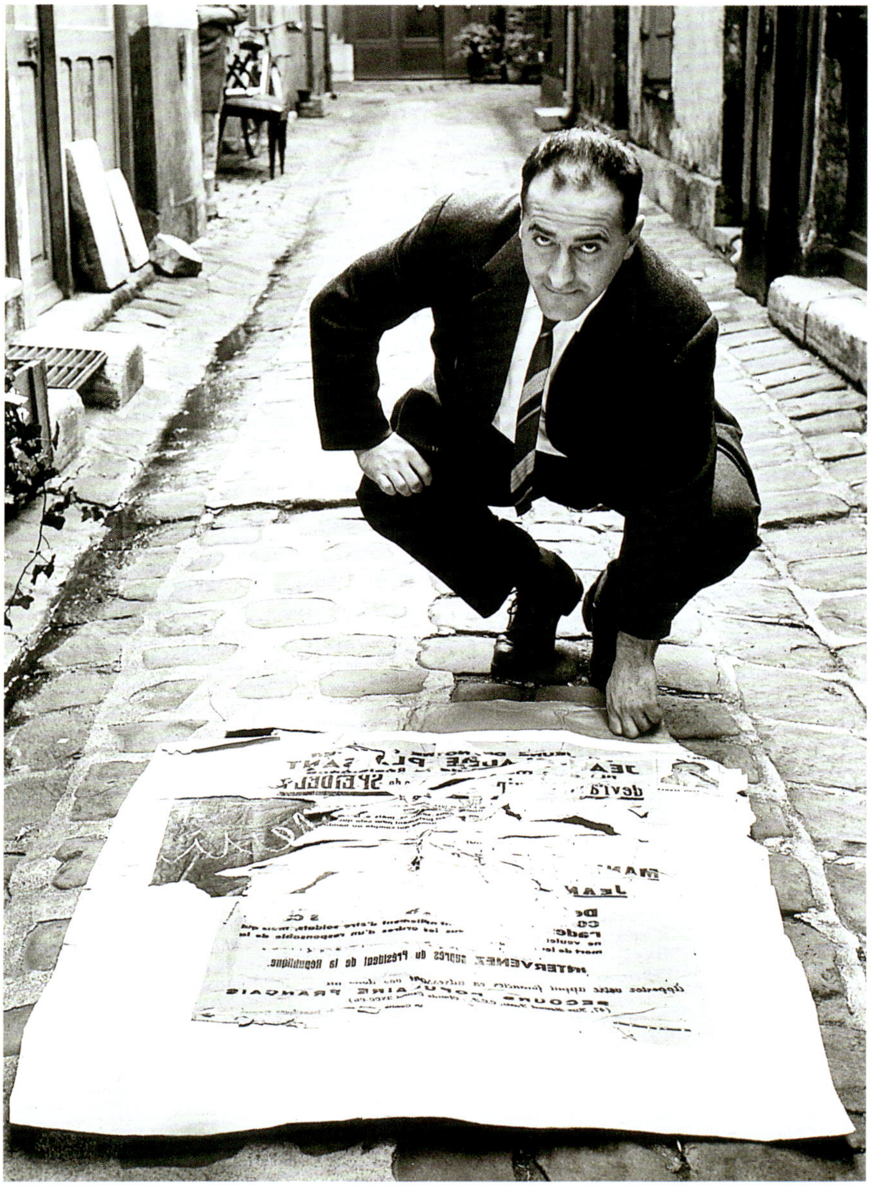

FRANCE DÉCHIRÉE : "La France déchirée," the title of an exhibition at Galerie J, in 1961, constitutes a special series in Hains's production. The twenty posters, two of them cosigned with Jacques Villeglé, stretch from 1950 to 1961—eleven troubled years of "sound and fury" related by posters carrying references to the war in Algeria, General de Gaulle, and the dramas of domestic politics. This "France torn apart" is hard to evaluate. Hains refused to sell it, but some of the posters have been scattered or shown in unexpected contexts (for instance, *Cet homme est dangereux*, like a portrait of an arsonist with SAFFA & SEITA matchbooks). Hains has never overtly stated any political positions. How could it be otherwise in the case of a man who describes himself as a "citizen of the world?" The red and the brown plaques both use the same techniques for aestheticizing politics. How could so-called engaged art avoid becoming a simple illustration of a *philosopheme* or a political thesis? Hains knew what happened to the surrealists when they went from "the surrealist revolution" to "surrealism at the service of the revolution." Artaud put a name on this transition: the surrealist "bluff," the suicide of art. Art feeding the ideological apparatus of politics becomes its own mimesis, cutting itself off from its critical function with regard to the established order. (CS)

below: *Carte d'identité de citoyen du monde* [Identification card of the citizen of the world], 2001.

RAYMOND HAINS'S FRANCE IN SHRED

TOM McDONOUGH

Late in 1961, New York's Museum of Modern Art held an important exhibition, "The Art of Assemblage," a survey of early twentieth-century collage and of what its organizer, William C. Seitz, described as its "unexpected extension" in recent artistic developments. His survey was international in scope, reviewing not only innovative American work, such as Robert Rauschenberg's "combine-paintings," but also European developments. It was in this context that Frenchman Raymond Hains would be introduced to an American audience. Hains, along with Jacques de la Villeglé and the Italian Mimmo Rotella, was presented as a practitioner of a new technique known as *décollage*, an art of lacerated or torn posters.[1] His contribution, an easelsize work entitled *De Gaulle compte sur vous, aidez-le* (De Gaulle is counting on you, help him [1961]), consisted of a field of half-torn placards removed from some Parisian wall; mutilating gestures reveal the accumulated layers of advertisements and form a dynamic abstract pattern. Seitz positioned works like this décollage as an extension of cubist collage—what had originated as the interpolation of nonart materials into a field still dominated by traditional techniques of oil painting, as the introduction of fragments of actuality within the "fictional environment" of the canvas, had become the artwork in its entirety. If Picasso, Braque, and company had originally "violated the separateness of the work of art, and threatened to obliterate the aesthetic distance between it and the spectator,"[2] Hains and the other artists of décollage took that violation to its extreme conclusion.

Such work would have been unimaginable without the mediation of Marcel Duchamp's readymades. Indeed, Seitz emphasized the Duchampian quality of décollage, calling it a form of "extreme actualism" through which art ceded its place to "the presentation of objects assembled in ordinary daily acts and without aesthetic intention."[3] Hains and his friend and colleague Villeglé (but not, it should be noted, Rotella) did not alter their lacerated posters but merely collected them, ripping them down as found on the city's walls, and then presented the results, untouched, as readymades of a sort. These artists were championed in France by critic Pierre Restany as one branch of the nouveau réalisme (the new realism), the movement he founded in 1960. Restany succinctly stated the basis of their strategy: "What they offer us is an entire aspect of the real, captured in its objective

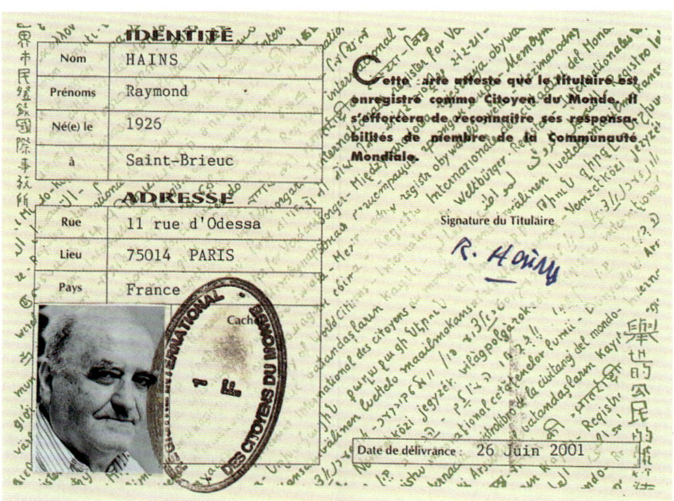

integrity, without transcription of any sort. Never at any moment is it a question of re-creation, but, on the contrary, of an expressive transmutation."[4] Transmutation, not transcription or re-creation, accident and choice, not "art," lay behind this work.

Restany's terms were another way of saying that Duchamp, with his indifferent selection of commonplace objects, was the relevant source rather than Kurt Schwitters, with his *Merzbilder* (those somewhat sentimental, nostalgic collages composed of rubbish picked up from the street), despite the evident morphological similarities between the latter and décollage. Those similarities were deceptive, since Hains and Villeglé refused the act of arrangement, the imposition of an individual sensibility, which accounted for the particular poetry of Schwitters's work.[5] Instead, the appropriation of found posters implied the elimination of the personal signature and a refusal of the romantic figure of the artist-creator, operations clearly at work in two salient aspects of these works: first, their collective production and exhibition (between 1949 and 1961, Hains and Villeglé often gathered and exhibited their décollages together, blurring if not obliterating distinct authorial identities); and second, in something approaching seriality (Villeglé's contribution to "The Art of Assemblage," entitled *6, bd. Poissonnière* (1957), featured the same iconically framed poster as Hains's contemporaneous *L'Humanité c'est la verité* (*L'Humanité* tells the truth [1957]), a pairing as critical of the myths of artistic originality as Robert Rauschenberg's *Factum I* and *II*).

The recourse to the Duchampian readymade must be seen however as a fundamentally ambivalent gesture, opening up certain avenues of critical practice but closing off others. Hains's contribution to the 1961 MoMA survey provides an excellent example: The curator was fully able—within the limits of the American artistic discourse available to him at the time—to discuss the internal critique of the work of art staged by this décollage, without any possibility of addressing its punctual character, its historical specificity for an original, French audience. For *De Gaulle compte sur vous, aidez-le* was nothing if not timely. Its title derived from the rectangular bill pasted near the top of the work, which various hands have tried to tear down: That small poster of January 1961 urged its readers to vote with the U.N.R. (the Union pour la Nouvelle République), the Gaullist party, in support of the president's policy of self-determination for the French colony of Algeria, in revolt since 1954. The vast majority of voters would indeed come to de Gaulle's aid, rejecting the positions of both the extreme Right and the communist Left in the January referendum and initiating the final chapter in the sordid history of France's colonial occupation of Algeria.

This is not to claim that the referendum on the future of Algeria constituted the "subject" of Hains's work but, rather, to suggest that the exclusive focus on the formal aspects of décollage—however radical—occluded its profound imbrication in a wider political history of France in these years. The two aspects are in fact inseparable, for if Hains's embrace of Duchamp ultimately focused on the reinvention of an indexical practice of artistic production,[6] then the specificity of décollage lay in what we might call its motivating of the indexical sign. That is, the lacerations that gave *De Gaulle compte sur vous* its form may have been anonymous, but they were not politically nonspecific; they were made, with intentional violence, by those who upheld the principle of *Algérie française*. Much the same could be said for Villeglé's *6, bd. Poissonnière* (1957), also in the "Assemblage" exhibition; that address is significant, informing us that these torn posters were collected on one of Paris's *grands boulevards*, in front of the building that housed the offices of the French Communist Party daily newspaper, *L'Humanité*. The placard that occupied almost the entirety of Villeglé's small work was, in fact, a letter from the editor of the newspaper, vaunting its reporting and urging readers to "make a daily appointment with the Truth!" Again, the "anonymous" tears were pointed: three gaping holes, like bullet wounds, deface the text; across the poster someone has scrawled "murderers"; and to the opening sentence, which reads, "*L'Humanité* tells the Truth about the war and the pacification" (referring, again, to the counterinsurgency in Algeria), "in Hungary" has been appended in barely noticeable ink—an ironic reference to the recent, brutal suppression by the Soviet Union of the 1956 uprising in that country, about which, of course, *L'Humanité* could write anything *but* the truth.

It may seem striking that the topical political references of these two works, chosen to represent the French artists of décollage to an American audience, should go completely unremarked, yet much the same was true of their reception in Paris at this time. The previous summer, Hains and Villeglé had exhibited a selection of their torn posters, collected between 1949 and 1961, that was exclusively concerned with political questions. The show, held at Restany's Galerie J, in Paris, was titled "La France déchirée" (France in Shreds),[7] a reference simultaneously to the state of the posters displayed and to the ideological divisions within the country to which they testified. With historical hindsight, one critic later could describe this series as unveiling "the psychological, political, and social chaos of French society,"[8] and in a recent essay Robert Fleck writes of their function as "witnesses":

They especially bore witness to this conflict between defenders and opponents of Algeria's independence that was ravaging the country like a civil war.... These "torn political posters" remain down to the present one of the few artistic testaments to this state of civil war in France during the "Algerian war," in which the generation of French philosophers who would later gain an international reputation (such as Jean-François Lyotard, Cornelius Castoriadis, and Gilles Deleuze) enlisted alongside the anticolonialist liberation movement just as their fathers (and the generation of Sartre and Camus) had enlisted in the Resistance before them.[9]

This is an interesting set of claims to make for "La France déchirée," in that it not only provides an explicitly documentary alibi for these works (they "bear witness," they are "artistic testaments" to a moment of national trauma) but also claims a clear political intention on Hains's part: He was an *artiste engagé* on behalf of the Algerian insurgents, taking up the Sartrean mantle of commitment.

To what extent can such claims be maintained? Just what was the context of the exhibition of these torn posters in the summer of 1961, and what were the ideological parameters circumscribing their potential reading by a Parisian audience at that time? Earlier that spring, French generals in Algiers, dissatisfied with de Gaulle's policies toward the colony, had attempted a putsch; their failure had strengthened the latter's hand, and in late May 1961, de Gaulle had opened negotiations in Évian with the provisional Algerian government. Algeria's independence was, by this point, a foregone conclusion, but, in the meantime, violence continued, not only in the colony but between pro- and anti-independence forces within Paris itself. The Algerian war was, in a sense, everywhere and nowhere, present daily in Parisians' newspapers as bulletins from the Évian conference and series of nighttime bombings against supporters of independence, but largely absent from their everyday lives.

These contradictory developments—the opening of peace negotiations and a heightened, secretive violence at home—were the immediate political context in which Hains would exhibit his work. Yet, what is striking today is the almost complete absence of this context from commentary about "La France déchirée" when it was shown that June. A critic in the daily *Le Monde* merely mentioned that the artist worked "in a completely personal and sarcastic atmosphere—or rather made the 'anonymous tearer' work, contenting himself with cutting out the poster with a razor to obtain the best possible layout."[10] This was a rather odd comment, given the explicitly public content of the placards on display; overall, the impression seems to have been one of an avant-gardist prank, a "sarcastic" demonstration of Hains's disregard for the niceties of artistic technique. Michel Ragon, in *Arts*, at least vaguely described the theme of the show ("torn election posters, framed by Raymond Hains"), but could only remark on his disappointment, without accounting for its causes: "The idea is excellent, but the reward is, in the end, rather meager."[11] His failure to justify this negative assessment—in other words, to accomplish the most basic task of the critic—signals that we are here dealing with some sort of avoidance or repression.

Perhaps Pierre Restany, the great promoter of (and apologist for) the nouveaux réalistes, set the tone in his brief text for the exhibition: "Let us turn over together these few pages shed from the diary of Paris's pedestrians," it read in part. "The dirty laundry of politics is that of a woman of good breeding who was having her monthly visitor. Our history is filled with enough blood, frills, and charms to make a bit of poetry, providing that one has a lucky hand and a pure heart."[12] To display these posters was to reveal something normally hidden or denied in polite society—Restany described them as "*les dessous de la politique*," meaning both the seamy side of politics and a woman's undergarments, soiled with blood in this case—and his euphemistic description captured the impossibility of openly or honestly discussing France's "dirty war." The telling conflation of feminine hygiene—the prefeminist disgust at the contrast between the seemingly clean "woman of good breeding" and her concealed menstruation—and state corruption, the apparent normality of French politics masking the murderous counterinsurgency in Algeria, was a rich metaphor for precisely what could *not* be spoken about the colonial conflict.[13] Indeed, what was most striking about this conflict was its virtual absence from public discourse; as historian Laurent Gervereau has remarked, its "peculiarity remained its lack of presence in postering, at least in the mother country."[14] Because, officially, there was no "war," Algeria seldom appeared on the walls of Paris outside of times of election, and when it did, the propaganda was primarily peaceful, emphasizing unity and fraternization between colonizer and colonized—a surface unanimity of tone shared by the government and by its far-Right opponents in the O.A.S. (the French paramilitary Secret Army Organization).

The works of "La France déchirée" ruptured this polite discourse and its sanguine repressions. To some extent, Fleck is quite justified in claiming that "during this period of emergency measures and censorship in France, this exhibition was an act of great courage" on the part of both Hains and Restany.[15] Significantly, that rupture took the form of a negation of meaning, whereby the clear message of the political poster—its propagandistic tone of assured positivity ("De Gaulle is counting on you...," "*L'Humanité* tells the truth...")—was voided of sense through the vandalism of anonymous passersby. Yve-Alain Bois characterizes this strategy as an "entropic deliquescence of language":

The stripped-off poster is only fragmentarily legible, at best. Moreover, we are not dealing with one poster but a veritable mattress of posters, myriad skins whose identity has been destroyed by irregular tearing (carried out over time): The strata merge into one another; the lettering grafts together; the words cannibalize one another; information is little by little reduced to undifferentiated noise.[16]

Entropy is, of course, a state of indifferentiation, and this term seems most apt to describe the décollages of "La France déchirée": Tearing has rendered their messages unreadable, one clearly indistinguishable from the next; but the posters themselves, in grouping together the most disparate political agendas on the two-dimensional plane of the wall, appear to propose their own variety of indistinguishability. Together, the centrifugal tendencies of French politics at the end of the fifties and the opening years of the sixties constituted their own "noise," a din of strident voices from Left and Right, Communist and Gaullist, pro-F.L.N. (the Algerian National Liberation Front) or pro-O.A.S., each advancing its incompatible program.

Or so the Galerie J exhibition would have it. Hains's title for the show in fact echoed that of a book published only four years earlier—"La France déchirée"—by political journalist Jacques Fauvet, who had diagnosed the ailing nation's condition in the closing months of the Fourth Republic. For Fauvet, the ideological divisions of France were

no more a matter of Algeria than of Indochina or any other contemporary drama. These dramas have distressed France, torn apart the French, threatened the Republic, but their outcomes will not alter the essential imperatives of the French problem.[17]

That problem lay not in the country's "elites or its regimes" but in "its history and its geography," which have placed France at the crossroads of different peoples, religions, and cultures, and have led to the loss of a coherent, unified national ideology. Bereft of a sense of collective identity, "France will remain torn apart, awaiting one or several revolutions."[18] By removing responsibility for France's polarization from its ruling elite and the latter's disastrous colonial policies—where responsibility truly lay—and placing it instead with a deterministic view of a national "fate," Fauvet had emptied the rhetoric of both ends of the ideological spectrum of any substance, reducing them to indistinguishable noise.

His solution for France had been equally apolitical: "A desperate effort to recover its cohesion and restore its personality" was required,[19] one that would ultimately rely on the lowest common denominator of liberal democratic politics, the exhausted notion of humanism. "European civilization," Fauvet had concluded,

must rediscover that awareness of the human person and respect for it by which it is distinguished from the new as from the old Islam, the "Islam" of Moscow as the Islam of Mecca. Apart from strictly religious beliefs, this is the only chance for our civilization to regain its spiritual unity. Men of good will, Christian or not, can meet on the common ground of Western humanism.[20]

Such a response to the polarized politics of these years in France must be seen as typical of a certain bourgeois intelligentsia that believed it possible to resolve the material conflicts of disparate class interests on the "higher" level of ideological reconciliation—by unifying a population around the subtly racist concept of "Western humanism," for instance.

Fauvet's illusory resolution of a concrete set of contradictions had a parallel in Hains's aesthetic practice. Although the coincidence of titles should not lead us to an oversimple alignment of their agendas, nevertheless we may locate a shared set of petit bourgeois principles at work behind both. Hains and Fauvet were operating within the same terrain of centrifugal political tendencies, and, more important, both operated from the assumption of the bankruptcy of radical programs of social transformation. This was clear in Fauvet's case, but it should be no less so in that of Hains: Benjamin Buchloh speaks of a sense of "political confinement" among the artists of Hains's circle who suspected that the revolutionary politics of interwar dada and surrealism had been rendered obsolete by "the experiences and consequences of World War II"; moreover, any striving toward politico-aesthetic synthesis "had been once and for all discredited by these failed efforts."[21] The result was a spirit of disillusionment and skepticism that could lead to an outright reactionary position, in the case of an artist like Yves Klein, but could also result in a retreat to an outdated bourgeois liberalism oddly linked with a program of aesthetic transgression, as with Hains.[22]

Recourse to Duchamp and the readymade was an integral part of this paradoxical position: The anonymity of the torn poster, the cutting off of producer from object in the operation of the index, functioned to create the illusion of Hains's distance from these works. He could, in other words, appear above the fray, implicated by neither side in these debates; he was merely the melancholic collector of the evidence of "France in Shreds," documenting the violence done to the symbolic body of the Republic. That such a studied neutrality implied its own politics was noted by the one reviewer of "La France déchirée" who addressed, in his short notice, the public nature of these torn posters: "Since it is often a question of the Algerian war and of the regime that it has entailed, I would prefer that the artist express more clearly his way of 'seeing things.' This is completely natural amidst such confusion."[23] Instead, Hains chose to remain within the prevailing social confusion of the moment, focusing on the material aspects of his procedure of décollage and delighting in the plays of words and phrases that resulted. "In which case," the reviewer concluded, "to speak politely, it amounts to indecency."[24] The ground on which politics and aesthetics might meet had fundamentally shifted by 1961, as others in France were recognizing at this moment (one thinks of the transformations through which the Situationist International was passing at this time[25]), and Duchampian transgression lent itself as easily to petit bourgeois retrenchment as to "the postulates of a revolutionary artist."[26]

So, when William Seitz included *De Gaulle compte sur vous* in his "Art of Assemblage" exhibition that fall, with no mention of the public, political implications of this work's sources or form, he was not being fundamentally dishonest to the artist's intentions. This was not a case, as so often occurred, of the American headquarters of institutionalized modernism emptying the meaning from an avant-garde practice in order to preserve its calcified, formalist shell. Back in Paris, Hains had *already* opted to position himself above the contending political forces that were indeed tearing France to shreds (even if we must admit that phrase contains a good deal of melodrama), situating himself, on one hand, as the ironic artist mining the city's walls for felicitous juxtapositions and double meanings, and, on the other, as the disenchanted humanist seeking to reconcile opposites. That this would prove an untenable position was evidenced by his abandonment of *décollage* in the following years and his search for less fraught aesthetic terrain. The works of "La France déchirée" did indeed speak of what postwar France had wished to keep silent, but they did so with a vocabulary destined to return their subjects to quiescence.

ENDNOTES

1. Seitz defined *décollage* as the antithesis of collage: Meaning, literally, "unsticking" or "taking off," he noted, "it refers to works made by removing materials already pasted," as in the tearing or mutilating of posters; see William C. Seitz, *The Art of Assemblage* (New York: The Museum of Modern Art, 1961), 150–55.

2. Ibid., 23.

3. Ibid., 83, 82.

4. Ibid., 82–83, Pierre Restany, quoted from an unpublished manuscript (Paris, 1961).

5. The relation of décollage to the antinomies represented by Duchamp and Schwitters was the subject of some confusion to its first American audience. If Seitz, for one, was clear in positioning this work within a Duchampian paradigm, others seemed less certain. For instance, in their book on collage Harriet Janis (wife of the owner of the Sidney Janis Gallery, which exhibited Hains's torn posters in its "New Realists" show of late 1962) and Rudi Blesh doubly characterized this work "as sentient and as memoried as the *Merzbilder*" and as a species of readymade—two rather mutually exclusive possibilities. See their *Collage Personalities, Concepts, Techniques* (Philadelphia: Chilton, 1962), 173, 175. The relation of décollage to the work of Schwitters is discussed critically in Benjamin H. D. Buchloh, "From Detail to Fragment—Décollage Affichiste," in *Décollage: Les Affichistes* (New York: Zabriskie Gallery, 1990), 5–6; a revised version of this essay appeared in *October*, no. 56 (Spring 1991), 98–110.

6. On the indexical sign and Duchamp's practice, see Rosalind E. Krauss, "Notes on the Index: Parts 1 and 2," in *The Originality of the Avant-Garde and Other Modernist Myths* (Cambridge, Mass., and London: MIT Press, 1985), 196–219.

7. "La France déchirée: Affiches lacérées de Raymond Hains," Galerie J, Paris, June 14–28, 1961. (Billed as a solo exhibition of Raymond Hains, Villeglé contributed a handful of works as well.) The gallery, directed by Jeanine Restany (Pierre Restany's wife), had opened the previous month with an important group exhibition of the Nouveaux Réalistes, "40° au-dessus de Dada," [40° above Dada], and would champion these artists until its closure in 1966.

8. Alain Jouffroy, "The Paris International Avant-Garde," trans. Norbert Guterman, in *New Art around the World* (New York: Harry N. Abrams, 1966), 84.

9. Robert Fleck, "Raymond Hains," in *Raymond Hains: Akzente 1949–1995/Accents 1949–1995* (Vienna: Museum moderner Kunst Stiftung Ludwig, 1995), 67.

10. M.C.L., "A travers les galeries," *Le Monde*, 23 June 1961: 9.

11. Michel Ragon, quoted in Raymond Hains, *J'ai le mémoire qui planche*, ed. Pierre

27 this page: *Comité pour la paix en Algérie* [Committee for peace in Algeria], 1961. Collection Éric Fabre, Brussels.
next page: Untitled, 1960. Collection Jean-Pierre Raynaud, La Garenne-Colombes.

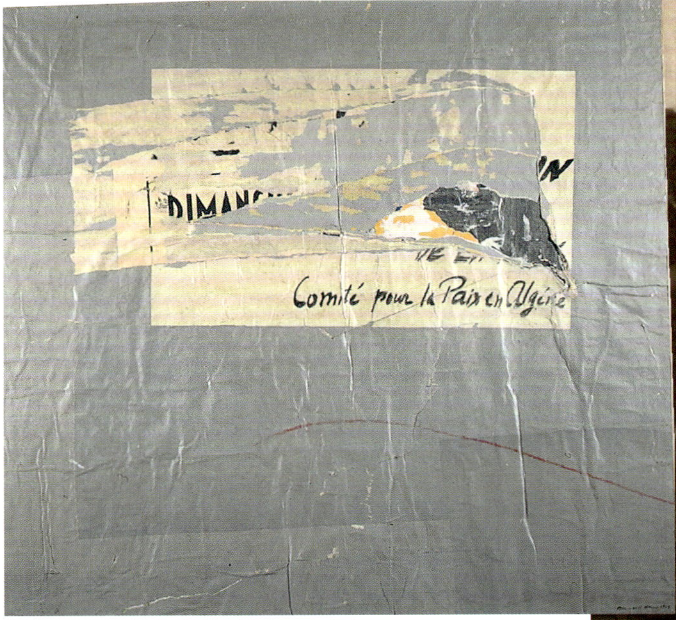

Leguillon (Paris: Éditions du Centre Georges Pompidou, 2001), 210.

12. Pierre Restany, quoted in *1960: Les nouveaux réalistes* (Paris: MAM/Musée d'Art Moderne de la Ville de Paris, 1986), 81.

13. French cultural historian Kristin Ross has discussed the cult of cleanliness and its relation to colonial politics in these years; see her extremely insightful *Fast Cars, Clean Bodies* (London and Cambridge, Mass.: MIT Press, 1995), 71–122.

14. Laurent Gervereau, "Africains et colonisation dans l'affiche politique française," in *Images et colonies*, eds. Pascal Blanchard and Armelle Chatelier (Paris: ACHAC and Syros, 1993), 66; see also his *La Propagande par l'affiche* (Paris: Syros Alternatives, 1991), especially 132–33.

15. Robert Fleck, "Raymond Hains," 67.

16. Yve-Alain Bois, "Ray Guns," in Yve-Alain Bois and Rosalind E. Krauss, *Formless: A User's Guide* (New York: Zone Books, 1997), 178. Earlier, Bois had elaborated on the role of "noise" within information theory in his essay, "Thermometers Should Last Forever," in *Edward Ruscha: Romance with Liquids, Paintings 1966–1969* (New York: Rizzoli International/Gagosian Gallery, 1993), 12–15.

17. Jacques Fauvet, *La France déchirée* (Paris: Librairie Arthème Fayard, Coll. "Les idées et la vie," 1957), 8. It was translated into English as *The Cockpit of France*, trans. Nancy Pearson (London: Harvill Press, 1960).

18. Ibid.

19. Ibid., 148 (151 in trans.).

20. Ibid., 149 (152 in trans.). Fauvet tellingly had used "Islam" as a synonym for all fanatical or absolutist belief systems—as, in other words, the very opposite of "nonideological," liberal bourgeois thought. Written at the height of the Algerian war, this was a very tendentious use of the term, with its own uncanny echoes of our own moment.

21. Buchloh, "From Detail to Fragment," 4. Hence, Hains's ultimate distance from Guy Debord, driving force behind the Situationist International, despite their shared experiences in a marginal Left Bank bohemia of the early fifties.

22. This linkage had been effected in the previous artistic generation by Jean Dubuffet, with whose work Hains had engaged on several fronts. On Dubuffet's humanistic position, see Aruna D'Souza, "'I think your work looks a lot like Dubuffet': Dubuffet and America, 1945–1962," *Oxford Art Journal* 20, no. 2 (1997), 61–73.

23. Raoul-Jean Moulin, quoted in *Raymond Hains, J'ai le mémoire qui planche*, 210.

24. Ibid.

25. The Situationist International's (S.I.) fourth conference, held in London in September 1960, devoted itself largely to resolving the extent to which the S.I. considered itself a political organization, upon which social forces it could rely, and under what conditions. The conference, and the subsequently published "Manifesto" drafted there, marked the S.I.'s turn from aesthetics to politics. For this history, see, among other sources, Jean-François Martos, *Histoire de l'Internationale situationniste* (Paris: Éditions Gérard Lebovici, 1989), 134–36.

26. As Alain Jouffroy described Hains, with considerable wishfulness; in "Paris International Avant-Garde," 84.

AUTHOR

Tom McDonough is assistant professor of art history at Binghamton University, New York. He is a regular contributor to *Art in America*, and his essays have appeared in *Documents* and *October*, among other journals. His anthology on *Guy Debord and the Situationist International: Texts and Documents* was recently published by MIT Press.

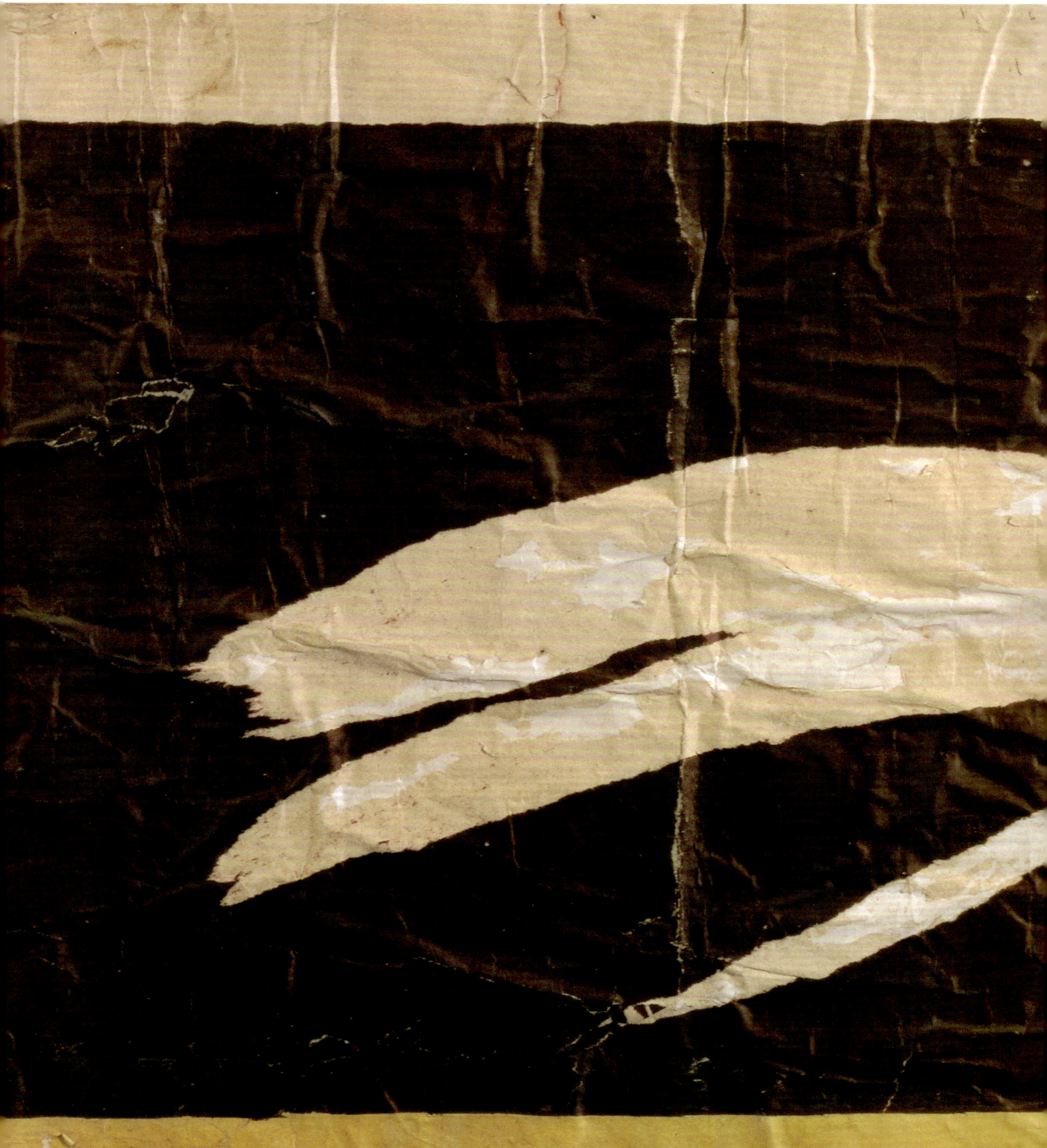

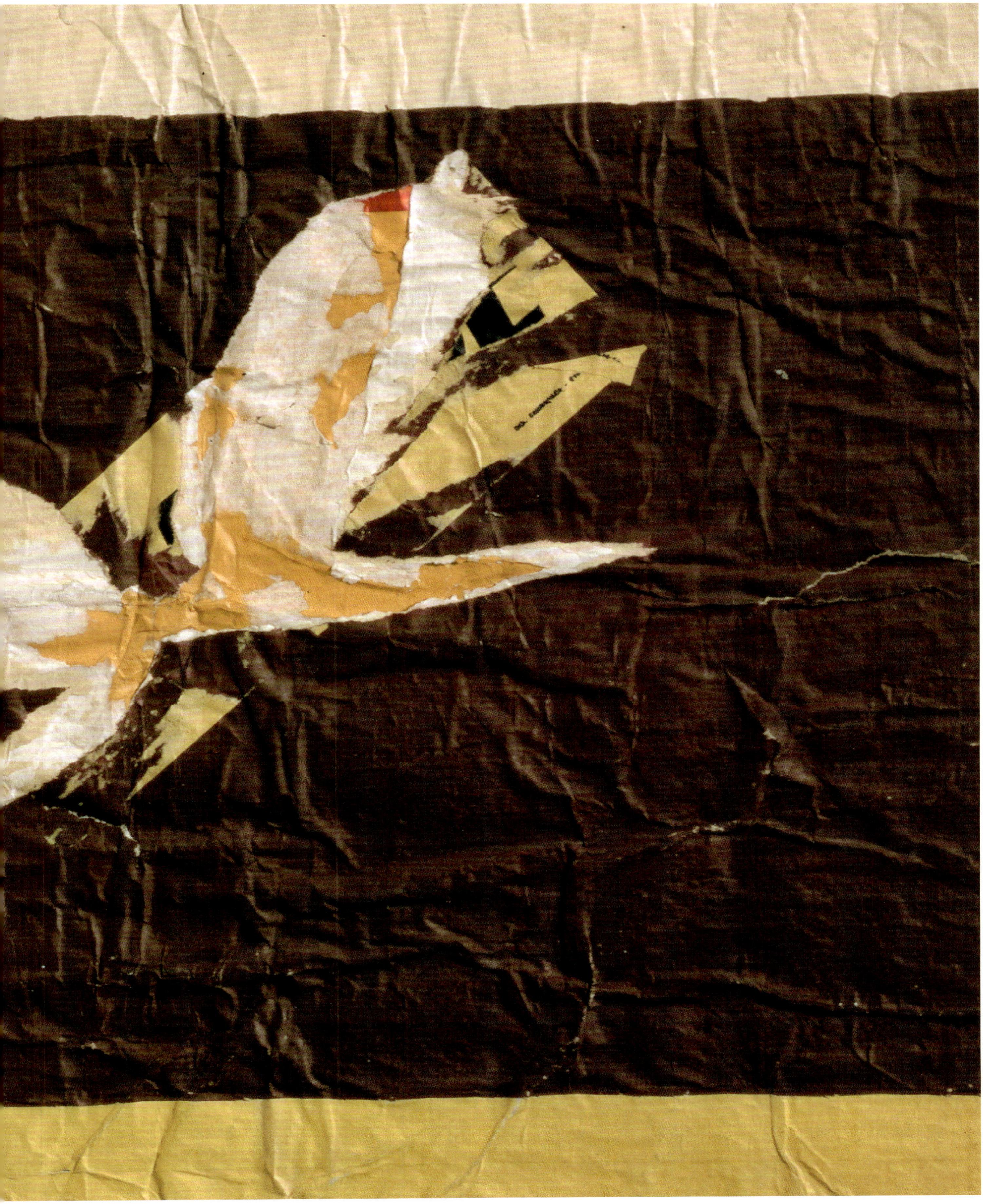

 this page, left: page from *J'ai la mémoire qui planche, Raymond Hains*, exhibition catalog, Centre Pompidou, Paris, 2001.
this page, right: *Cet homme est dangereux* [This man is dangerous], 1957. Collection Ginette Dufrêne, Michel Marcuzzi, Paris.
facing page: *L'Humanité c'est la vérité* [*L'Humanité* tells the truth], with Jacques Villeglé, 1957. Collection Ullmann, Paris.

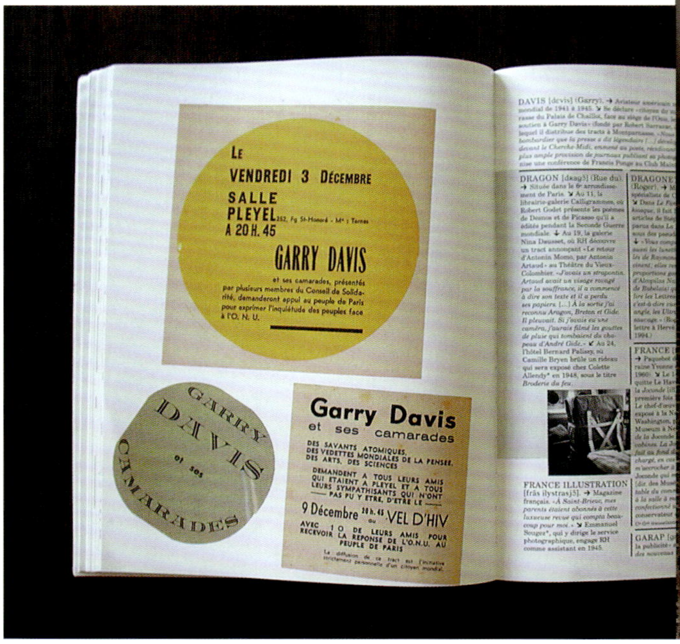

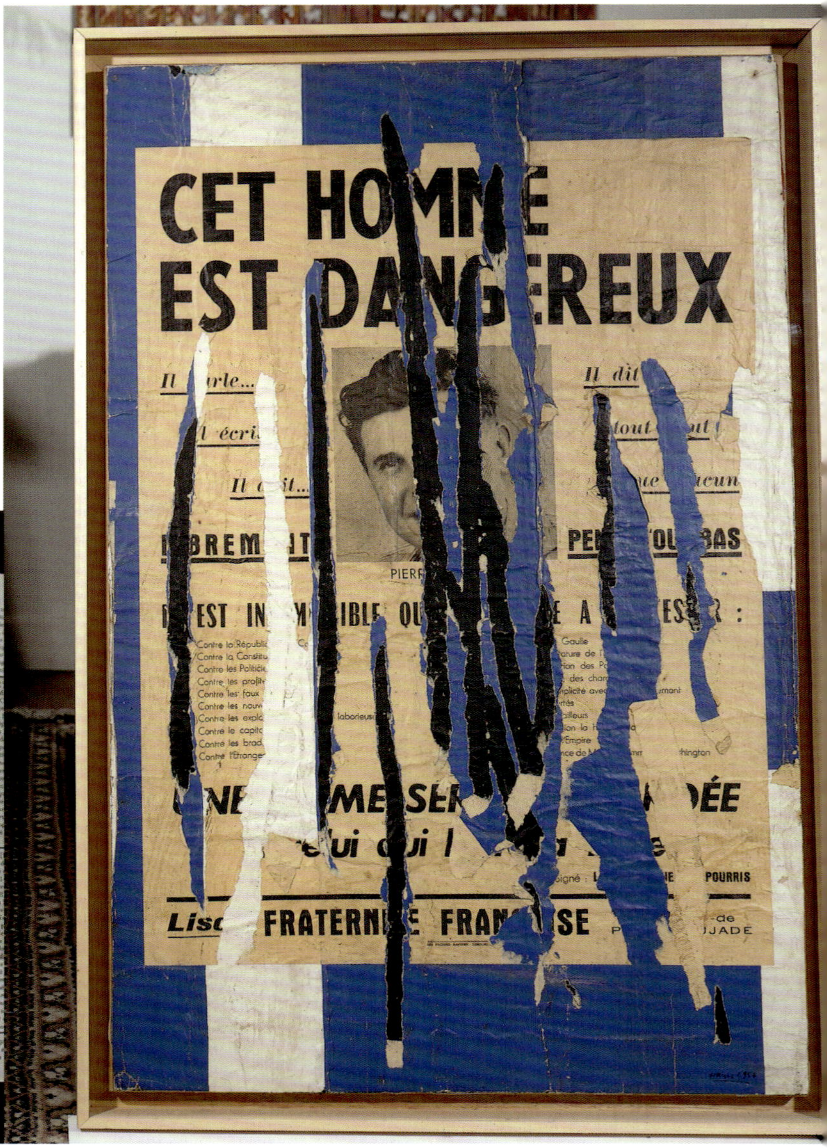

GARRY DAVIS : In May 1948, while on holiday in Saint-Brieuc, Raymond Hains read in the newspaper that a young American bomber pilot, Garry Davis, "having become a killer against his will," had symbolically handed in his passport to the United States embassy in Paris. Now stateless, he was pitching his tent outside the Palais du Trocadéro, where the General Assembly of the United Nations was being held, and declaring himself a "citizen of the world," a term coined in the eighteenth century by Fougeret de Monbron. A month later, French intellectuals, rallied by Robert Sarrazac, came to manifest their support. A support committee was formed, its first signatories being Breton, Sartre, Gide, the Abbé Pierre, Camus, and Vercors. Hains also signed. In February 1949, the surrealists addressed a letter to Davis pledging their support and saying that they, too, felt themselves to be "citizens of the world" and "abhorred nationalism." On July 10, 1949, the town of Cahors declared itself a "City of the World" (*Cahors Mundi*). Soon, it inaugurated the "road of Citizens of the World," which it marked with a milestone at the entrance to the Pont Valentré. In 1999, as a guest at the Printemps de Cahors festival, Hains made his *Cahors Mundi Macintoshages* showing images of a later, identical copy of the milestone, now kept in a private collection at Saint-Cirq-Lapopie. In 2000, he made his *Monnaies raymondines* (chocolate money, based on Cahors's medieval coins). (CS)

Rather than being a creator, I see myself as existing within an encounter. When I stop in front of a torn poster, it's because I'm crazy about it. Instead of removing posters from walls, I could have photographed them. But I became the Brassaï of posters. I never wanted to see the posters disappear, so I took them and hung them in my room. I was an image hunter, and I became a poster-raptor. Given that I was taking posters that were created and printed by others, then torn up by strangers, my first move was not to say, "I am going to put my signature on them"—I was just happy to save the pieces. It was a sort of archaeological kidnapping that forced my contemporaries to have to look at the "yes" and "no" votes of a referendum, in the same way we look at the inscriptions of Pompeii. | Raymond Hains from Otto Hahn, "Raymond Hains," BEAUX-ARTS MAGAZINE, **April 1986.**

I am an inaction painter. The paradox of torn posters is that the less the poster comes from me, the more Hainsian it is. When I am struck by a poster in the street, I find it more authentic than if I had tinkered with it. What interests me is the street-corner encounter: My workers are the passersby, who, for any reason at all, peel away at the posters that are glued there. They are like assistants, or living paintbrushes, like the young women that Yves Klein dipped in blue. | Raymond Hains interview with Aude Bodet, May 22, 1983.

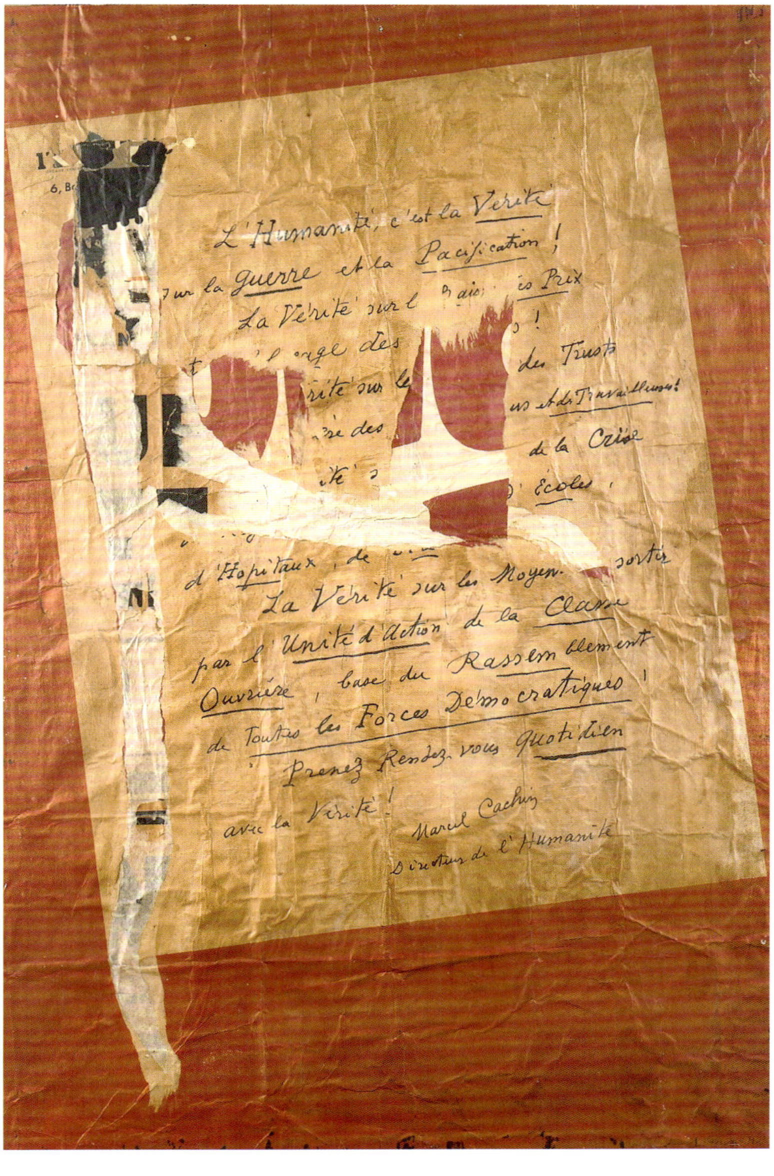

this page, left: *Borne kilométrique Cahors, Paris, New York* [Milestone Cahors, Paris, New York], June 1950. Collection Alain Prillard, Saint-Cirq-Lapopie.
this page, right: Untitled, from *Cahors Mundi/Cahors, ville du monde* [Cahors, city of the world] series, 1999. Collection National Contemporary Art Fund, Ministry of Culture and Communication, Paris.
facing page, top: *Les Raymondines* [Raymondines], 2000.
facing page, bottom: *Euros en chocolat* [Chocolate Euros], 2000.

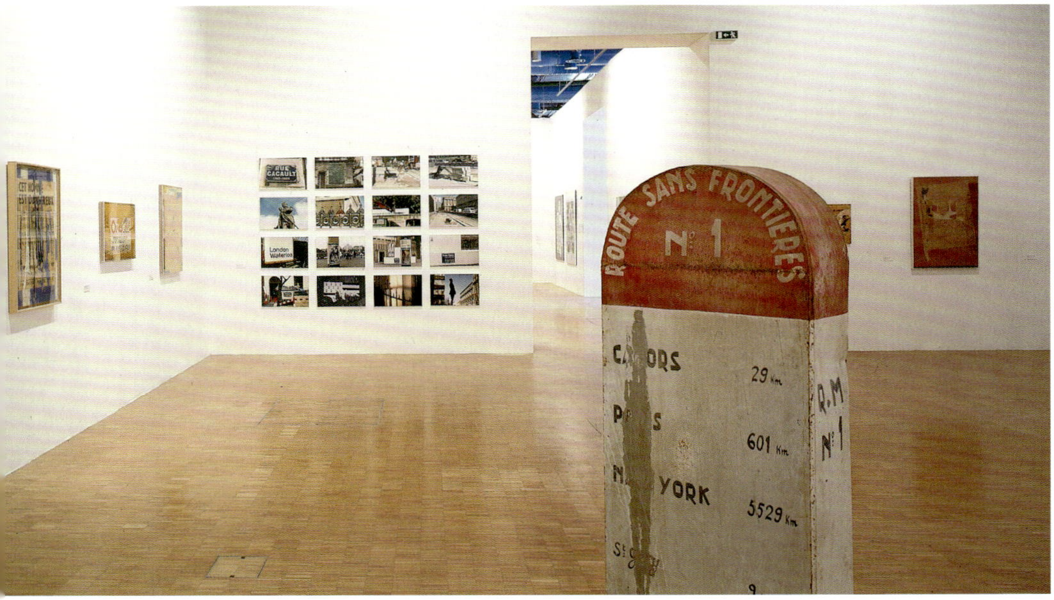

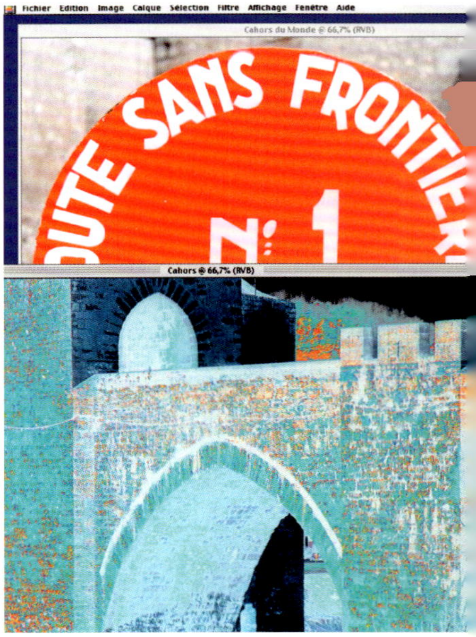

I was already invited to the Cahors Spring Festival last year. It brought back memories, because Cahors had declared itself "International City" in 1947. Some people looked through the newspaper archives and found articles about it. For instance, this is how I found out that Orson Welles and André Breton had inaugurated, with a series of milestones, the Route without Borders—which went from the Pont Valentré, the medieval bridge of Cahors, to Saint-Cirq-Lapopie, where André Breton was living. At the time of the centenary of Breton's birth, his wife uncovered one of these milestones. So, I had been given various documents, photos, press clippings about it, which I was able to make good use of by transforming them with the help of a computer, to create what I call MACINTOSHAGES.

This year my participation is very different, for I am not playing a direct role. It was also discovered that there had been bankers in Cahors during the Middle Ages, and that one of them had these very beautiful coins called RAYMONDINES, **because his name was Raymond. Last year, the pastry shops that were supposed to come out with chocolate Raymondines didn't have the time to do it. So, that is what we are doing here. Because my name is Raymond, too. This time around, I am not exhibiting anything. I am represented by these** RAYMONDINES, **which can be found at the patisserie Périn.**

All of this is even funnier when you consider that I've always been so bad in money matters. I don't know how much of the Manet "menu" or the Monet "menu," or how much of Cézanne or Victor Hugo, you have to give to get a flower from Giverny. I don't know the value of artistic works. Not even mine, like the PALISSADE **at the Pompidou Center workshop. I even had this little expression about it: If my** PALISSADE **is in the pawn shop, my aunt has been pawned, too.* Yves Klein had an aunt who owned a pharmacy and she was his patron. My aunt, she had a little souvenir stand, and sold bits of lace....**

All of this is a way of saying that I have seen everything under the sun, when it comes to art and money. Now we're about to enter the era of the euro, and I find it quite appropriate to be coming out with RAYMONDINES. **Everyone is asking me to do retrospectives, but I consider that I spent good parts of my life without the means to do what I wanted to do. So, here I am, just having a good time making Chocolate** RAYMONDINES. **I do hope that the chocolate will be digestible.** | **Raymond Hains from Henri-Francois Debailleux, "Raymond Hains,"** LIBÉRATION, **June 16, 2000.** | ***Hains uses two archaic expressions for the pawnshop here:** LE CLOU **(the nail), and** LE MONT-DE-PIÉTÉ **(Mount Piety).**

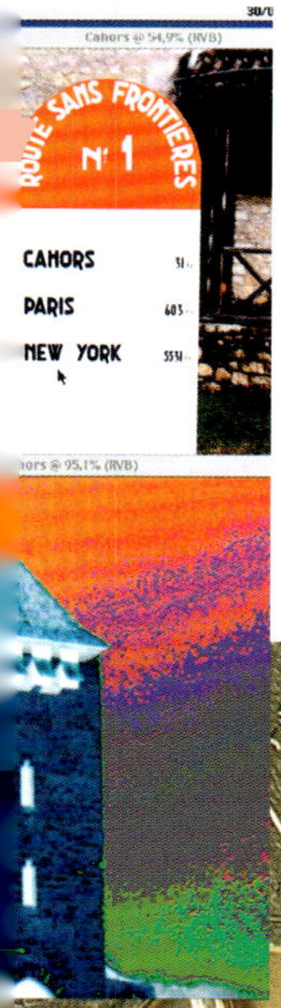
ROUTE SANS FRONTIÈRES
N°1
CAHORS
PARIS
NEW YORK

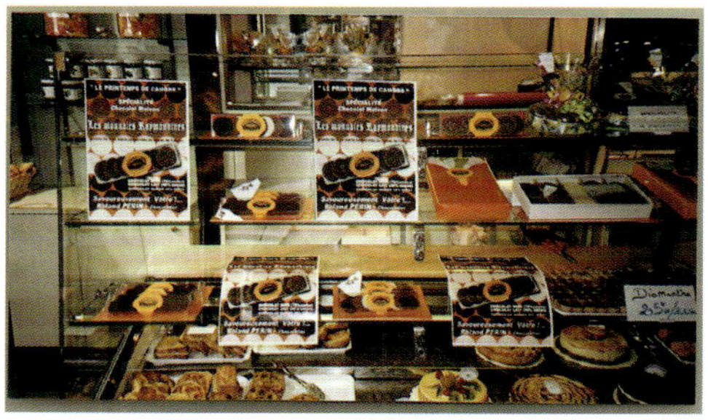

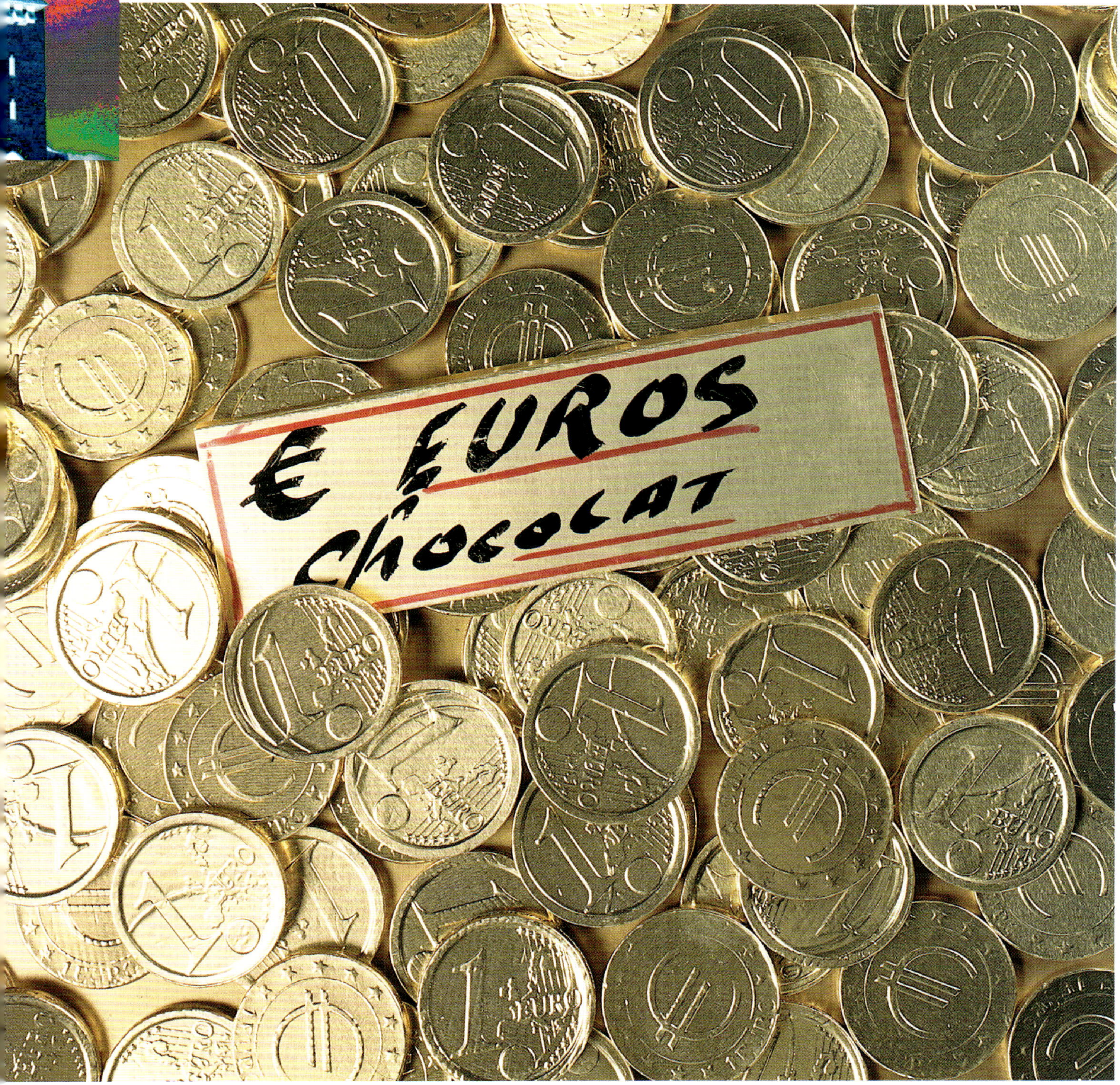
€ EUROS
CHOCOLAT

this page: *La Chimère d'Arezzo* [The Chimera of Arezzo], 1947. Collection Musée National d'art Moderne, Centre Pompidou, Paris.
facing page: Essay by Raymond Hains as published in *Photo Almanach Prisma*, no. 5, 1952. Collection Agnès de Gouvion Saint-Cyr, Paris.

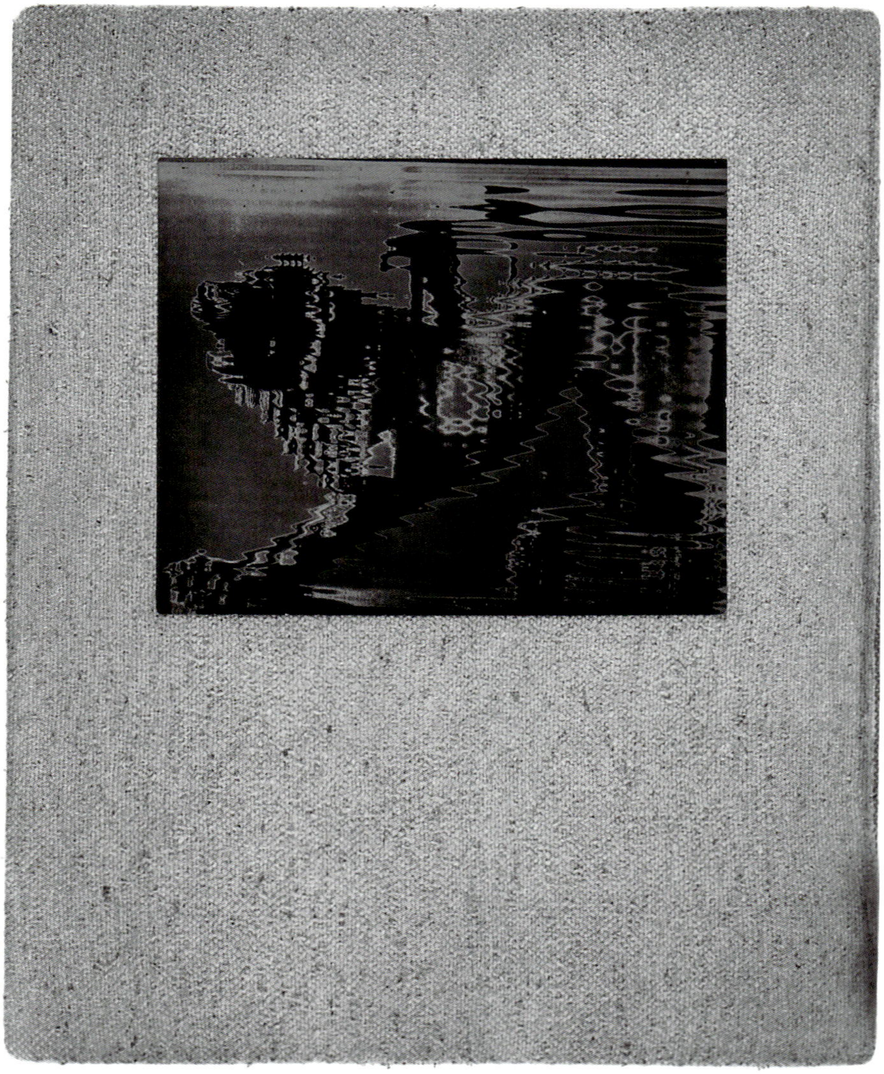

HYPNAGOGIC PHOTOGRAPHS

RIBBED GLASS : "There's some glass in the glazier's workshop that might be of use to you." It was Hains's father who led him to discover ribbed glass. Looking at the Chimera of Arezzo through a piece that he had picked up, Hains experienced "a kind of dizziness due to the letter's going from visible to invisible. I could have called this dizziness reading and nothingness (Hains's words, "la lettre et le néant," are a pun on Sartre's *L'être et le néant* [Being and Nothingness])." In his article "Graphic Art in Photography: When Photography Becomes an Object" (*Photo Almanach Prisma*, no. 5, 1952), Hains explained the new artistic procedures that ribbed glass made possible, wresting photography away from its mimetic tendency: "It is a matter of producing rather than reproducing." Hains said that he was looking for "unfamiliarity" from the repetitions, play of mirrors and prisms, overprinting and deformation. He was looking for a "graphic" style of photography that could be presented "as an object." Hypnagogic photography was "another reality." It was also known as abstract photography. (CS)

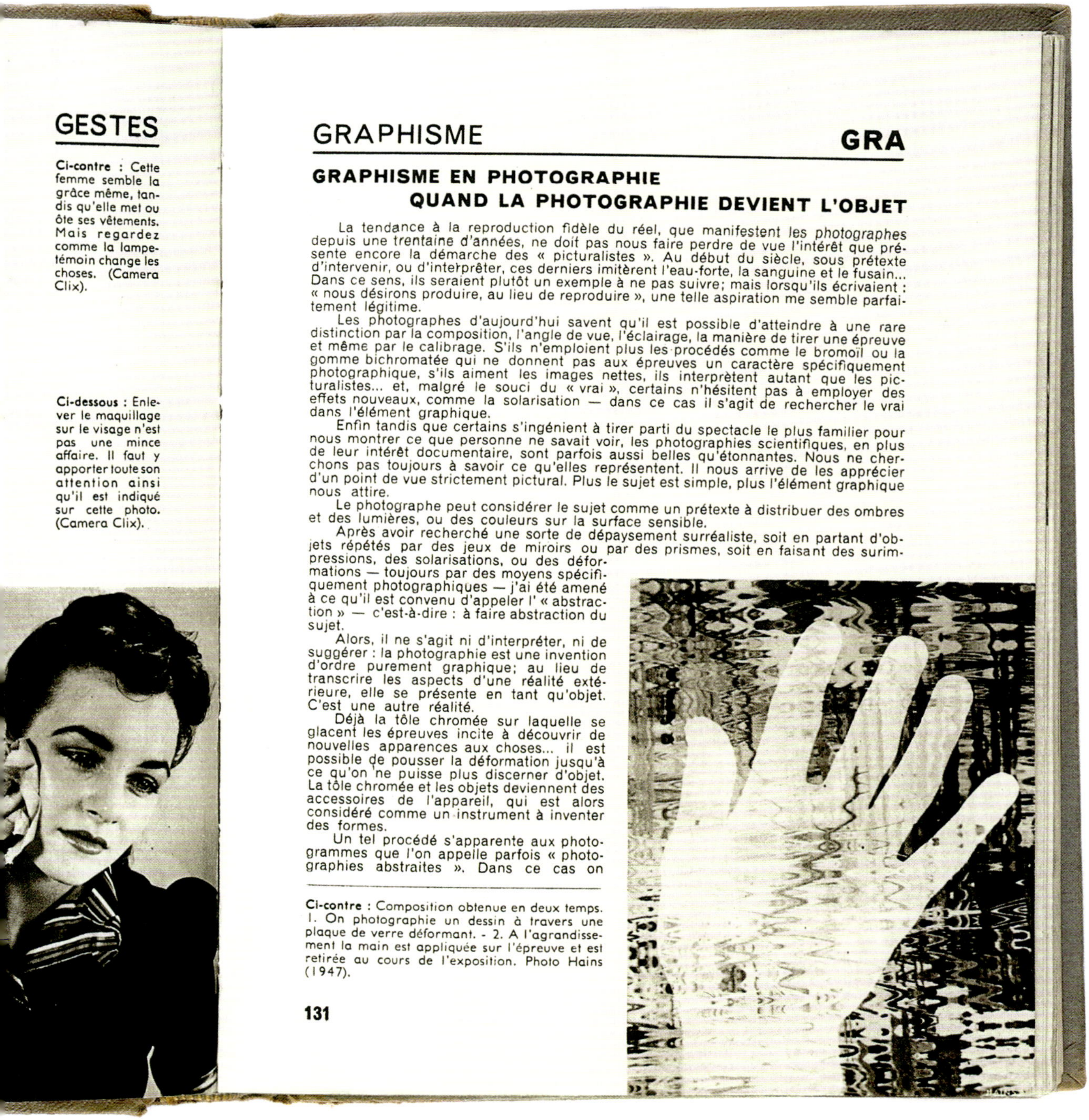

GESTES

Ci-contre : Cette femme semble la grâce même, tandis qu'elle met ou ôte ses vêtements. Mais regardez comme la lampe-témoin change les choses. (Camera Clix).

Ci-dessous : Enlever le maquillage sur le visage n'est pas une mince affaire. Il faut y apporter toute son attention ainsi qu'il est indiqué sur cette photo. (Camera Clix).

GRAPHISME **GRA**

GRAPHISME EN PHOTOGRAPHIE
QUAND LA PHOTOGRAPHIE DEVIENT L'OBJET

La tendance à la reproduction fidèle du réel, que manifestent les photographes depuis une trentaine d'années, ne doit pas nous faire perdre de vue l'intérêt que présente encore la démarche des « picturalistes ». Au début du siècle, sous prétexte d'intervenir, ou d'interpréter, ces derniers imitèrent l'eau-forte, la sanguine et le fusain... Dans ce sens, ils seraient plutôt un exemple à ne pas suivre; mais lorsqu'ils écrivaient : « nous désirons produire, au lieu de reproduire », une telle aspiration me semble parfaitement légitime.

Les photographes d'aujourd'hui savent qu'il est possible d'atteindre à une rare distinction par la composition, l'angle de vue, l'éclairage, la manière de tirer une épreuve et même par le calibrage. S'ils n'emploient plus les procédés comme le bromoil ou la gomme bichromatée qui ne donnent pas aux épreuves un caractère spécifiquement photographique, s'ils aiment les images nettes, ils interprètent autant que les picturalistes... et, malgré le souci du « vrai », certains n'hésitent pas à employer des effets nouveaux, comme la solarisation — dans ce cas il s'agit de rechercher le vrai dans l'élément graphique.

Enfin tandis que certains s'ingénient à tirer parti du spectacle le plus familier pour nous montrer ce que personne ne savait voir, les photographies scientifiques, en plus de leur intérêt documentaire, sont parfois aussi belles qu'étonnantes. Nous ne cherchons pas toujours à savoir ce qu'elles représentent. Il nous arrive de les apprécier d'un point de vue strictement pictural. Plus le sujet est simple, plus l'élément graphique nous attire.

Le photographe peut considérer le sujet comme un prétexte à distribuer des ombres et des lumières, ou des couleurs sur la surface sensible.

Après avoir recherché une sorte de dépaysement surréaliste, soit en partant d'objets répétés par des jeux de miroirs ou par des prismes, soit en faisant des surimpressions, des solarisations, ou des déformations — toujours par des moyens spécifiquement photographiques — j'ai été amené à ce qu'il est convenu d'appeler l' « abstraction » — c'est-à-dire : à faire abstraction du sujet.

Alors, il ne s'agit ni d'interpréter, ni de suggérer : la photographie est une invention d'ordre purement graphique; au lieu de transcrire les aspects d'une réalité extérieure, elle se présente en tant qu'objet. C'est une autre réalité.

Déjà la tôle chromée sur laquelle se glacent les épreuves incite à découvrir de nouvelles apparences aux choses... il est possible de pousser la déformation jusqu'à ce qu'on ne puisse plus discerner d'objet. La tôle chromée et les objets deviennent des accessoires de l'appareil, qui est alors considéré comme un instrument à inventer des formes.

Un tel procédé s'apparente aux photogrammes que l'on appelle parfois « photographies abstraites ». Dans ce cas on

Ci-contre : Composition obtenue en deux temps. 1. On photographie un dessin à travers une plaque de verre déformant. - 2. A l'agrandissement la main est appliquée sur l'épreuve et est retirée au cours de l'exposition. Photo Hains (1947).

131

GRAPHIC ART IN PHOTOGRAPHY: WHE

RAYMOND HAINS

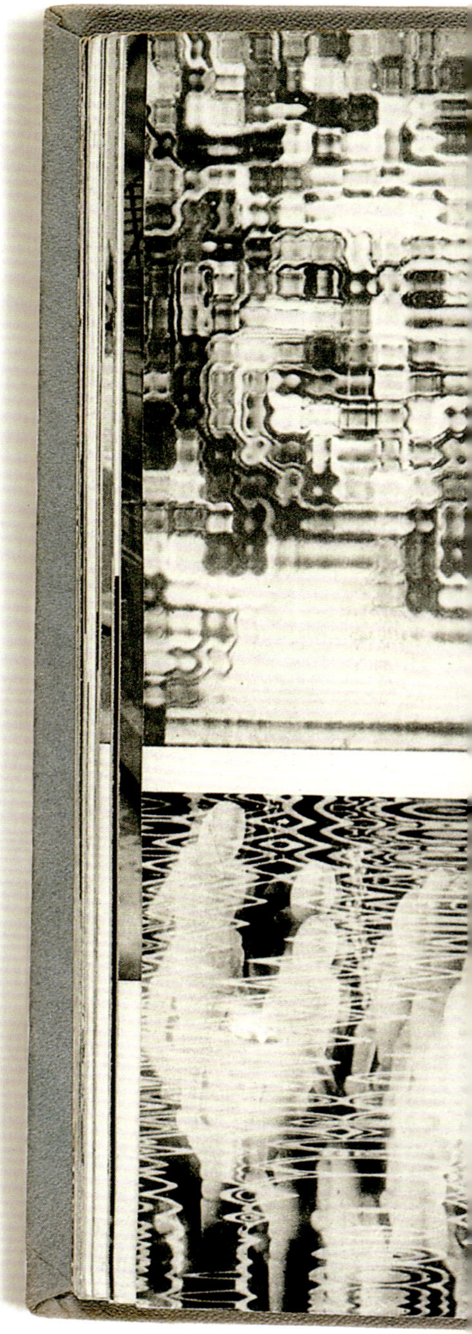

The tendency to reproduce faithfully the real, manifested by photographers over the last thirty years or so, should not lead us to overlook the continuing interest of the pictorialist approach. At the turn of the twentieth century, the pictorialists, claiming to intervene or interpret, imitated the techniques of etching, sanguine, and charcoal. In this sense, theirs is more an example to be avoided, but when they wrote that "we wish to produce, rather than reproduce," such an aspiration may seem perfectly legitimate.

Photographers today know that it is possible to achieve a rare degree of distinction by the way they organize the composition, angle, and lighting, and make and even calibrate the print. They no longer use such procedures as bromoil or gum bichromate, which do not give prints a specifically photographic character; if they have a preference for sharp images, they still interpret just as much as the pictorialists did, and, in spite of their concern with "truth," some of them readily make use of new effects, among them solarization. In such cases, it is a matter of looking to the graphic element for truthfulness. Although some strive to treat the most familiar sights in ways that reveal things to us that nobody has ever seen before, scientific photographs, in addition to their documentary interest, can be as beautiful as they are surprising. We do not always try to find out what they represent. Sometimes, we appreciate them from a strictly pictorial point of view. The simpler the subject, the more we are attracted by the graphic element.

The photographer can consider the subject as a pretext for distributing light and shade or colors on the sensitive surface. After seeking a kind of surrealist exoticism, either by repeating objects through the play of mirrors or prisms, or by using overprinting, solarization, and distortion—but always in ways that are specifically photographic—I came to what is conventionally known as abstraction—that is, abstracting the subject.

Here, it is no longer a matter of interpreting or suggesting—photography, in this case, is a purely graphic invention; instead of transcribing the appearances of an external reality, it is presented as an object in itself—as another reality.

For starters, the chrome sheet on which the prints acquire their gloss encourages us to see things in a new light. It is possible to take the distortion to the point that we can no longer make out the object. The chrome plate and the objects become accessories of the apparatus, which is now considered as an instrument for inventing forms.

HOTOGRAPHY BECOMES AN OBJECT

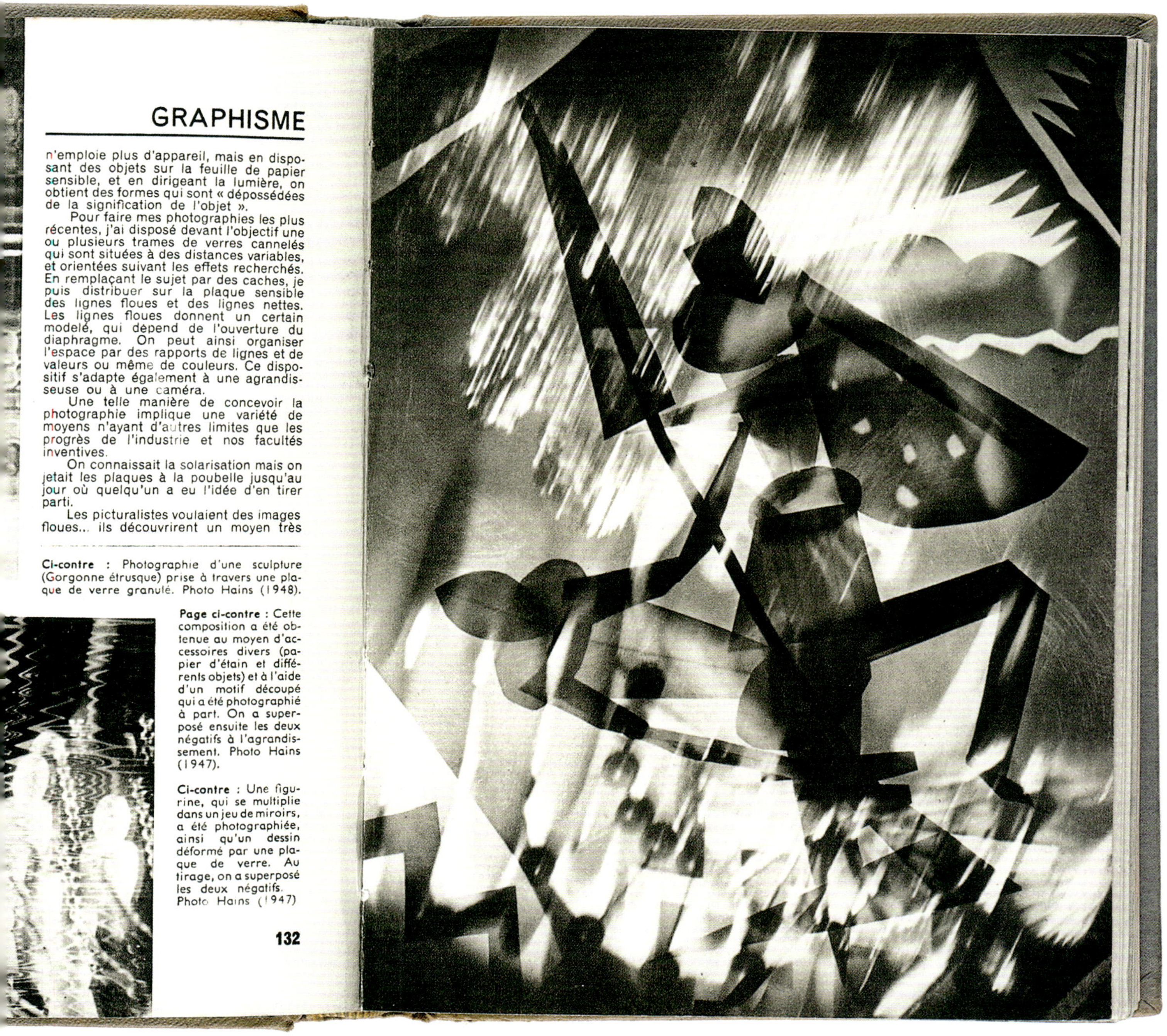

GRAPHISME

n'emploie plus d'appareil, mais en disposant des objets sur la feuille de papier sensible, et en dirigeant la lumière, on obtient des formes qui sont « dépossédées de la signification de l'objet ».

Pour faire mes photographies les plus récentes, j'ai disposé devant l'objectif une ou plusieurs trames de verres cannelés qui sont situées à des distances variables, et orientées suivant les effets recherchés. En remplaçant le sujet par des caches, je puis distribuer sur la plaque sensible des lignes floues et des lignes nettes. Les lignes floues donnent un certain modelé, qui dépend de l'ouverture du diaphragme. On peut ainsi organiser l'espace par des rapports de lignes et de valeurs ou même de couleurs. Ce dispositif s'adapte également à une agrandisseuse ou à une caméra.

Une telle manière de concevoir la photographie implique une variété de moyens n'ayant d'autres limites que les progrès de l'industrie et nos facultés inventives.

On connaissait la solarisation mais on jetait les plaques à la poubelle jusqu'au jour où quelqu'un a eu l'idée d'en tirer parti.

Les picturalistes voulaient des images floues... ils découvrirent un moyen très

Ci-contre : Photographie d'une sculpture (Gorgonne étrusque) prise à travers une plaque de verre granulé. Photo Hains (1948).

Page ci-contre : Cette composition a été obtenue au moyen d'accessoires divers (papier d'étain et différents objets) et à l'aide d'un motif découpé qui a été photographié à part. On a superposé ensuite les deux négatifs à l'agrandissement. Photo Hains (1947).

Ci-contre : Une figurine, qui se multiplie dans un jeu de miroirs, a été photographiée, ainsi qu'un dessin déformé par une plaque de verre. Au tirage, on a superposé les deux négatifs. Photo Hains (1947)

132

HYPNAGOGIC : The adjective "hypnagogic" comes from nineteenth-century mental pathology. The French "hypnagogique" is not featured in the authoritative *Grand Robert* dictionary. Emile Littré includes it in his *Dictionnaire de médecine* (1855), where he gives the Greek etymology as *hypnos*, sleep, and *agogos*, which induces. The example given is hallucination or hypnagogic delirium, which can occur when one is half awake, half asleep—about to drop off. The exhibition "Photographies hypnagogiques, Raymond Hains" was held at Galerie Colette Allendy (vernissage, Wednesday, June 30, 1948). According to an anonymous plan of the exhibition, twenty photographs dating from 1947 and 1948 were exhibited. The term "hypnagoscope" comes from the Greek *hypnos*, sleep, and *agogos*, something that leads to, and *skopein*, to observe. This is an instrument conceived by Raymond Hains, designed to allow the observation of the fragmentation of images and letters, or the creation of images, thanks to the interposition of ribbed glass between the lens and the camera. The ribbed-glass spectacles are a portable version of this. The plans were drawn by Jacques Villeglé, but the hypnagoscope was never made. In his two drawings of the hypnagoscope, Villeglé gave five examples of deformation. The name of Camille Bryen, the name Hains partially deformed, and tests on *Hépérile*. (CS)

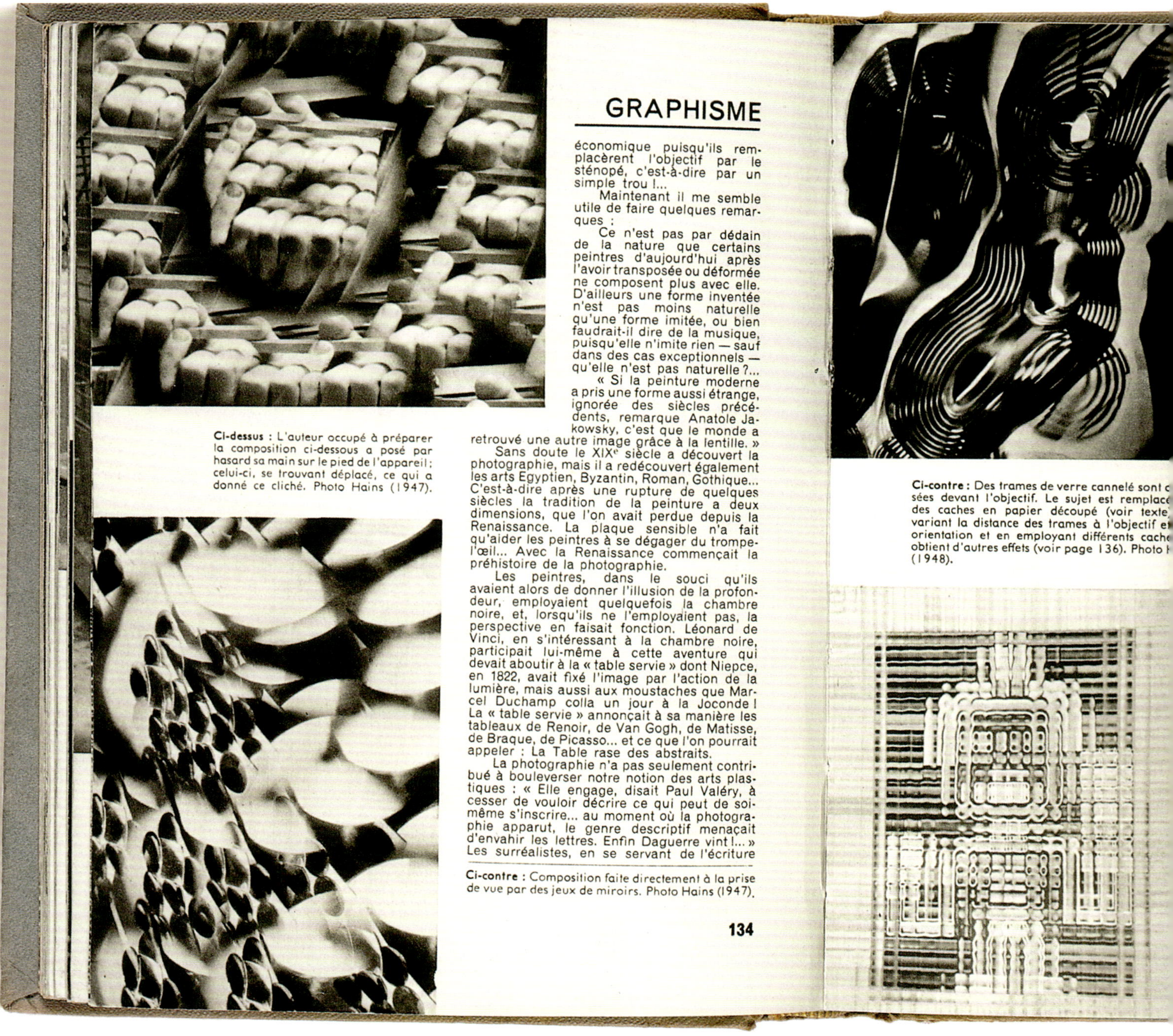

GRAPHISME

économique puisqu'ils remplacèrent l'objectif par le sténopé, c'est-à-dire par un simple trou !...

Maintenant il me semble utile de faire quelques remarques :

Ce n'est pas par dédain de la nature que certains peintres d'aujourd'hui après l'avoir transposée ou déformée ne composent plus avec elle. D'ailleurs une forme inventée n'est pas moins naturelle qu'une forme imitée, ou bien faudrait-il dire de la musique, puisqu'elle n'imite rien — sauf dans des cas exceptionnels — qu'elle n'est pas naturelle ?...

« Si la peinture moderne a pris une forme aussi étrange, ignorée des siècles précédents, remarque Anatole Jakowsky, c'est que le monde a retrouvé une autre image grâce à la lentille. »

Sans doute le XIXe siècle a découvert la photographie, mais il a redécouvert également les arts Egyptien, Byzantin, Roman, Gothique... C'est-à-dire après une rupture de quelques siècles la tradition de la peinture a deux dimensions, que l'on avait perdue depuis la Renaissance. La plaque sensible n'a fait qu'aider les peintres à se dégager du trompe-l'œil... Avec la Renaissance commençait la préhistoire de la photographie.

Les peintres, dans le souci qu'ils avaient alors de donner l'illusion de la profondeur, employaient quelquefois la chambre noire, et, lorsqu'ils ne l'employaient pas, la perspective en faisait fonction. Léonard de Vinci, en s'intéressant à la chambre noire, participait lui-même à cette aventure qui devait aboutir à la « table servie » dont Niepce, en 1822, avait fixé l'image par l'action de la lumière, mais aussi aux moustaches que Marcel Duchamp colla un jour à la Joconde ! La « table servie » annonçait à sa manière les tableaux de Renoir, de Van Gogh, de Matisse, de Braque, de Picasso... et ce que l'on pourrait appeler : La Table rase des abstraits.

La photographie n'a pas seulement contribué à bouleverser notre notion des arts plastiques : « Elle engage, disait Paul Valéry, à cesser de vouloir décrire ce qui peut de soi-même s'inscrire... au moment où la photographie apparut, le genre descriptif menaçait d'envahir les lettres. Enfin Daguerre vint !... » Les surréalistes, en se servant de l'écriture

Ci-dessus : L'auteur occupé à préparer la composition ci-dessous a posé par hasard sa main sur le pied de l'appareil ; celui-ci, se trouvant déplacé, ce qui a donné ce cliché. Photo Hains (1947).

Ci-contre : Composition faite directement à la prise de vue par des jeux de miroirs. Photo Hains (1947).

Ci-contre : Des trames de verre cannelé sont
sées devant l'objectif. Le sujet est remplac
des caches en papier découpé (voir texte
variant la distance des trames à l'objectif e
orientation et en employant différents cach
obtient d'autres effets (voir page 136). Photo
(1948).

134

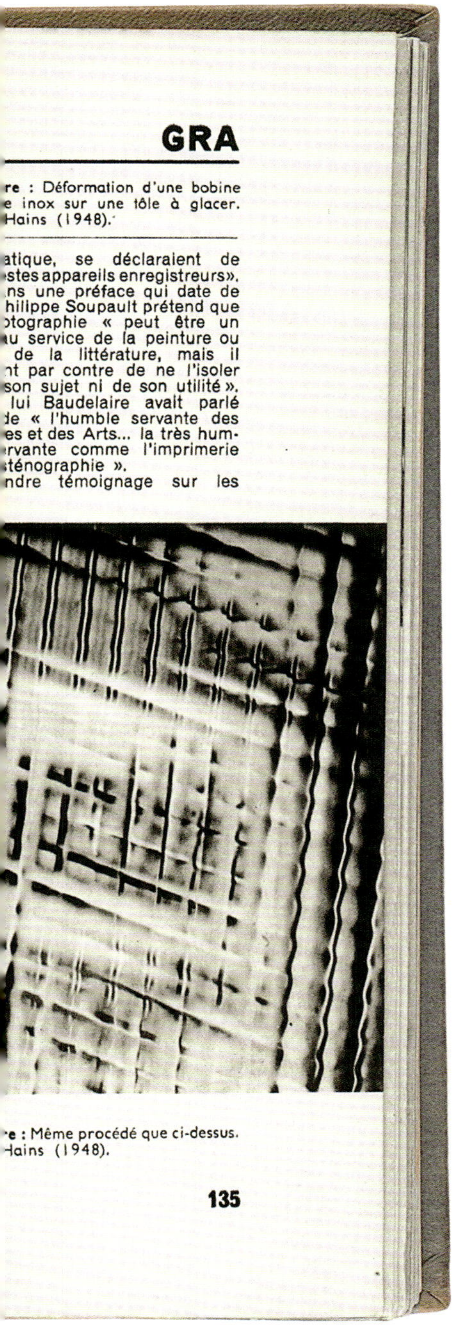

GRA

re : Déformation d'une bobine
e inox sur une tôle à glacer.
Hains (1948).

atique, se déclaraient de
stes appareils enregistreurs».
ns une préface qui date de
hilippe Soupault prétend que
otographie « peut être un
u service de la peinture ou
de la littérature, mais il
nt par contre de ne l'isoler
son sujet ni de son utilité ».
lui Baudelaire avait parlé
de « l'humble servante des
es et des Arts... la très hum-
rvante comme l'imprimerie
sténographie ».
ndre témoignage sur les

re : Même procédé que ci-dessus.
Hains (1948).

135

39 Essay by Raymond Hains as published in *Photo Almanach*, no. 5, 1952. Collection Agnès de Gouvion Saint-Cyr, Paris.

Such a procedure is akin to that of photograms, which are sometimes called abstract photographs. Here, the camera no longer plays a role; instead, objects are laid out on sheets of sensitive paper so that, by directing the light, one obtains forms that are "dispossessed of the signification of the object."

To make my recent photographs, I laid one or several sheets of ribbed glass in front of the lens, placing them at varying distances and directing them in accordance with the desired effect. By replacing the subject with masks/filters, I can distribute blurred and clear lines on the photosensitive plate. The blurred lines afford a certain degree of modeling; this depends on the aperture of the diaphragm. One can, therefore, organize the space in terms of the relations between lines and values, or even colors. This apparatus can also be fitted onto an enlarger or a movie camera.

This way of conceiving of photography suggests a variety of resources, whose only limits are those of industrial progress and our own inventive faculties.

We knew about solarization, but we used to throw away the plates, until someone had the idea of putting them to good use.

The pictorialists wanted hazy images. They discovered a very economical method: They replaced the lens with a pinhole—with a simple hole! It may be useful now to make a few observations.

It is not out of disdain for nature that some of today's painters, after transposing and distorting nature, no longer make use of her. In fact, an invented form is not less natural than an imitated one. Otherwise, would we not have to say that music, which, apart from the odd exception, imitates nothing, is not natural?

"If modern painting took such a strange form, one unknown in previous centuries," notes Anatole Janowsky, "it was because, thanks to the lens, the world had acquired a new image."

It is true that the nineteenth century discovered photography, but it also rediscovered Egyptian, Byzantine, Romanesque, and Gothic art. And it did so after a break of several centuries with the tradition of two-dimensional painting, which had been lost since the Renaissance. The photosensitive plate simply helped painters get away from the trompe l'oeil. The Renaissance marked the beginning of the prehistory of photography.

In their efforts to create the illusion of depth, painters in those days sometimes made use of the camera obscura, and, when they did not, perspective played the

this page: Essay by Raymond Hains as published in *Photo Almanach Prisma*, no. 5, 1952. Collection Agnès de Gouvion Saint-Cyr, Paris.
facing page, top: *Mon encyclopédie Clartés* [My own "clarity" encyclopedia], 2001, for website visible on www.centre.pompidou.fr, designed for Raymond Hains by Opixido, Paris.
Lit-clos breton [Breton cupboard bed], 1663. Collection Musée de Bretagne, Rennes.
facing page, right, and next page: Untitled, c. 1946. Collection Musée National d'art Moderne, Centre Pompidou, Paris.

I myself am a kind of Web. I am working on a spider's web, or a piece of Brittany lace. | Raymond Hains, interview with Christine Macel, 2000.

same role. Leonardo da Vinci, who also took an interest in the camera obscura, was one participant in this adventure that culminated in "la table service," whose image Niepce fixed using the action of light, but also in the mustache that Marcel Duchamp one day affixed to the Mona Lisa! The "laid table" was, in its way, a harbinger of the paintings of Renoir, van Gogh, Matisse, Braque, and Picasso, and of what we could call the tabula rasa of the abstracts.

Photography did more than help revolutionize our idea of the visual arts. As Paul Valéry said, "It incites us to stop trying to describe that which is able to inscribe itself. When photography made its appearance, the descriptive genre was threatening to overwhelm the arts. And then along came Daguerre!" In their use of automatic writing, the surrealists presented themselves as "modest recording machines."

In a preface that dates from 1931, Philippe Soupault argues that photography "can be a motif in the service of painting or even of literature, but it is important not to isolate it either from its subject or from its use." Before him, Baudelaire, too, had spoken of the "humble servant of the Sciences and the Arts ... the very humble servant such as printing and stenography."

The fact of bearing witness to the most diverse aspects of a universe, one that we are constantly rediscovering—and that we say is "expanding"—does not prevent photographers from understanding the word *realism* in both senses. They can strive to introduce into life what Apollinaire called new realities. In conjunction with older techniques like painting or sculpture, photography also offers unexpected resources.

Radio technicians and musicians are also trying to compose "mechanical" music. Thus, their apparatus, which were originally designed to record images and sounds, are now being used to discover new images and sounds.

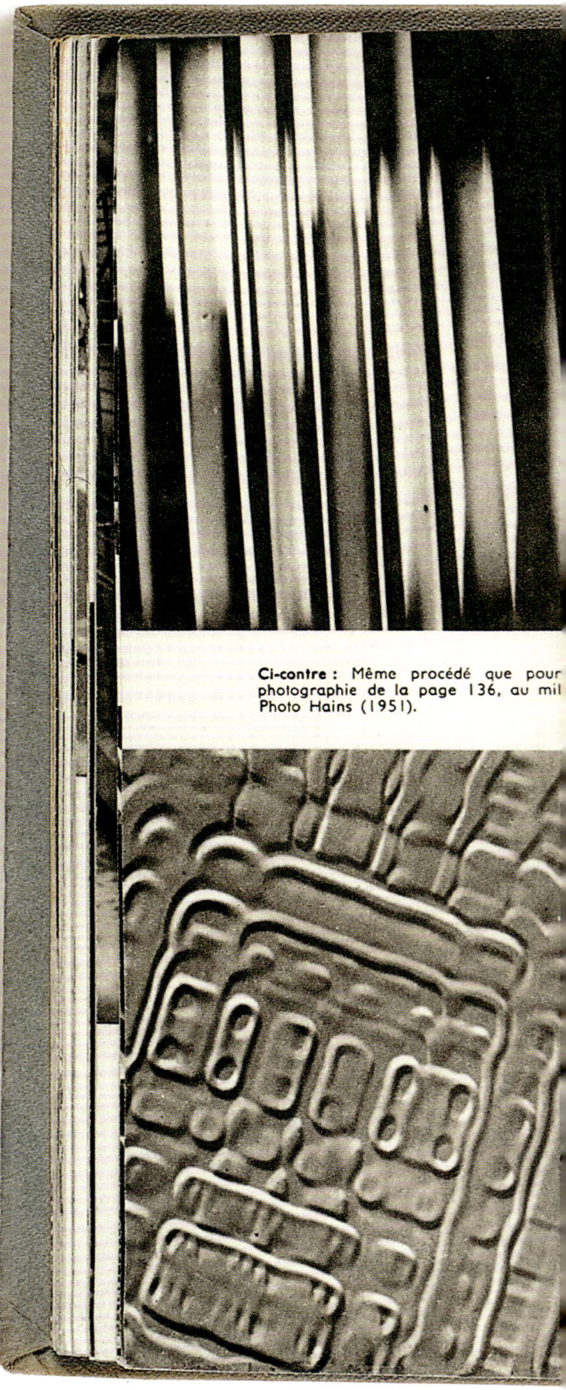

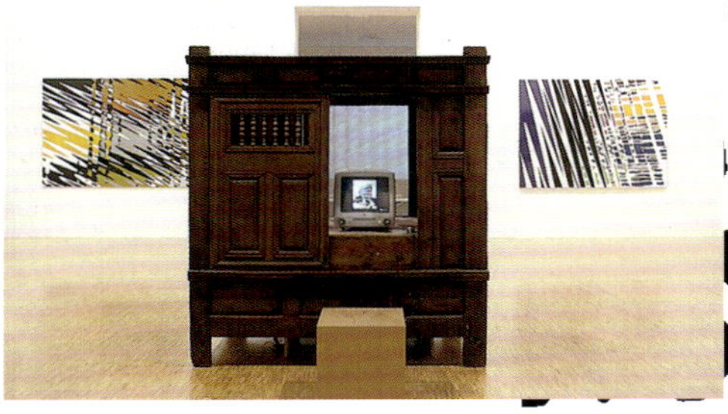

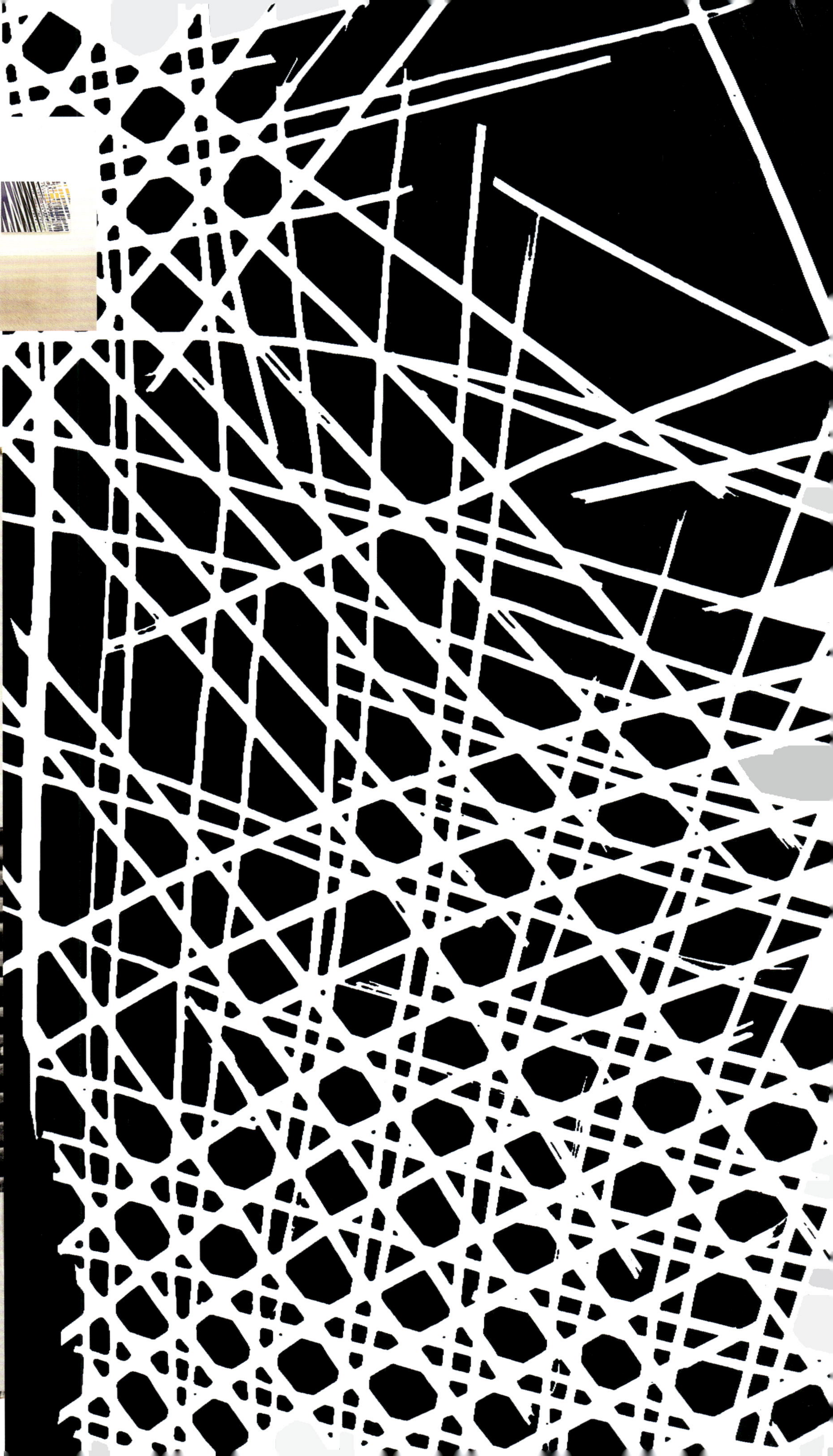

GRAPHISME

Même procédé que pour la photographie
: 136, au milieu. Photo Hains (1949).

es plus variés d'un univers, que nous
is de découvrir — et que l'on dit « en
» — n'empêche pas les photogra-
itendre le mot réalisme dans deux
peuvent s'efforcer d'introduire dans
qu'Apollinaire appelait des réalités
. En s'ajoutant à des techniques plus
s comme la peinture ou la sculpture,
raphie ne manque pas d'offrir des
s imprévues.
echniciens de la radio et des musi-
efforcent aussi de composer une
« mécanisée ». Ainsi les appareils,
d'abord à enregistrer les images et
servent aujourd'hui à découvrir
images et d'autres sons.

Raymond HAINS.

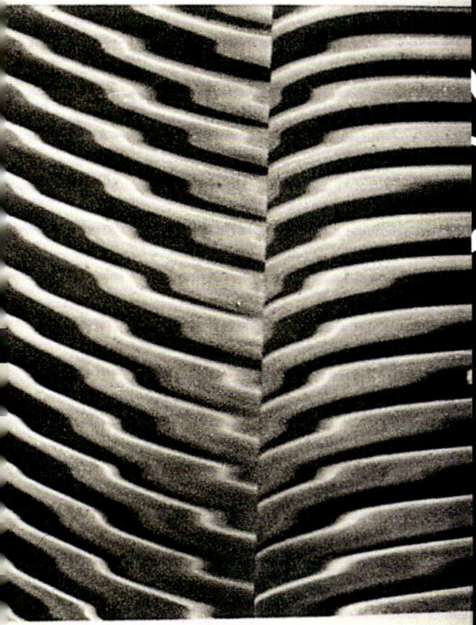

: Superposition au tirage d'un négatif et
f légèrement décalés d'une partie de la
a page 135, en bas. Photo Hains (1950).

ntre : Images. Treizième prix Enfants
A.P. 4. Rollei. F : 8, Eclatron. Photo
rgevin.

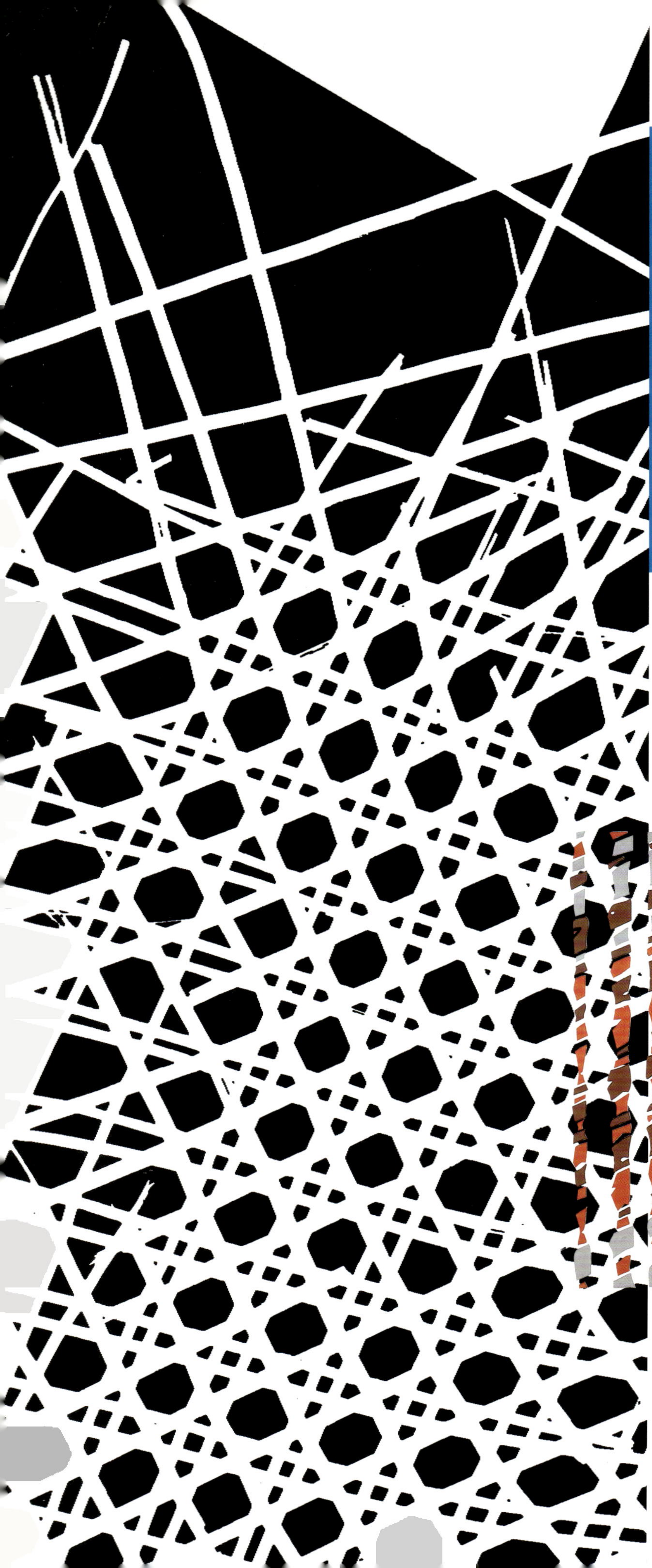

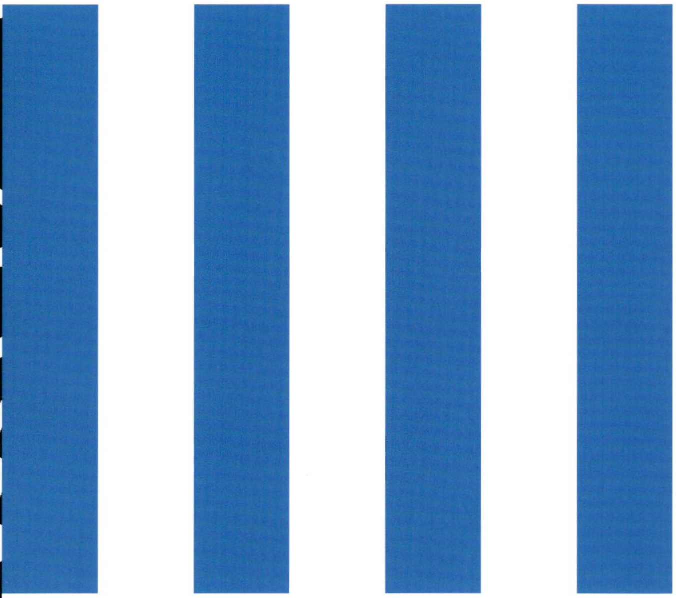

PÉNÉLOPE

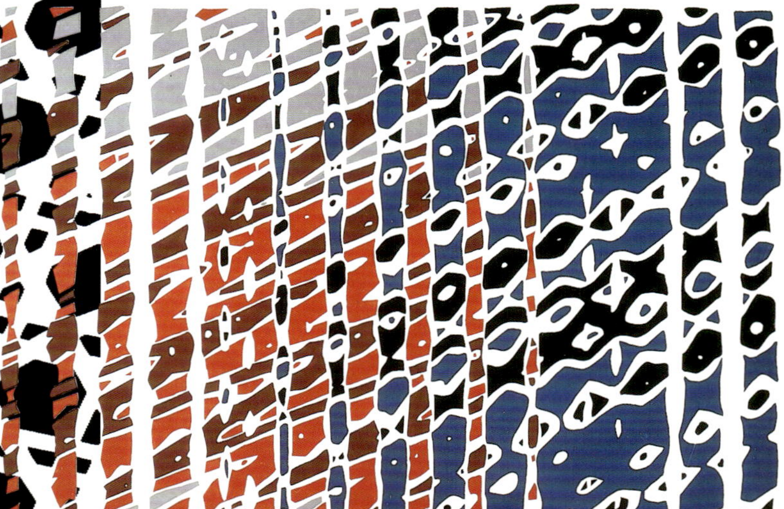

43 facing page, right, and this page: *Pénélope*, with Jacques Villeglé, 1954/1981. Shot 1950–1954, edited by Jean-Michel Bouhours, 1981. Collection Musée National d'art Moderne, Centre Pompidou, Paris.

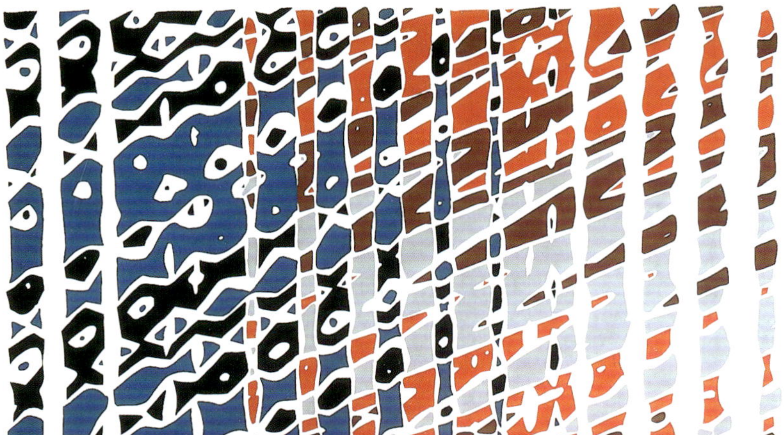

 this page, and facing page, left: *Pénélope*, with Jacques Villeglé, 1954/1981. Shot 1950–1954, edited by Jean-Michel Bouhours, 1981. Collection Musée National d'art Moderne, Centre Pompidou, Paris. facing page, right: Untitled, c. 1950–54. Preparatory drawing for *Pénélope*. Collection Musée National d'art Moderne, Centre Pompidou, Paris.

PÉNÉLOPE : *Pénélope* is the title of an abstract film that was deformed and fragmented by the lines of the ribbed lenses. It was made by Hains and Villeglé between 1950 and 1954 and edited only in 1981. Pierre Schaeffer wrote a soundtrack for a particular part of it, which became the *Étude aux allures*. But, here, we need to consider the implications of the name. In the *Odyssey*, Homer makes Penelope an embodiment of patience. As a result of her ploy of unraveling by night the part of the tapestry that she has just woven by day, her endless handiwork provokes the impatience of the suitors seeking to usurp Odysseus's position. The work of Penelope, a Penelope who "weaves and unweaves (herself)," could also be a way of being and doing things and a strategy for the artist. The parallel between Penelope and *Margot La Ravaudeuse*, the author of which, Fougeret de Montbron, considered himself a "citizen of the world," is particularly significant here. If, as is possible, we were to consider Hains in relation to the tradition of oral literature, we might then ask if he himself is not "mending." We need only bear in mind the *rhapsode*, the speaker who went from one Greek city to another speaking anthologies of poetry. Etymologically, the *rhapsode* was the person who weaved and unweaved, sewing together fragments of stories and songs, including those of the *Iliad* and *Odyssey*. (CS)

ÉTUDE AUX ALLURES : Between 1950 and 1954, Hains made a number of films, including *Pénélope*, *Loi du 29 juillet 1881*, and *Défense d'afficher*. Jacques Villeglé took a hand in preparing the fragmented letters that Hains began photographing through a ribbed glass lens in 1947 and in the film *Pénélope*. A first film was shown in 1960 by the Centre de Recherche Image at the RTF (French Radio and Television corporation) and distributed under the name *Étude aux allures*, the name of the music-concrête piece written by Pierre Schaeffer as a soundtrack for this short 16mm extract. In a letter, Schaeffer presents this *Étude* as a "fortuitous encounter between two experiments: one acoustic, the other visual, these 'studies' encountering the hazards of Hains's piece, playing on the ribbed lenses in order to create a mobile, colorful graphic effect. Villeglé named the full-length version of the film, which has no soundtrack, *Pénélope*, because of its southern colors and its incompleteness, the result of Hains's way of working. It was shown thirty years later, in 1981, by Jean-Michel Bouhours at the Pompidou Center. (CS)

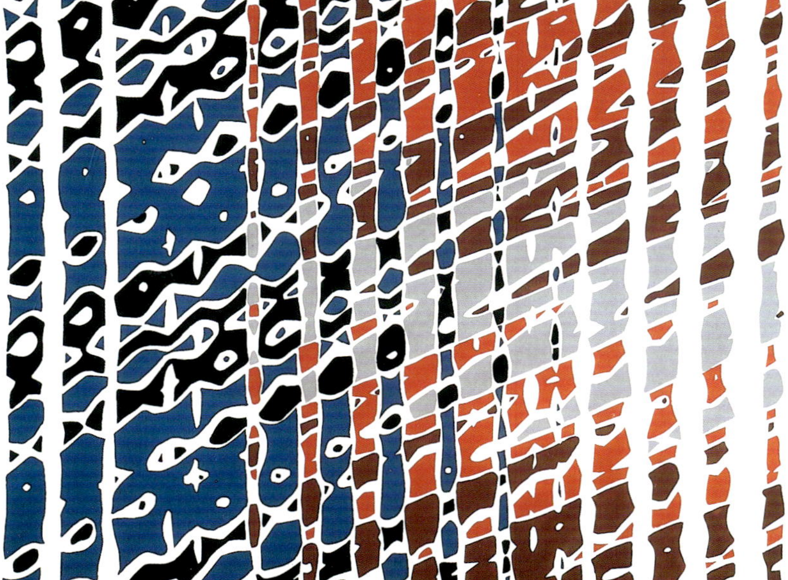

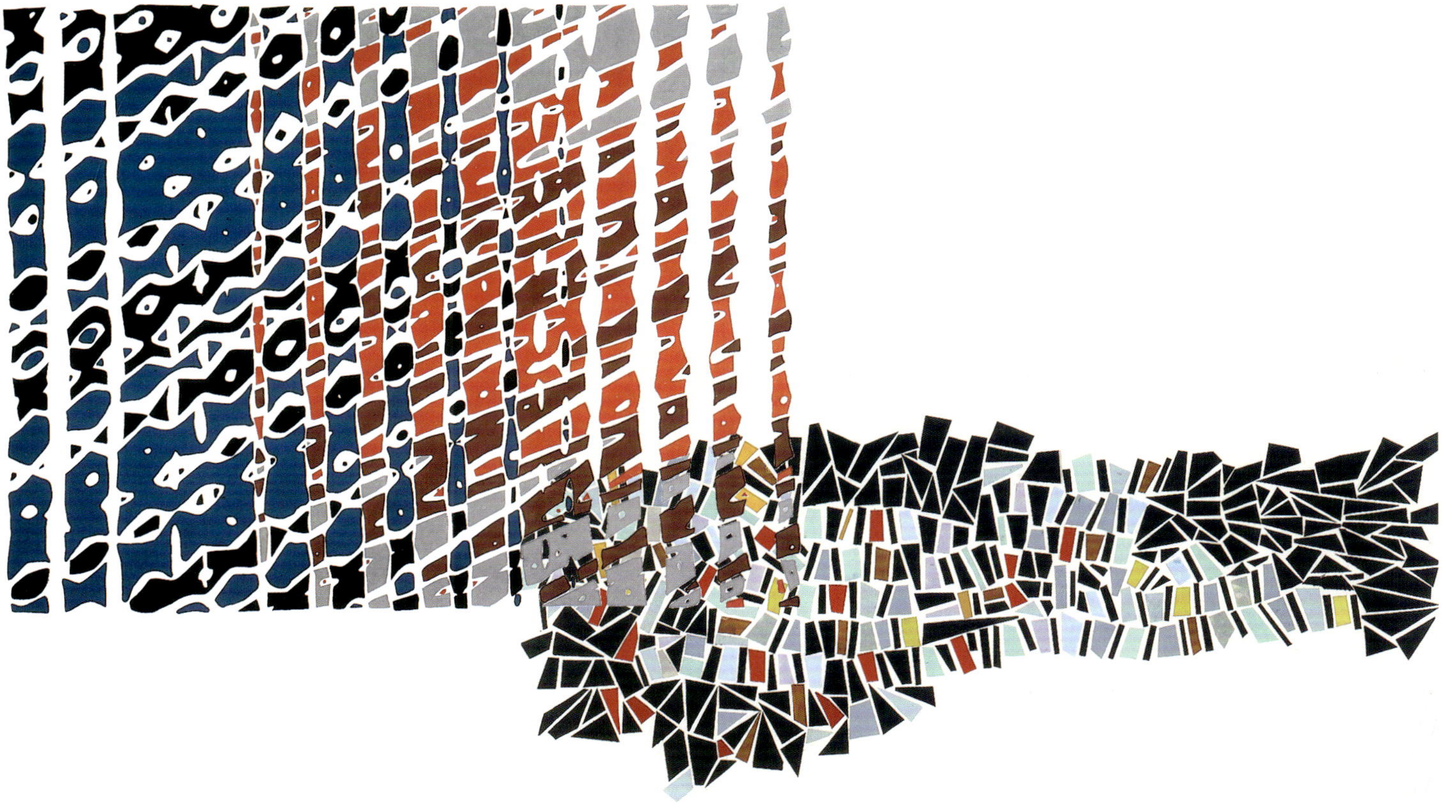

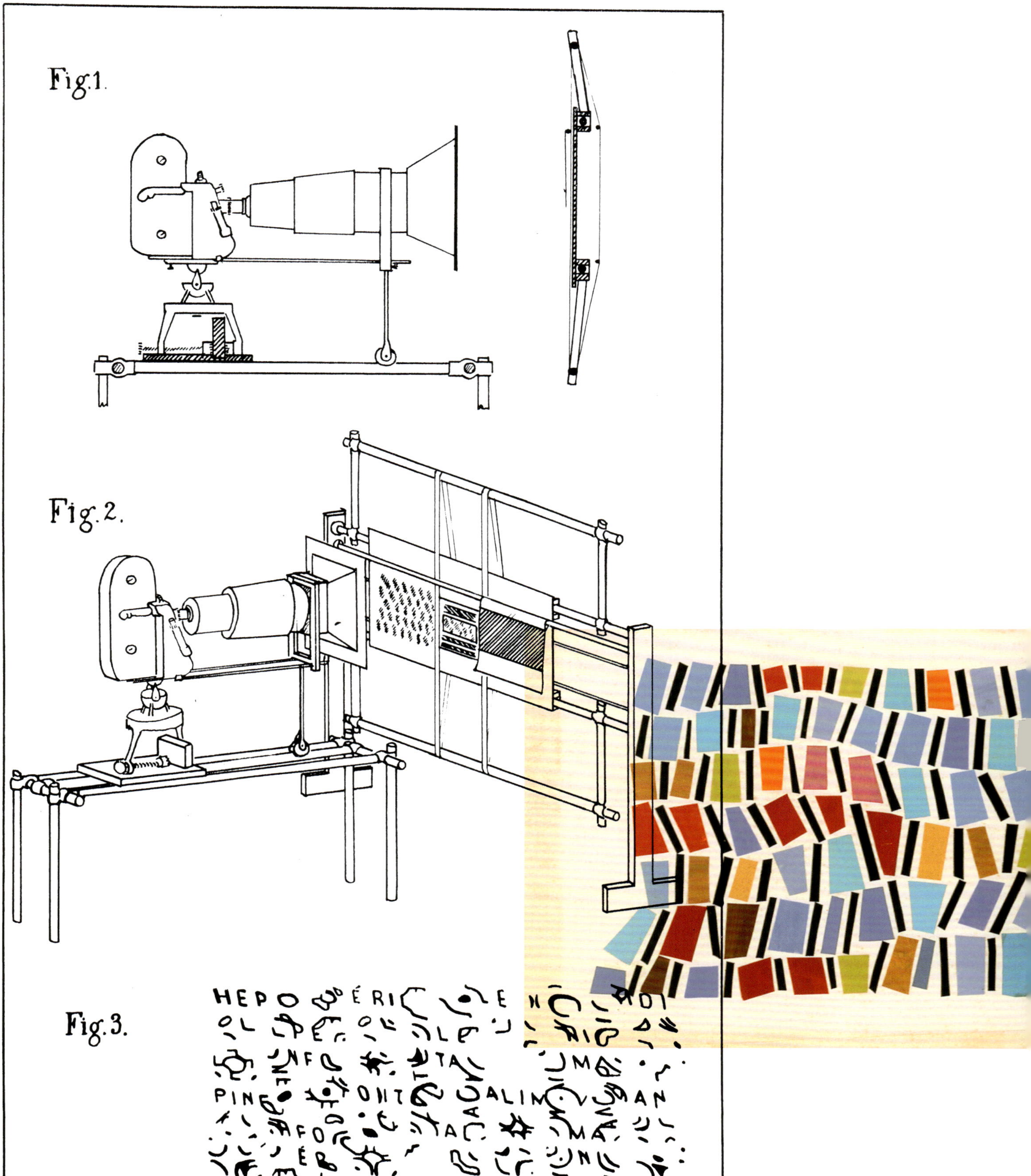
Fig.1.
Fig.2.
Fig.3.

 facing page: Jacques Villeglé, Untitled *(L'Hypnagogoscope)* [Hypnagogoscope], 1952. Collection the artist.
this page: Untitled, c. 1950/1954. Preparatory drawing for *Pénélope*. Collection Musée National d'art Moderne, Centre Pompidou, Paris.

JACQUES VILLEGLÉ : Hains and Villeglé met at the Beaux-Arts school, in Rennes, in 1945. In January 1947, Villeglé enrolled at the architecture school in Nantes, where Hains then went to visit him. In his book *Urbi & Orbi*, Villeglé has some fine pages on the spirit of those years and on his friendship with Hains. "We used to walk round the town, with the transporter bridge ahead of us, when the shadowless winter light transformed the sheds along the banks of the Loire into an unconventional architecture by erasing the details of their disorderliness. The noise of electric saws from the boatyards, the movement of the cranes in the harbor, presented us with a visual, auditory, and moving whole that, without need of retouching, formed a complete spectacle that we thought at first we should film and record." In 1949, Hains and Villeglé embarked on the adventure of the torn posters and the *Lacéré anonyme* (Villeglé). Some of the works from those early years were cosigned: the posters *Ach Alma Manetro* (February 1949), *M* (1949), two posters for the exhibition "La France déchirée" at Galerie J in 1961, *Et quand vous dites Soviétique Patrie est notre plus juste histoire de lard* (1950), and *L'Humanité c'est la vérité* (1957), and the film *Pénélope* (1950–54). Villeglé has been Hains's faithful friend ever since those early student days—a lifelong companion. (CS)

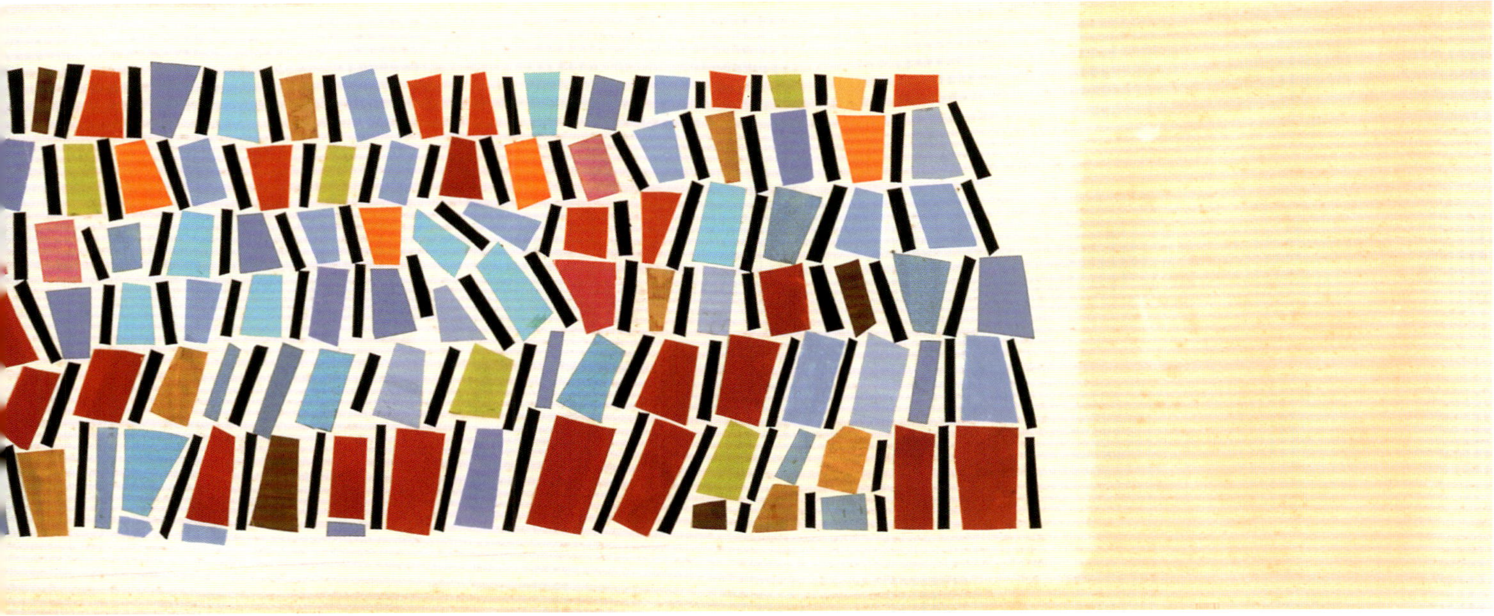

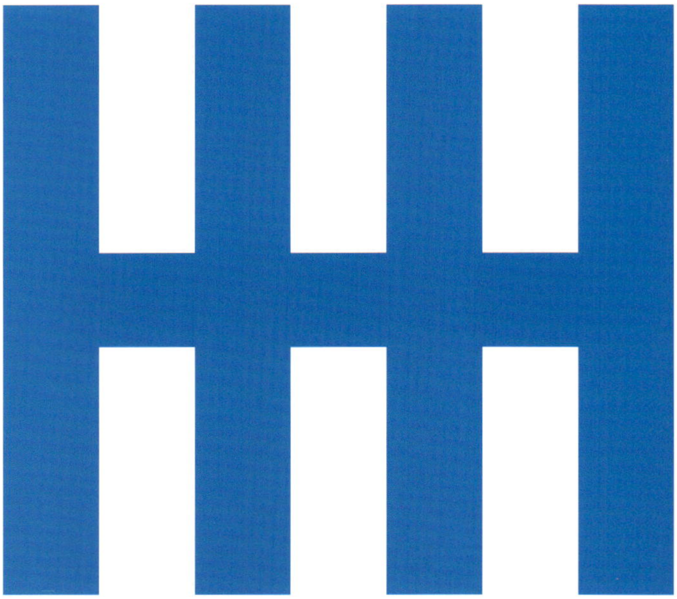

LES VÉRITÉS DE LA PALISSE

LA PALISSE : In 1959, when he was doing his wordplay on boardings/fences, Hains came across a shop window displaying the new *Encyclopédie Clartés*, open to a page showing a cream tart called the "Entremets de La Palissade" (Dessert of La Palissade). Then, at a dinner, he met Genevieve de Chabannes la Palice, a descendent of La Palice. In 1963, when he made his first trip to Lapalisse, in the Allier (department of central France), he found that the local specialty was a sweet called "Vérités de la Palisse" (Truisms). These he later photographed (1988). In 1975, Hains read Michel Pêcheux's book *Les vérités de La Palice*, published by François Maspero. The experience was as invigorating as he might have hoped. The author set out to "give Monsieur de la Palice the position he deserved as the patron saint of semanticists." He recalled La Palice's famous song: "On Friday he died/the last day he was alive/On Saturday had he gone/His life had been more long." (CS)

My raw material is every bit as much the name of an art dealer as it is the paper of a poster. Things have surprising links with one another through their names. | Raymond Hains interview with Aude Bodet, March 25, 1985.

 left: *Palissade à De Feugas* [Billboard/fence in De Feugas], 1959. Collection Musée de l'Objet, Blois.
L'Entremets de La Palissade [La Palissade dessert], 1964. Collection the artist.

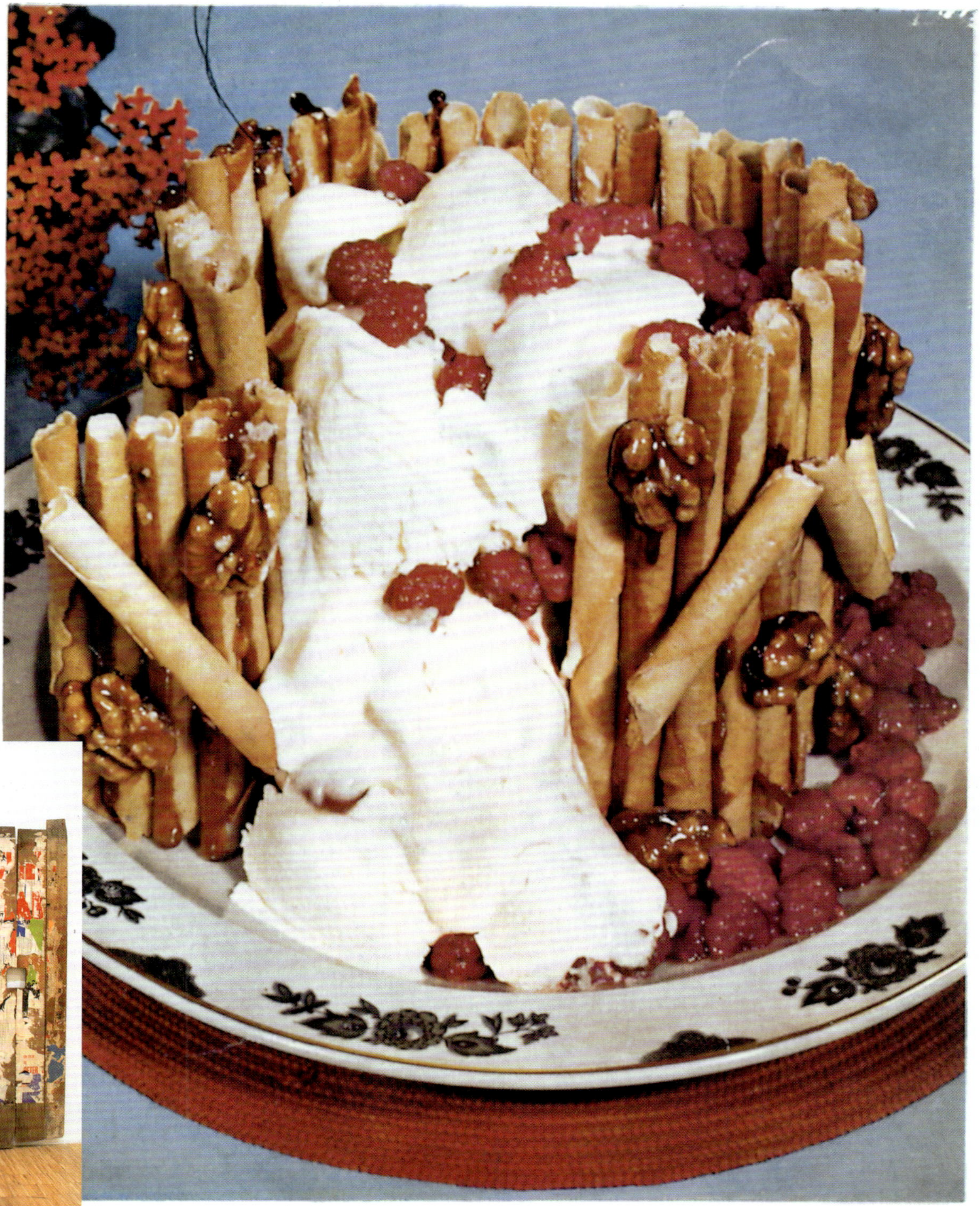

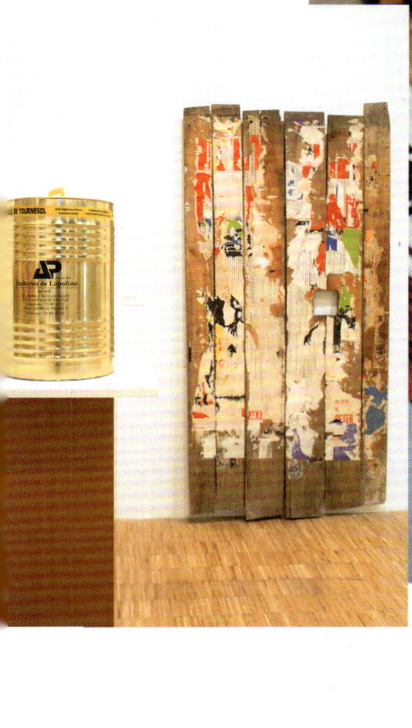

"La palissade"

(Photo Karl Egli)

5278

top and bottom: *Les Vérités de La Palisse* [Truisms of La Palisse], 1987. Collection FRAC Champagne-Ardenne, Reims.
facing page: *La foire aux skis* [Ski fair], 1988. Collection National Contemporary Art Fund, Ministry of Culture and Communication, Paris.

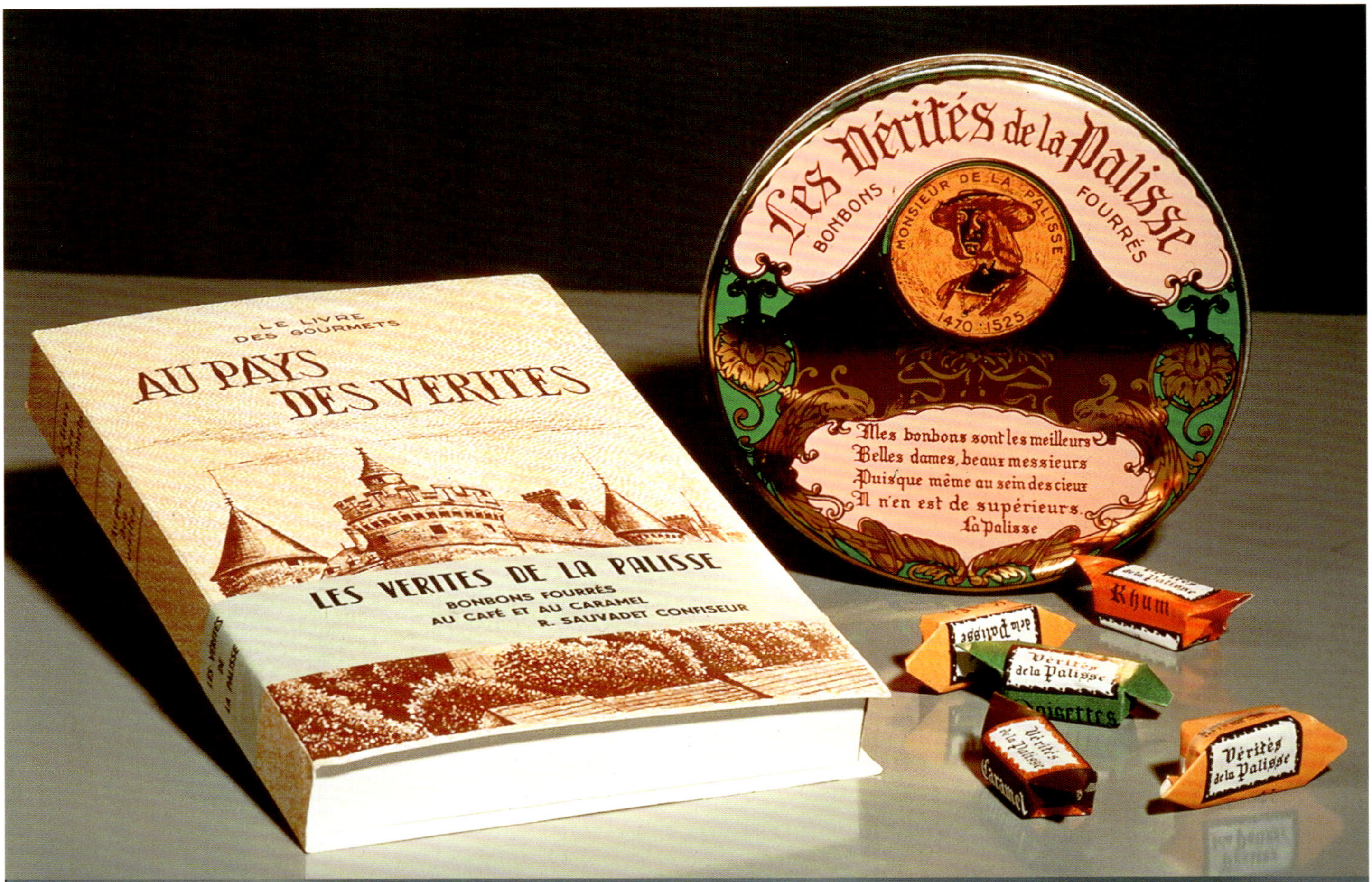

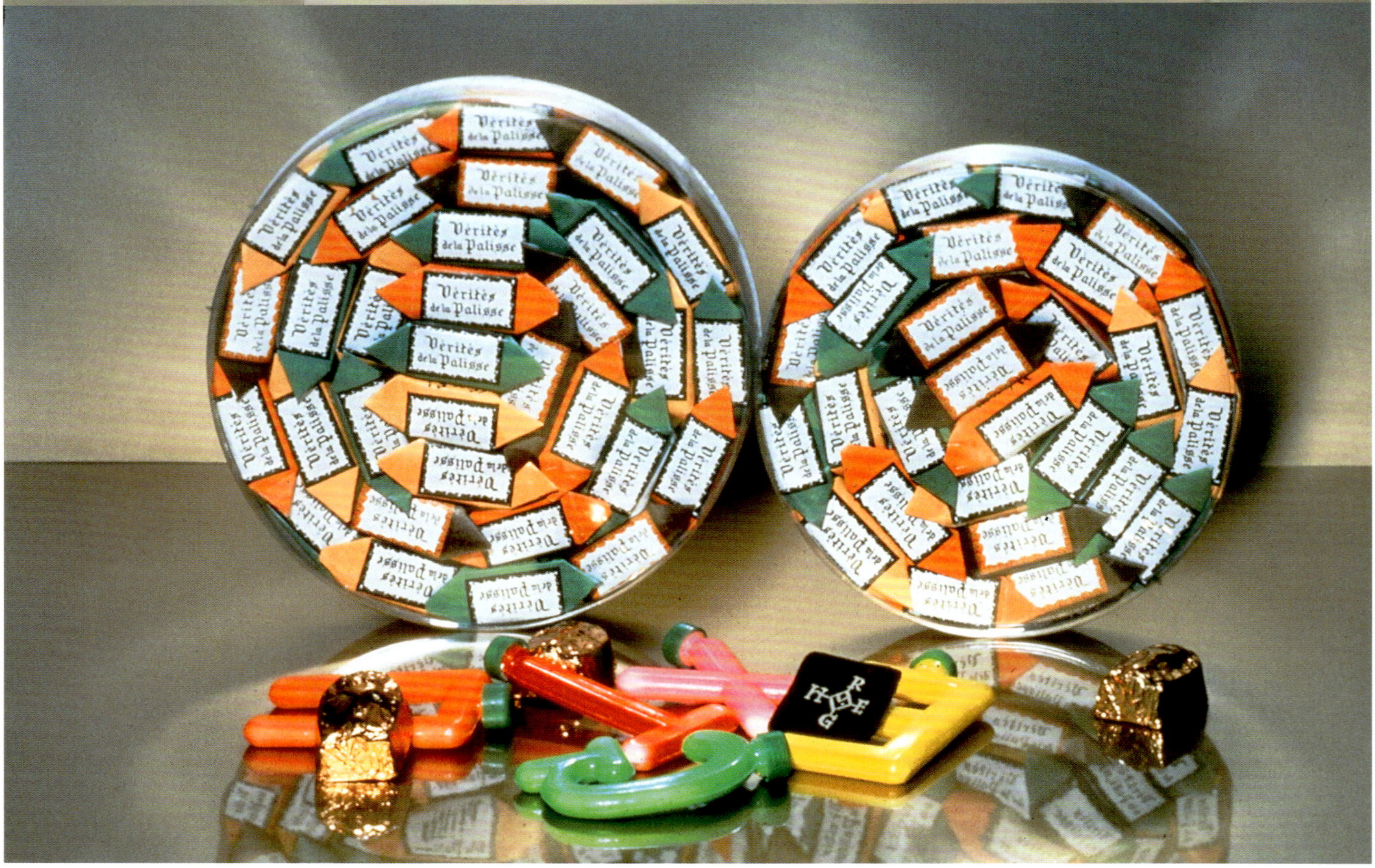

IMPROMPTU IN EIGHT FRAGMENTS

CHRISTIAN SCHLATTER

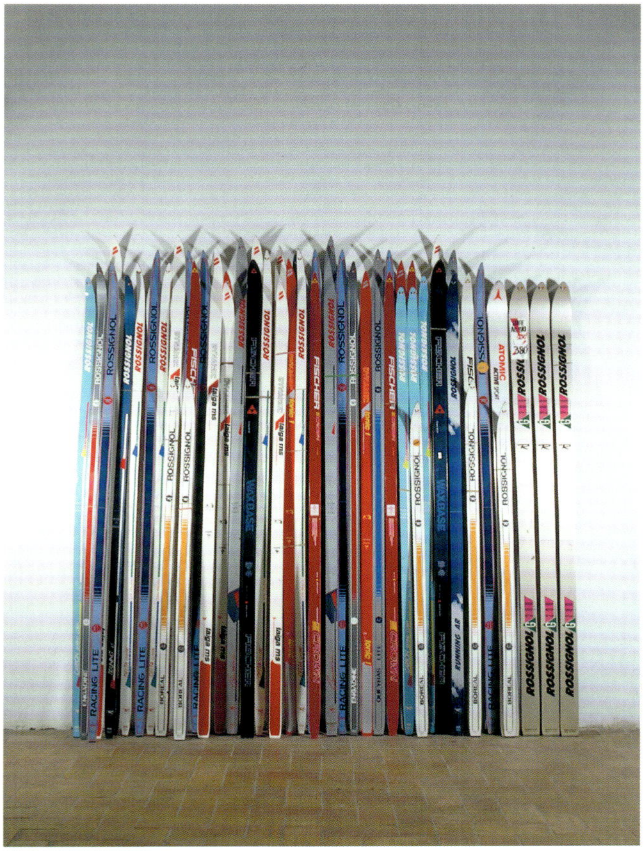

Something crazy happens with language. Something bizarre, something suspicious. There are extremely weird coincidences. This is why I have become a structuralist, mustachist, dialectician of idiot's truths.* I am trying to give order to it. | Raymond Hains from "The 3 cartiers. From the Grand Louvre to the 3 Cartiers," Cartier Foundation for Contemporary Art, Paris, 1994. | *LAPALISSADE: another French idiomatic word for a VÉRITÉ DE LA PALICE.

In 1959, when I was making up puns about PALISSADES, I found myself looking at a cream pie in the window of the offices of the Encyclopedia Clartès.... Was this a troublesome or reassuring strangeness? | Raymond Hains from "The 3 Cartiers. From the Grand Louvre to the 3 Cartiers," Cartier Foundation for Contemporary Art, Paris, 1994.

1. H, R, hain. The man who has long proclaimed that he is "the man who bugs the critics,"[1] as if attaching an epithet to his name, carries no *demotic* patronymic or initials; once unfolded, opened, and explained, his epithet expresses this artist's demonic questioning. It is interchangeable as a proper name with that of Raymond Hains. But, then, since this artist is interested in proper names, tacking a few additions onto his own is not making too much of the thing but making to measure. There is such a thing as a *hain*, but what is it exactly? In his *Dictionnaire de la langue française*, Emile Littré informs us that it is a fishing term, used for a kind of hook. "Hain is most used by sea fishermen on the Normandy coast, but also in other provinces." Without hains, the lexicographer points out, mustering quotations in support, not only would "it not be possible to catch fish" but, as we learn from seventeenth-century French, there would be no "charms" and "graces." The *hain* is lost only to the dictionary *Le Robert* and its *Supplément*. Raymond Hook, Raymond of the Hooks? This meaning cannot be dismissed when it comes to the artist's physiology. Now, if we look at the initials of the artist's given and family names, the *H* and the *R*, can we not decipher the hieroglyphs of his artistic position and procedures? These letters gave rise to a unique bit of speculation by a philologist. This "lover of language" was Charles Nodier, and the book, his *Dictionnaire raisonné des onomatopées françoises*[2]; his undertaking was to go back to the "root language," the one that makes it possible to depict and thus to show, to listen and to say, that the "properties of names are inscribed in their initials." What, then, does Nodier say about the *R*? That "the rolling palatal *R* painted to the ear the character of all the signs wherewith one rendered the idea of continuity, of repetition and renewal in the multiplicity of actions." And what does the letter *H* signify? This "indeterminate vowel" is a "special sign of aspiration, but, taken in its relation to its spirit, there is about it something of haste, of an impatient rapacity; it is used to represent ideas that have to do with the action of *seizing* or snatching away." Nodier illustrates this *H* with the word "hook" (*hameçon*) and with the word "Houyhnhnm," invented by Swift for Gulliver's voyage to the land of the horse people. But that, for Hains, is another story.

2. Matches and glasses. Two bars/measures on Martial. The master of the Latin epigram composed an opening for his volume of pithy statements that was so singular, it embarrassed his publishers into giving it a title distinct from the rest of the work—*Liber Spectaculorum*, or "book of spectacles." Without undue exaggeration, could we not say that the Eternal City of Rome thereby became the city of the "spectacle," and Martial, through the epigrams he fired off at it, a protosituationist? Rome flaunted itself shamelessly, and with it, since Rome was universal, so did the world. It manifested the universality of a society that had become a spectacle and in which everything now had a price, where everything was for sale, and everything was merchandise under the unbridled reign of universal fungibility. In this book, Martial describes a character who plies one of the menial trades that exist in the poor districts, a peddler who exchanges "yellowish matches" (*pallentia sulphurata*) for "broken glass" (*fractis vitris*). Second bar/measure: The epigram is a barb, whether based on a pun, a double entendre, a new meaning, an analogy, or an ingenious alliteration. Everytime, the words seem to fit so snugly, no others would do. It is hard not to have the same impression when we listen to Hains. Martial warns Caesar that he is "material for [his] witticisms" (*materium dictis*), for his epigrams, and assures him that this will do him no harm. Whereas, Louis XV was not "material" for the Marquis de Bièvre[3], who insisted, punningly, that "the King is not a subject." This witticism is quoted by Freud, except that now we have shifted to another register, that of *Witz* (a key word for the first school of German romanticism, at Iena), which, for the time being, can be translated as "witty remark" or "linguistic sally." Hains reversed the exchange offered by Martial's peddler, starting with his *grooved glass* and, after many a trick and manner, ending up as a master of matches, via the artists SAFFA and SEITA, invented when he happened to need them.

3. Scaffolding, arachnean beauty and aesthetic modernity. In his *Curiosités Esthétiques, XIII*, "Painters and Etchers," Baudelaire, the inventor of the term "modernity," set out to analyze the contents of the "natural solemnity of a great capital." He found it in "the obelisks of industry vomiting their coalitions of smoke against the firmament" and in the "prodigious scaffoldings of monuments under repair, applying to the solid architectural body their open architecture with its arachnean and paradoxical beauty." This idea can be likened to other manners explored by Hains—his billboards, scaffoldings, photographs of work sites, and pavement sculptures. Less immediate, more subterranean, is Baudelaire's allusion to the "Lydian art of weaving" and to the adjective "arachnean," with its reference to spiders. A spider's web? T. W. Adorno has a very fine passage on spiders' webs in *Minima Moralia*, where they image the hidden architecture of a text: "Properly written texts are like spiders' webs: tight, concentric, transparent, well-spun, and firm. They draw into themselves all the creatures of the air. Metaphors flitting hastily through them become their nourishing prey. Subject matter comes winging towards them." Here, Adorno is laying down the highest requirements for written texts, whose architecture must fear abstractions more than anything else and seek to capture "concretudes" or "concretions." Do not Hains's *Macintoshages* provide a way of manifesting this work of capturing groupings and resemblances and the infinite analogies whose murmur can be heard in the artist's words, one that takes up all the portmanteau words, the books closed on margins filled with texts copied out by the artist, and libraries in cases left on work sites that are never finished because they are always open to events? The *Macintoshages* are more than just an incisive way of using a technology without becoming subservient to instrumentalization, more than a way of using it to find the right form. We have the impression that he was able to see it, to wait for it, almost, in order to manage, as Hains often puts it, to "explain [which, here, means to exhibit, to show] something of all these stories without which nothing can be understood."

4. Example. Diplopia, double vision. Sunday, June 3, 2001, Raymond Hains is sitting in Le Dôme, a restaurant, saying that not long ago, a couple came in and sat down just near this table. The silhouette of the young man brought back an image of his older brother (five years his senior), an image/sensation of the days when he was on board *La Découverte*. Hains says that these memorial images come to him often, a collision of past and present busting suddenly into his perception of the world. They produce no "disturbance," induce no feeling of paramnesia or *uncanniness*. Such images bring him "back to a question of reality," or, more precisely, what Freud, in his 1936 homage to Romain Rolland, on the occasion of his seventieth birthday, *A Disturbance of Memory upon the Acropolis*, calls a "question of reality." Reaching the top of the Acropolis, Freud "took in the scene," and, as he did so, a strange idea came to him: *"So all this really does exist, just as we learnt at school!"* Is what we rather absentmindedly term "reality" always deceptive? Another traveler, to Venice this time, says exactly the opposite, while making the same reservations about reality. In Proust's *Remembrance of Things Past*, the narrator expresses disappointment, but this time because the imaginary Venice had preceded the real one and created in his mind a Venice that was very different from the one that he was, at last, able to look at. Hains has brought some books with him. He is reading Louis Aragon's *Henri Matisse, roman* ([Paris: Gallimard "Quarto," 1998] 19–27) and stops to consider some of the marginalia—the words that he copies out (his *fiches*, or notes) in the margins of books: "If you want to understand what I do, you must gather a few documents, read and look, and then things will be clear." For instance, he explains, to understand the "abstract films" he made with Jacques Villeglé, one needs to have seen Matisse's *La Blouse Roumaine*, for the film borrowed some of its patterns and colors. "I always pay my debts." But the interesting thing about this *Blouse* is that it went through several states, the only trace of which are the black-and-white photographs reproduced in the Aragon book. Since Matisse was constantly painting over the canvas, all we have is the definitive state, while the erasures and earlier states are known only from the photographs taken at the painter's request. In those same pages, Hains was struck by Aragon's note requesting Matisse's permission to enlarge the drawings on a letter he had sent the poet ("shell from the front" and a "shell from the back") for reproduction in the journal *Poésie 42*. He then reads the conclusion to this first chapter, "Matisse or Grandeur": "That drawing is writing is something that School has long since forgotten, and that the Master of Cimiez, Henri Matisse, our pride, has taught us anew." Hains comments: "Those words could be by [Francis] Ponge." But Matisse's shells were of no interest to him on their own. They were to be related to Sartre's article on Ponge, "Man and Things" (*Situations 1*), in which Sartre speaks of the writer "who delights in imagining object-words like empty shells." Ponge, the author of *L'Ecrit Beaubourg*, saw the Centre Pompidou as a "great idea housed." In 1947, Hains attended Ponge's talk "Tentative orale," at which he said that, as he saw it, "If he had decided to write, it was precisely in opposition to the spoken word." It is reported that, at the end, the speaker bent down and kissed the table.

5. On wit; combinatory Witz. It is hard to shake off the shock of Hains's impromptus, improvised discourses, and artistic productions. In what aesthetic sky does this strange constellation belong? This question should not surprise us. It is put because there is no alternative to putting it and because it, therefore, calls for an aesthetic position. It is deadly for (engaged) art to present itself as the illustration of a philosopheme. Witness political art. The same can be said for any reduction of an artwork to a philosopheme, an aesthetic without art. Still, we cannot separate artistic production from the relations within which it is constituted and with which it communicates, even in the lexemes of its language. Why? No philosophical tendency is an isolated phenomenon. It represents a subject's positions with regard to the world—fundamental experiences seeking expression through the medium of thought. This position explains the parallels between the early romanticism of Iena and the artist considered here. It may be that certain fragments by Novalis, Schlegel, or Schleiermacher can, if formulated programmatically, be seen as taking effect in this artist's discourse and production. The force at work here is that of the romantic Witz with all its tensions and polarities, in which the most brilliant victories are threatened by the most destructive dissolution, as wrought by humor and irony. This aesthetic motif, which is the encrypted center of the first romanticism, has here been displaced onto Hains, an energizing force that has to do with the artist's wit, wordplay, lightning-quick thought, and conversational improvisation (this catalog bears witness to that). The ramifications are certainly complex, but also linked to precise thought processes and objectives. We can say: This is the serious part, the signified, and those are the leaps, the surprising turnabouts, the brilliant digressions with their sidetracks, all the surprising productions of the same combinatory Witz. What figure fits this artist? *Raymond the Abstract*, according to Guy Debord; *Shatterer, Poster Artist, Sheet-metal worker*,[4] *SAFFA, SEITA, the Sigisbée of the critics*, according to Claude (Stella) Rivière, for instance, but none can pin him down. He has deliberately sought to escape from each of these figures, to run away[5] and avoid being locked into a personified abstraction, like Klein with *Yves the Monochrome*. This is the sign of a twofold allergy. The first is to all so-called power-sharing by artists, and not only those of Nouveau Réalisme. Any serious aesthetic cannot fail to note that any "appropriation" ends up turning into its redoubtable contrary, the subjection and, therefore, alienation of the artist by what he thought was his territory. The second allergy concerns the freedom against incompetence: "There is no Nouveau Réalisme, there is only a Tinguely-type movement of which we are the *rotellas* (in Italian, small wheels, and evoking the can of Rotella machine oil), and this movement that is our glory machine would become our shame machine if we failed to stick a nail in the tree of liberty" (interview at the Hotel Carlton, June 1992). If we speak of this artist's behavior or attitude, then we must deal in the flesh of examples.

On the day of June 3, as mentioned earlier, in his thinking about personified abstractions and Nouveaux Réalistes, Hains came round to wondering if, by virtue of the transparent metal mesh used for the Louvre's pyramid extension, the architect I. M. Pei had not become a kind of "lozenge" artist. He then continued with the subject already broached, allowing for a distinction: "This brings us back to Matisse, who said that the worst thing for an artist is to be a prisoner of his manners. What, then, is an artist's style? In 1961, when I was showing my palissades and Jean Tinguely was presenting his painting machines, they had just published Claude Lévi-Strauss's book of conversations with Georges Charbonnier. One very important passage is where Lévi-Strauss speaks of the 'extraordinary profusion of manners in the work of a given painter,' which we see throughout the work of Picasso. That radical change of manner, that constant change of manner, seems to me to be directly related to the individuation of artistic production." Without wishing to overstate the importance of these *Entretiens* [Conversations], published in December 1960, or of Lévi-Strauss himself (to whom he refers, notably his book *The Savage Mind*) in the archaeology of the artist's cultural formation, this reading functions as an implicit injunction to change manners. Hains is a modal artist, and in this sense he is similar to Loki and his figures, as described by Georges Dumézil (whom Hains also read, back in 1945–46).[6] What Dumézil says about Loki can be applied to this artist: He is versed in metamorphosis; he is ingenious, inventive, wily; he has an insatiable curiosity as an observer, questioner, and explorer, and is alert to new developments. The procedure of an *assemblage* artist? The *Macintoshages* are the recent version of what the artist has been doing for many years now. With them, he is exhibiting his practice of scaffolding, concentrating, gathering, abridging, and shifting textual and visual fragments that have been around for a long time already. Like a spider's web, he lays traps. Hains is patient and can wait. He is constantly linking, binding, assembling, weaving together fragments, readings, words, names, encounters—the woof of his very life.

6. History from the viewpoint of the vanquished? It is hard not to note an affinity between Hains's attitude and one of Walter Benjamin's *Theses on the Philosophy of History*—on the need to write a history written from the viewpoint of the vanquished, in opposition to the history hitherto written from the winner's viewpoint. Adorno sees an aesthetic equivalent for this reversal in Erik Satie's position with regard to Schönberg's Viennese school, leaving by the wayside such sentimental, naive, and humorous pieces as the *Préludes Flasques (pour un chien)* [Flaccid preludes (for a dog)], *Choses Vues à droite et à gauche (sans lunettes)* [Things seen right and left (without glasses)], *Sonatine Bureaucratique* [Bureaucratic sonata], the waltz *Je te veux, En Habit de cheval* [I want you, in horse outfit], *Pièces Froides* [Cold cuts], the *Sonnerie de la Rose + Croix* [Rose + crucian bell], the *Gnosiennes*, and other *Musiques pour Ameublement* [Musical furniture], eclipsing them like so many traces of a lived experience that the Viennese school can only know as an idea. Certainly, Hains's constellation is peopled by "world-historical individuals" (Hegel), ones that Herder calls "the golden line of creators." But, at the same time, and staying with the terminology of aesthetic modernity, Hains affirms a very particular taste for what Baudelaire calls *poetae* and minor artists (*minores*). On the margins of history recounted from the winner's viewpoint, his world is peopled by multifarious modest names, places, events, and books by little-known authors, which are all like actors in *his* story. Here, we find Bernini, but also Lemot, a sculptor from Lyon. We find Georges Palante and Louis Guilloux who, by the associations of his own Witz, lead us via *Cripure*[7] to Kant, the "old ape of Königsberg," as Nietzsche once put it, and from him to "us philologists" and, as Hains planned to add in one of his exhibition projects, "de la Garenne-Lemot." Getting our bearings by these few names, we need to note and generalize the artist's position: All of them (great and small) play equal roles in his words and productions. And, more precisely, in his life, his story—in regard to history? Yes, providing that we grasp this other fragment from Novalis (*Poeticism*, no. 187, Freiberg): "Life must not be a novel that we are given but one that we make."

7. Romanticize or new realism? What is it that Hains so proudly summons up, and en masse, to confront the contested booty of history written from the viewpoint of the winner? A quick response is needed, so let us go straight to Novalis: "Everything around us—everyday events, our life's habitual relationships and habits—has an influence on us that is continuous and, because of that, impossible to observe, but also of the utmost importance (Freiberg Manuscript, II [Poetry], § 31). So much for the reference. This fragment should be set alongside the beginning of chapter six of *Henry von Ofterdingen*. Novalis distinguishes two character types: for the *contemplative* types, these little things are considered unimportant, insignificant, ephemeral—coincidence, but not for the *active* sort, who knows how to take them, pick them up, to metamorphose them by means of that *magical idealism* wherein "all chance events are transformed into stories, and their [the active person's] life is an unbroken series of memorable and brilliant, complex and strange events." These two texts can, no doubt, serve to define the specific sphere that Hains is attentive to, and his way of endlessly exploring it. But this aspect is not enough. We also need to go to what sounds like an authentic rallying cry for an avant-garde of radical art, whose precepts Novalis sought to realize: "The world must be romanticized." This is none other than an operation of qualitative potentialization enacted in sovereign fashion by the *subject*: "When I endow the ordinary with an elevated meaning, the common with mystery, the known with the dignity of the unknown, the finished with the appearance of infinity, then I am romanticizing them" (Freiberg Fragment [Poeticisms], § 105).

This *gestus* of absolute sovereignty, which comes long before Malevich and the epistemology of Bachelard, has a name. It was first written by Friedrich Schlegel, when he called for a "new realism." This, in fact, sounded the knell of all realism, since no philosophy could be contained within it. The philosophy of the day was idealism. By positing the sovereignty of the subject, it recognized the perpetual alternation of the subject's being out and in the self: "Each thought, each production is none other than the result of this activity" ("Discourse on Mythology"). One idiosyncratic trait of the artist, emphasized here, is the difficulty of "working with him." This apparent difficulty could well be immanent, within the general character. If we modify the inflection slightly, fragment 375 in Schlegel's *Athenaeum*, we come back to the *active* character evoked by Novalis, here termed "energetic." Schlegel contrasts two different types, the "virtuoso, the man of genius," the man who is determined to achieve a precise objective and whose primary concern is to "create a form," and the *energetic* type, who knows nothing of these "gesticulations" and "does nothing but use the *moment*. He is always ready, of infinite plasticity. Either he has an *incalculable number of projects* or he has none." This definition of the energetic type could easily correspond to one of Hains's manners or statements. Energy is more than a basic, plastic agility, it is an active force, out beyond, as indicated by Schlegel's *new realism*: a force whereby the *sovereign Self* is formed and acts.

8. "Am I deceived, or is this indeed real?" Ludwig Tieck, *Sternbald*. Everything that Hains comes across, hears, sees, and reads, he relates to himself, gathers up in a story, and, in these strange embraces, is constantly coming into contact with in his own life, his story. "Witz is creative, it produces resemblances" (Novalis, *Allgemeinen Brouillons*, § 732). He makes resemblances, analogies, and associations. Hains does not create, in the strict sense, but forges relations between things (here, keeping "thing" to designate his sphere of attention); he knots and assembles in a combinatory art and an arachnean practice, as described earlier. But, if we read Schleiermacher, we can no longer speak of finds and coincidences in the trivial sense: "Many of the inventions of Witz are like unexpected reunions after a long separation between two friendly thoughts" (*Athenaeum*, § 37). Not that these "separated entities" always existed elsewhere or in an exteriority; their separation had its duration in waiting, it is necessary, for it is in the patience of this waiting that "friendly thoughts" can be reunited. As one of Hains's sayings explicitly states, "We'll see where all this leads." The discovery, with its "friendly" association, always takes the form of a reunion. The address of a bank manager opens up a Bonaparte love affair, the homophony of a proper name and a place name reopens the Descartes question, a letter by David to his protector, the Marquis de Bièvre, about his *Oath of Horatii*, restores the pertinence of the artist's critical distance vis-à-vis institutions and galleries, and, from there, everything falls provisionally into place. Raymond Hains is not a solipsism without doors or windows; his fist is not clenched. Our artist could be slipped into Tieck's text commenting on the impact of events on the young painter Sternbald. It is from his text in the *Almanach Prisma* that Hains gets stuck in reality. When Hains opens his fist, he does not risk being threatened by what he has caught there, but the viewer does risk being engulfed by an aesthetic experience that, ultimately, turns out to be the experience of reality itself.

ENDNOTES

1. The French term "asticoteur de la critique" uses the double meaning of "asticoter"—to harry and nag, or to bait a line with a larva, an *asticot*.
2. Charles Nodier, *Dictionnaire raisonné des onomatopées françoises (1808 and 1802)*, preceded by "La nature dans la voix," by Henri Meschonnic, reprint (Toulouse: T.E.R., 1984).
3. Two of Hains's favorite books are the *Marquis de Bièvre's Vercingentorixe* (Paris: Jean Jacques Pauvert, 1961) and Freud's *Jokes and Their Relation to the Unconscious*.
4. In French, tôlard (sheet-metal worker) sounds the same as taulard, jailbird.
5. The French slang expression for running away, "se tailler," connects with many other meanings. See diagram in Aude Bodet's essay.
6. On Loki, the Nordic divinity who, though without a specific cult or function, was a highly active god, Georges Dumézil has written authoritatively, notably in the revised edition of *Loki* (Paris: Flammarion, 1986).
7. Cripure is the name of the philosophy teacher in Louis Guilloux's *Le Sang noir*. One of his models is Georges Palante, a Nietzschean whose frequent references to Kant prompted his students to nickname him "Cripure," a contraction of *Critique of Pure Reason*.

AUTHOR

Christian Schlatter holds degrees in psychology, sociology, and philosophy, and a doctorate in esthétique-science de l'art from the Paris I-Panthéon-Sorbonne, Paris. He teaches seminars on aesthetics for the Union Centrale des Arts Décoratifs, Paris, and serves as director of research for advanced studies in architecture and design.

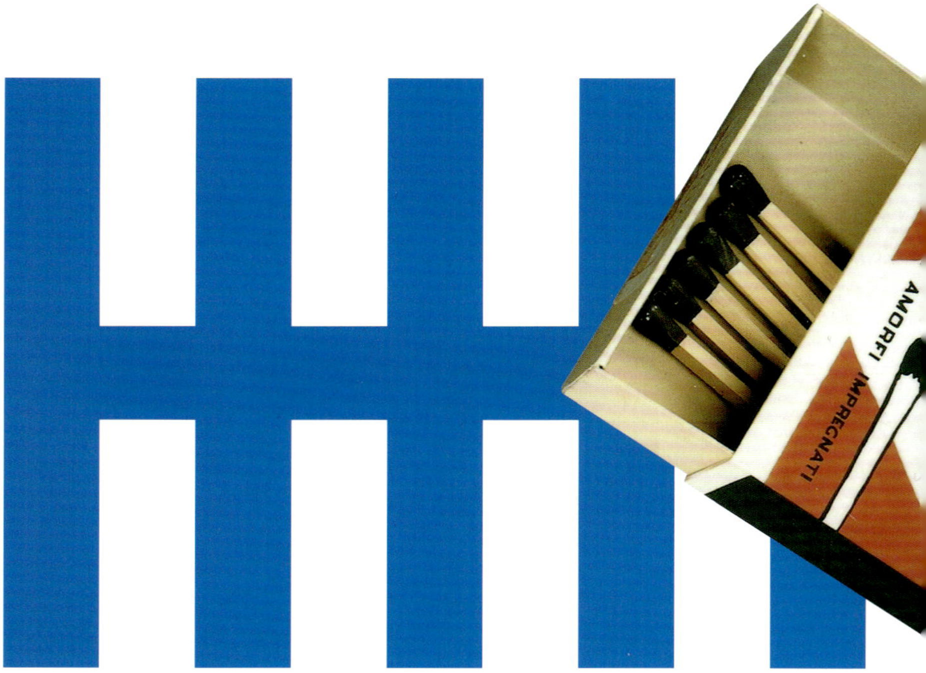

SAFFA & SEITA

SAFFA & SEITA : The initials of the French and Italian state-owned tobacco monopolies were used by Hains as the names of twin artists whose works he presented in his exhibitions. Hains readily compared them to the good twins Castor and Pollux. Hains put their names to certain works and exhibitions, just as SAFFA and SEITA could sign works by Hains. Thus, on October 12, 1965, "Under the high inspiration of the French and Italian tobacco companies, Iris Clert "presented" 'SEITA & SAFFA, copyright by Raymond Hains.'" Here, Hains exhibited his "super matchboxes": "Today's artist is simply a mythological character who takes up a fragment of reality and uses it as a mask." After all, did not Duchamp style a urinal "Fountain" and sign it "R. Mutt"? (CS)

I had been looking at a matchbook put out by the French state tobacco authority,* a matchbook lying on the table, just like that, while I was drinking in cafés around town. It had a picture of La Fontaine's fable THE DONKEY DRESSED IN THE LION SKIN on it. And while I was turning it over and over, I had the idea that it would be fun to have these matchboxes enlarged and hung on the wall. This was at the time of the 1964 Venice Biennale and the pop art exhibition. So, I was inspired by Oldenburg's idea.
In Italy, they have pink matches with yellow tips, in rather vibrant colors that come close to Klein or Matisse. In restaurants, L'Angelo or La Colomba, for instance, there were photographers taking pictures of people while they were eating their dinner or having dessert, and the photographers would come back to the diners with their photo glued onto a matchbox. That explains how I came up with this whole thing. I imagined two artists, each of whom had a monopoly on these matchboxes. It was a trick to help illustrate what I thought of Nouveau Réalisme, which could have been called abstractions personified. | Raymond Hains interview with Marc Bormand, February 16, 1999. | *LA RÉGIE FRANÇAISE [The French Authority] = SEITA.

 SEITA & SAFFA, copyright Raymond Hains. iris.time, no. 21, 12 October 1965. Documentation Musée National d'art Moderne, Centre Pompidou, Paris.

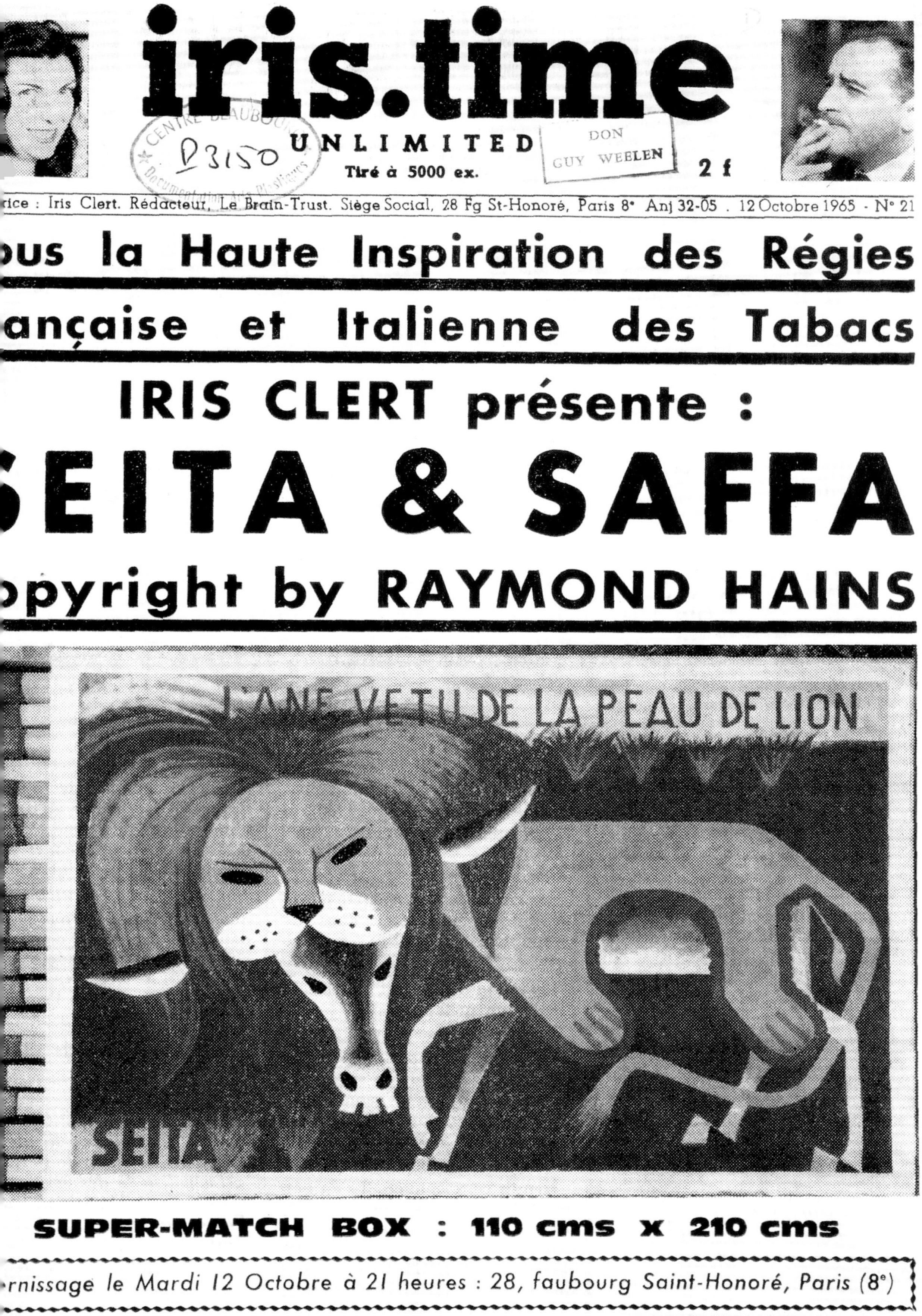

iris.time

UNLIMITED

Tiré à 5000 ex.

2 f

…rice : Iris Clert. Rédacteur, Le Brain-Trust. Siège Social, 28 Fg St-Honoré, Paris 8e Anj 32-05 . 12 Octobre 1965 - N° 21

…ous la Haute Inspiration des Régies
…ançaise et Italienne des Tabacs

IRIS CLERT présente :

…EITA & SAFFA

…opyright by RAYMOND HAINS

SUPER-MATCH BOX : 110 cms x 210 cms

…rnissage le Mardi 12 Octobre à 21 heures : 28, faubourg Saint-Honoré, Paris (8e)

this page, and facing page: *SEITA & SAFFA, copyright Raymond Hains. iris.time*, no. 21, 12 October 1965. Documentation Musée National d'art Moderne, Centre Pompidou, Paris.
facing page, right: *SAFFA*, 1964. Collection Daniel Pérel, London. Courtesy Galerie Georges-Philippe and Nathalie Vallois, Paris.

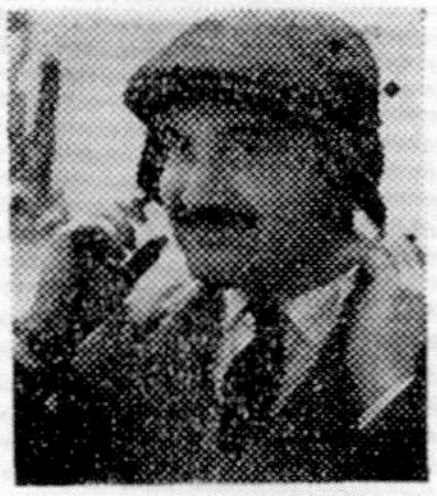

LE BRO - NOTES

La Pyromanie Un Sport Populaire

Un jour, en allant consulter un de mes amis qui s'occupait d'enfance délinquante, j'avisai un petit garçon à l'air futé, qui courait partout comme un écureuil.

Je demandai : « Et qu'est-ce qu'il a fait, celui-là? »

On me répondit: « Il a mis le feu à l'usine de son père ».

Jusqu'à une date récente, seules les classes élevées de la société ont pu se payer ce luxe à la Néron.

Dieu merci, aujourd'hui, grâce à l'émancipation des masses, grâce à l'automobile, grâce aux congés payés, la pyromanie n'est plus un privilège de classe.

Le plus modeste des campeurs, muni d'une bicyclette et d'une pochette de la Régie à cinq centimes, peut voir flamber des hectares.

Ainsi la France, toujours première partout, aura bientôt paysage lunaire sur la côte d'Az ce qui lui évitera les coûteu expériences spatiales.

René Brô

Phrase de feu

« J'espère que mes couleurs provoqueront un incendie qui dépassera les exigences d'une allumette ». (Lanskoy).

« Ces peintres vous parlent: l'œil du temps ».

Cordier, c'est pas fini !

Hervé Villard, le nouveau poulain de Daniel Cordier, n'ira plus à Capri; Cordier est revenu à Paris.

LE POINT DE VUE D'IRI

Qui est Raymond Hains

Né à Saint-Brieuc-les-Choux (Côtes-du-Nord) en novembre 1926, il est Breton jusqu'à l'os et Celte délirant.

Emigré à Paris en 1946, il expose ses premières photos abstraites chez Colette Allendy en 1948.

Sa pensée, depuis, n'arrête d'évoluer et de proliférer dans de gigantesques méandres analogiques.

Raymond Hains est le roi du calembour métaphysique.

Vers 1952, avec l'aide de Villeglé, il se lance dans le cinéma et fait un film abstrait en se servant du procédé des verres cannelés. Ce film, pour des raisons techniques et financières, n'ayant jamais été terminé, se dénomme Pénélope.

Depuis cette époque, il s'est bâti une mythologie personnelle, et de fil en aiguille et d'exposition en exposition, est devenu le « SIGISBEE DE LA CRITIQUE » ainsi que le « CHEF DE LABORATOIRE DES FRERES LISS DE L'ILLISIBLE ».

Puis de palissades (1) en La lissades, il en est arrivé à la Ré Française des Tabacs qu'il a vo immortaliser en même temps q la Régie Italienne en créant personnes emblématiques de :

SEITA et SAFFA (2),

que j'ai la joie de vous présen dans ma galerie le 12 octobre 19 en attendant la grande affaire sa vie : LA BIENNALE ECL TEE qui aura lieu l'année p chaine.

Iris CLERT.

(1) *Exposition des Affiches l cérées chez Colette Allendy, 19 Première Biennale de Paris, 19 « La palissade des emplaceme réservés ». Exposition de France déchirée à la Galerie* 1961.

(2) *Exposition à la Galleria Leone* 1964.

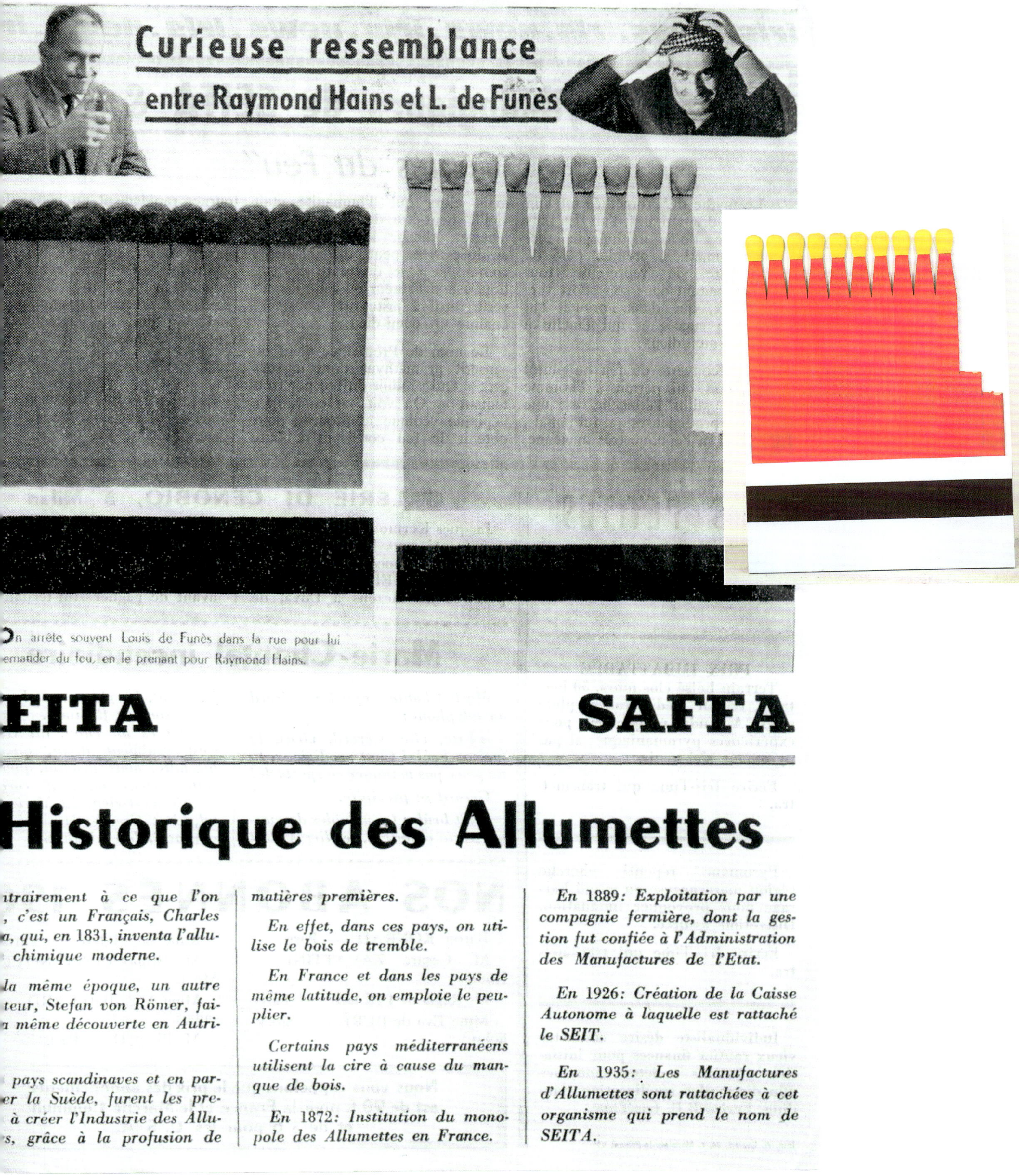

Curieuse ressemblance

entre Raymond Hains et L. de Funès

n arrête souvent Louis de Funès dans la rue pour lui
emander du feu, en le prenant pour Raymond Hains.

EITA

SAFFA

Historique des Allumettes

ıtrairement à ce que l'on
, c'est un Français, Charles
a, qui, en 1831, inventa l'allu-
chimique moderne.

la même époque, un autre
teur, Stefan von Römer, fai-
ı même découverte en Autri-

pays scandinaves et en par-
er la Suède, furent les pre-
à créer l'Industrie des Allu-
s, grâce à la profusion de
matières premières.

En effet, dans ces pays, on uti-
lise le bois de tremble.

En France et dans les pays de même latitude, on emploie le peuplier.

Certains pays méditerranéens utilisent la cire à cause du manque de bois.

En 1872: Institution du monopole des Allumettes en France.

En 1889: Exploitation par une compagnie fermière, dont la gestion fut confiée à l'Administration des Manufactures de l'Etat.

En 1926: Création de la Caisse Autonome à laquelle est rattaché le SEIT.

En 1935: Les Manufactures d'Allumettes sont rattachées à cet organisme qui prend le nom de SEITA.

 SEITA & SAFFA, copyright Raymond Hains. iris.time, no. 21, 12 October 1965. Documentation Musée National d'art Moderne, Centre Pompidou, Paris.
facing page: *L'âne vêtu de la peau de lion* [The donkey dressed in the lion skin], 1967. Collection Musée National d'art Moderne, Centre Pompidou, Paris.

iris.news.iris.news.iris.news.iris.news.ir

Origines mythologiques de SEITA & SAFF

"Génies du Feu"

Le mythe de Prométhée est l'un des plus dramatiques, l'un des plus complexes de la mythologie grecque. Prométhée, premier père de l'humanité, la représente tout entière, autant dans son effort vers le mieux, que dans l'orgueil qui vient du succès et qui l'incite à s'égaler aux dieux.

La découverte du feu ou plutôt l'invention qui permit à l'homme de faire jaillir l'étincelle, est une des plus prodigieuses qui fut jamais, celle qui, à l'époque très ancienne, mais alors que l'humanité était vieille peut-être de plusieurs millénaires, change le cours de ses destinées. Elle peut être considérée comme la base de toute civilisation. Aussi l'auteur de cette découverte fut-il à juste titre considéré comme un demi-dieu.

Le nom de Prométhée vient du sanscrit prâmathyus dont le sens est : « Qui produit du feu par frottement ». On voit, en effet, qu'à l'époque védique le procédé pour obtenir le feu consistait à faire tourner rapidement un bâton da un trou pratiqué lui-même da une pièce de bois. En faisant ce opération on invoquait le di Agni; le bâton était comparé l'organe mâle, le trou à l'orga femelle. C'est ce qui explique confusion qui, de l'inventeur feu, fait le modeleur de l'homm

Les Dieux du Paganisme Henri de Vibraye — Editeur Em Hazan.

NOS PETITES ANNONCES

PRIX IMBATTABLE

Terrain boisé clos murs, 50 hectares, région Méditerranée, plein soleil. A vendre uniquement pour expériences pyromaniaques si pas pyromane s'abstenir.

Ecrire Iris-Time qui transmettra.

Pyromane repenti cherche région marécageuse ou grand barrage pour provoquer inondation. Discrétion assurée.

Ecrire Iris-Time qui transmettra.

Individualiste désire contacter vieux routier finances pour initiation mystères sociétés anonymes afin dissimuler amélioration standing. Ecrire B.P. Iris-Time.

GALERIE DI CENOBIO, à Milan

Jacques Kermoal (dit Kérozène) a présenté sous le titre « Nuovo Realismo a Fuoco » un hommage à SAFFA et SEITA : trente-huit peintres de Mezens à Dova, de Peverelli à Rotella et d'Azur Kliko Yoslinda ont pris thème : l'allumette. Gros su l'exposition part pour Loca avant de gagner Amsterdam.

Marie-Chantal incendiaire

Marie-Chantal appelle Gérard au téléphone:

« Vite, vite, Gérard, viens, la maison brûle! C'est prodigieux, tu ne peux pas manquer ce spectacle!

Gérard se précipite.

Tout brûle: les meubles de marquetterie crépitent, les livres d'art flambent, les rideaux et les t series sont en flammes.

« Tu es un chou, dit Gé c'est vraiment divin, quel incendie! mais, dis-moi, quell cette curieuse odeur de cara

« Ce n'est rien, dit Marie-C tal, c'est Grand-mère qui br elle avait le diabète. »

NOS ABONNÉS 196

Baron KONRAD — Paris.

M. Cesare ZAVATTINI — Rome.

M. Régis de POLEON — Paris.

Mme Eva de BURÈN — Stockholm.

Mme de MOHL — Paris.

M. Bruno CONTENOTTE Milan.

Mme Alice JUILLARD. — sailles.

M. PUECH — Paris.

Nous vous rappelons que le prix des abonnements est de 20 f. pour la France et le Marché Commun et de $ 6 pour les U. S .A.

Imp. A. Lapied, 24, r. Monsieur-le-Prince, VIe

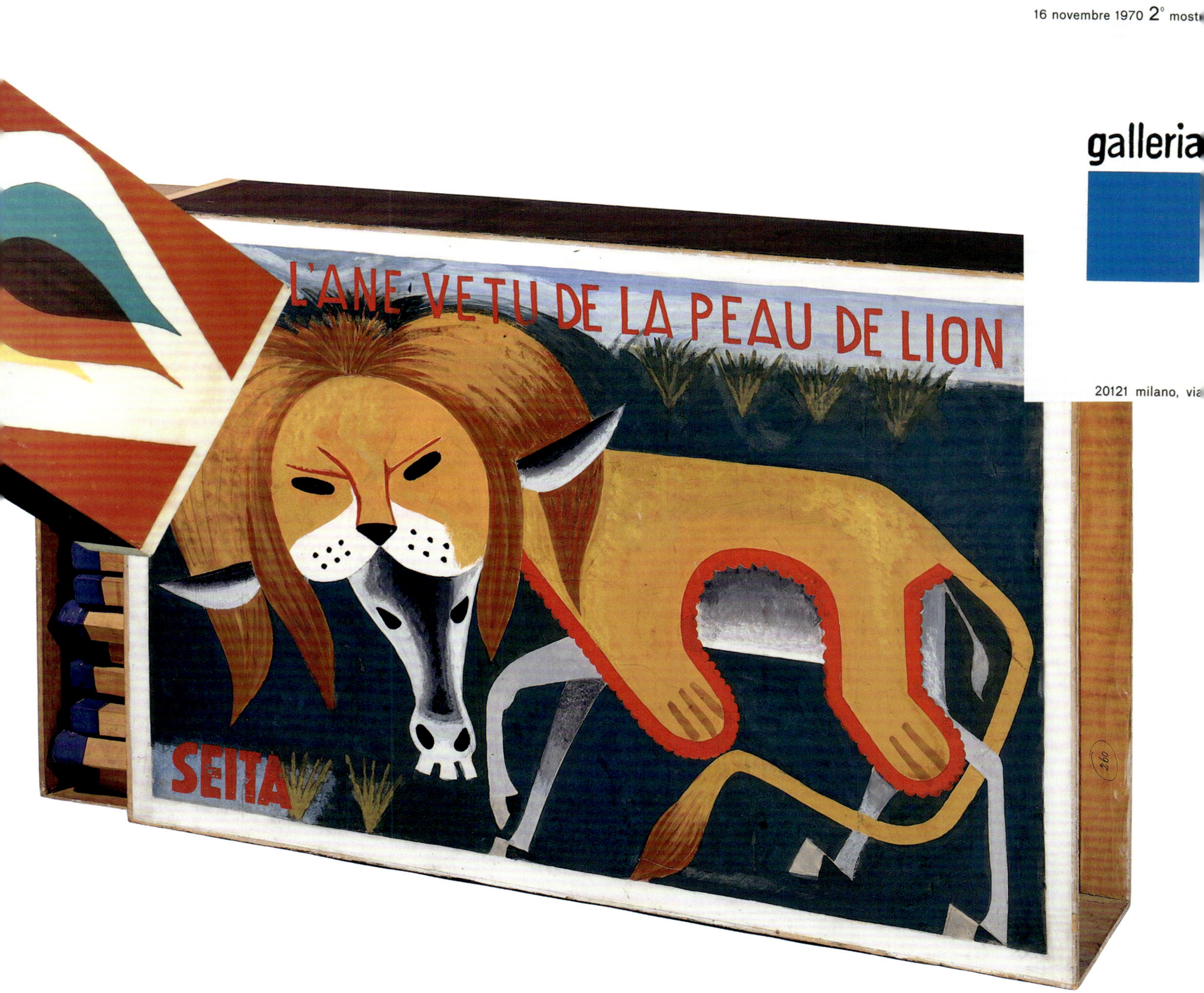

LEONE (GALLERIA DEL) : **In 1964, at the Galleria del Leone, in Venice, Raymond Hains exhibited a giant matchbox bearing an illustration based on La Fontaine's fable of the "ass dressed in a lion skin." He came back to this theme in 1966 for "La Biennale de Raymond Hains," taking the opportunity to evoke the artist's own bestiary and its cryptic meanings, working with the animal names of certain galleries (lion, tortoise, elephant, etc.). Hains used the name of the del Leone gallery to create an allegory of the artist and critic (the ass dressed in the lion skin). This was an artistic strategy for "escaping" or "getting out" after performing some kind of exploit. His bestiary drew on his reading of Apuleius's *Golden Ass*, Ovid's *Metamorphoses*, and Aesop's and La Fontaine's fables. What was most important to Hains were the metamorphoses of the actual artist figure, to which he gave a variety of names, including SEITA and SAFFA. This was how he hoped to avoid becoming pinned down, caught up in a "personified abstraction," or accused of appropriation.** (CS)

this page: *Disque bleu pour SAFFA* [Blue disc for SAFFA], 1970. Courtesy Galleria L'Elefante Treviso Italia.
facing page: *Iris Clert, la messagère des arts* [Iris Clert, messenger of the arts], 1997. Collection Éric Fabre, Brussels.

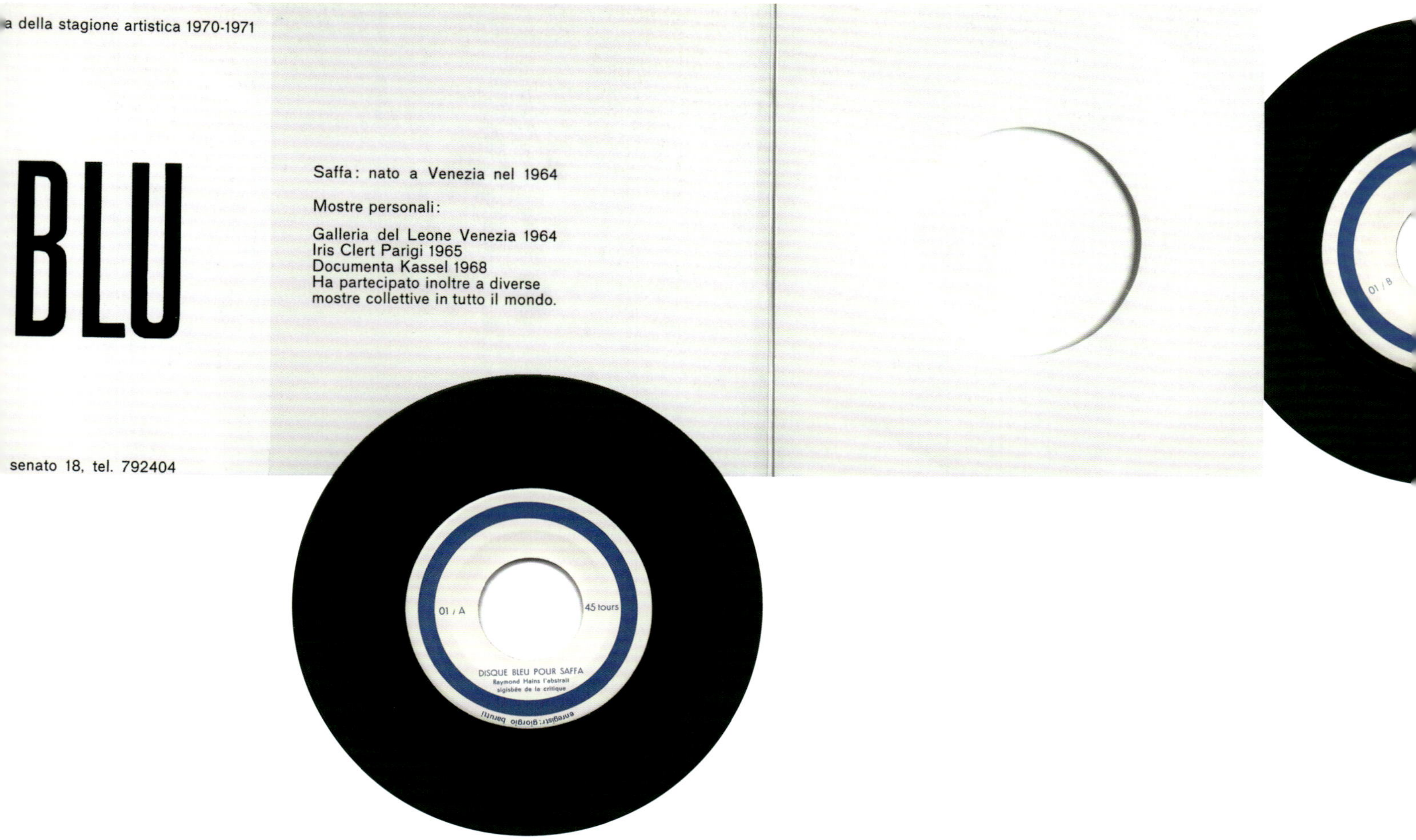

DISQUE BLEU : Milan, November 16, 1970. A Hains exhibition at the Galleria Blu. He shows and plays his *Disque bleu pour SAFFA*, a homophone of the French "Disque bleu" cigarettes. On the front: "sans filtre" [unfiltered]: "Yes, Mr. Penrose *c'est la vie*. Today we no longer know if the blue of the sky belongs to Monochrome Yves or to Georges Bataille. But as André Breton said, Osiris is a black god. And when SAFFA makes a contract with Palazzoli, it is a kind of disc/obolus, or a disque bleu, a magnanimous 45 rpm that we offer with all our heart, with postage and packing, over and above the painting market." On the "filter" side, Hains recites a piece of text, as if deformed by an echo. Inside the sleeve, Hains states that "SAFFA was born, in Venice, in 1964. Solo shows: Galleria del Leone, Venice, 1964; Iris Clert, Paris, 1965; Documenta, Kassel, 1968. Has taken part in various group shows all over the world." It is only on side 01/A of the disc that we can read "DISQUE BLEU FOR SAFFA, Raymond Hains the abstract, sigisbée of critics," and, on side 01/B, "DISQUE BLEU-FILTER—Raymond Hains the abstract." (CS)

I could have pursued a type of phonetic, musical, or poetic artistic research, and, indeed, this is the path that François Dufrêne was to take. It would have even been a natural thing for me to do, given that I had already put out a first record, then a second, with Yves Klein, which we had sent to François in Morocco. Perhaps it was Dufrêne who delivered me from the temptation of this phonetic work, just as Spoerri did, with cooking. | Raymond Hains interview with Christian Schlatter, POETING AND PAINTRY, Musées de Marseille, Réunion des Musées Nationaux, Paris, 1993.

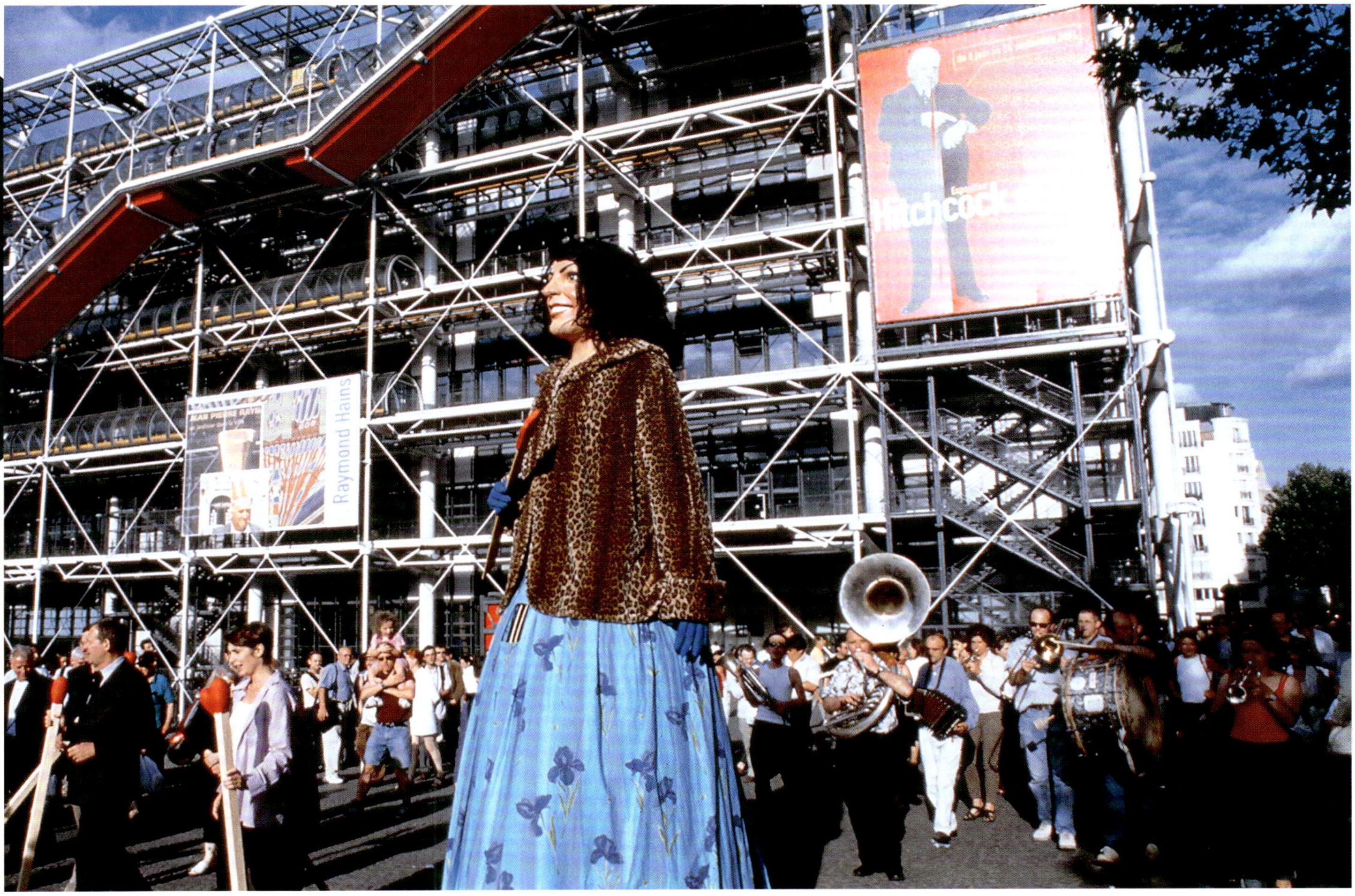

IRIS CLERT : In issue no. 21 of *iris.time*, dated October 1965, subtitled "Iris's point of view," we find Iris's answers to the question "Who is Raymond Hains?": He "is the king of metaphysical puns.... Ever since 1946, his ideas have unceasingly moved and proliferated in huge analogical meanders." Physically, Hains is likened to popular comic actor Louis de Funes by comparing photographs of the two men. Villeglé points out that the tone of all this reflected the taste of the day. When Iris Clert exhibited the matches, SAFFA & SEITA, she invited Parisian firemen. The seventies broke with this taste by inaugurating a more earnest spirit. Other invitations at the gallery: Camille Bryen's, in 1957, on the occasion of the Micro-Salon; then Yves Klein's *Le vide* (Emptiness) and *Immatériel* (April–May 1958), which invited visitors to honor the work "with their full affective presence the lucid and positive event of a certain reign of the sensible"; and finally, Arman's *Le plein* (Fullness), in October 1960, accompanied by an invitation to "come and observe in this fullness all the strength of the real compacted into an oneiric mass." (CS)

Giant Iris, Messenger of the Arts : I wanted the sister-city relation to take place between Kassel in Germany and Cassel in France, two cities with good reasons for making cultural exchanges....
Because Iris Clert was the messenger of the arts, and because the Giants of Cassel* are called REUZE MAMA and REUZE PAPA and can't be moved at all, and because they are figures made of papier-mâché, and quite fragile, I had the idea of commissioning a giant Iris, Messenger of the Arts, and she REALLY gets around. | Raymond Hains interview with Marc Dachy, HORSE-LANGUAGE AND FACTOR TIME, FRAC Champagne-Ardenne/Actes Sud, Arles, 1998 |
*Names of the traditional monumental "puppets" in the Lenten carnival of the Dunkerque area in the north of France. REUZE is a French deformation of the Flemish REUSCHE, meaning giant.

AUDE BODET

"I WOULD PREFER NOT TO (EXHIBIT)"

RAYMOND HAINS AND THE CRITICS

"I AM AN INACTION PAINTER" —R.H.

At the end of *Nadja*, albeit as a note, as if addressing only his more attentive readers, André Breton records a memory:

So, on the quayside of Marseille's Vieux Port, in an idle moment, not long before dusk, I observed a strangely scrupulous painter struggling on his canvas to outdo the dying light in skill and speed. The mark corresponding to the sun's own declined in keeping with the sun. At the end of it all, there was nothing left. All of a sudden, the painter felt he had fallen behind. He got rid of the red from a wall, dispelled one or two remaining glints on the water. His painting, which for him was finished and for me was the most incomplete picture in the world, struck me as very sad and very beautiful.[1]

It is not difficult to identify this fragment as an *ecphrasis*—that is, the embellished account of a painterly feat, in the tradition of Pliny and Vasari. All the rules of the genre are observed, but inverted as in a mirror. In a sense, the painter on the old harbor, in his touching inability to grasp the object of his painting—not unlike that of Frenhofer in Balzac's *The Unknown Masterpiece*—is the exact negative of Vasari's Giotto, who, resting his elbow on his hip, unfalteringly drew a circle so perfect that it would be remembered for centuries to come. Modernity reversed these perspectives; it stands things—and this is what many people think, but without seeing the beauty of the thing—on their head: Incompleteness, disarray, and impotence are now attributed a positive value. It was the letter of protest he wrote to Jacques Rivière, when the latter refused to publish his poems, that inaugurated Artaud's genius as a writer. Beckett's characters fail and stammer, but their distraction is, in fact, like the courteous inertia of Melville's Bartleby, a figure of omnipotence.

The fragment from *Nadja* celebrates the failure of painting—not only, as we might think, of painting that wrestles with the real but the failure of any enterprise that seeks, in whatever small way, to capture the flux of words and things—and illustrates the vocation of art in the twentieth century: to exalt incompleteness, the unfinished.

This figure of the paradoxical *ecphrasis*, or celebration of the nonevent, can be found in one of the most pertinent and funniest texts ever written about Raymond Hains, the one that Otto Hahn published in the catalog of the artist's first retrospective, at the Centre National d'Art Contemporain, in 1976. Its title, "Raymond Hains, l'homme le plus extraordinaire que j'ai rencontré" (The Most Unforgettable Man I Ever Met),[2] was a joking echo of the world-famous *Reader's Digest* formula. Hahn's text relates the making of a film on the Nouveaux Réalistes[3] in La Palice, and is therefore about the inventor of the *Palissades* (Palisades/Fences) and *Tôles galvanisées* (Galvanized Steel Sheets). The shoot soon turned into a slapstick chase. No sooner were the sound and camera ready than Hains would give them the slip, stammer, or run off to the restaurant. And just when Hains finally started talking, the card-carrying union team demanded a break. Try as they might—holding up a train, being as cunning as Sioux—when, by some miracle, they managed to reach an agreement, it had already been dark for hours and nothing could be done. This documentary debacle tells us only one thing: The artist is elusive, both literally and figuratively.

It is certainly true that Hains's modernity is, to a large

extent, bound up with a practice that is fractured, scattered in fragments that are difficult to fit into the categories of art, and that the camera itself is unable to capture.[4] His vagabond "work in progress," which is not literature or philosophy or painting or barroom banter, and yet is all those things and more, holds a special fascination for critics and induces an unusual mimetism (which I can vouch for, having succumbed to it on occasions myself). One need only look at the catalogs—and, although brilliant, the one produced recently by the Musée National d'Art Moderne[5] is no exception—to see that they are more like delegated artist's books than historical tomes designed to show the evolution of a body of work over time. In them, exegesis is more like an echo chamber—Otto Hahn's account is seminal in this respect. The phenomenon is so palpable that one might legitimately wonder if it is not implacably induced by Hainsian logic, and if the trap that is the mirror held up to critics is not plainly and simply a constitutive element of Hains's oeuvre.

If, for a moment, we allow ourselves to take a few liberties, we can say that there may in fact be *two* Raymond Hains. The first, the man of the abstract photographs of 1946–47, of the film *Pénélope* (with Jacques de la Villeglé), of the torn posters and metal sheets, can easily be affiliated to some of the firmly established traditions of twentieth-century art: photographic manipulation, as initiated by Moholy-Nagy and Man Ray; abstract film, in the manner of Viking Eggeling or Oskar Fischinger; collage, of course and, on the level of purely visual effects, *art informel*.

The second, the man of those visual supports for ricocheting wordplay that are the *objets-blasons* (objects/blazons) and *images cryptées* (cryptic images), is not easy to fit into contemporary history. In order to find equivalents for the works in this category, we need to go back to traditions that are both older and more marginal: those of the Marquis de Bièvre's "six yews,"[7] which Raymond Hains himself has often acknowledged, or, more seldom invoked, the illustrated jokes of *Les Arts incohérents*[8]: Marcel Lebrun's *Les Dix Manches gras* [literally *Ten Fat Sleeves*, homophonically dimanche gras, i.e., Quinquagesima Sunday]; the portrait of the chemist Géraudel entitled *Le Génie de la pastille* (pun on pastel/Bastille), the *Vénus des mille eaux* [Venus de Milo/thousand waters], Paul Bilhaud's famous *Combat de nègres dans un tunnel* [Negroes fighting in a tunnel], wrongly attributed to Alphonse Allais, who merely copied the theme—all these and many other combinations that we now know only from catalogs. What is significant here is not so much the wordplay—in that area, Hains's forebears are truly innumerable—as the specific question of translating that wordplay into visual terms or, better, integrating it into a system that includes visual representation as part of the game. It could be said that the burlesque constructions of the Marquis de Bièvre and the Incohérents are themselves distant heirs of Brueghel's *Flemish Proverbs*,[9] which play cleverly on the disjunction that arises when one attempts to put a real image onto an imagistic turn of phrase, such as "he is sitting in the ashes between two stools" or "throwing roses to the swine." For the first, Brueghel depicts a man trying to stand on his feet using two stools—for the second, someone throwing roses to the pigs pressing around him.

Of course, this distinction is both hypothetical and reductive. For instance, there are times when the torn posters themselves bear punning titles (see the 1961 series "La France déchirée" (France torn apart),[10] in which the tatters of papers evoke the metaphorical division of the country into two camps during the war in Algeria). Alternatively, objects whose main point is their multilayered homophonic resonance are presented as found objects. This is the case, notably, for his *Palissades* (a punning title referring both to fencing or boarding and to a droll truism), which no doubt represent the most obvious objects of transition between the "mute" works of the first Hains and the "talking" ones of the second. Formally, the object presented here is close to the torn posters, and is indeed taken from the same urban space, but its visual quality, while not something Hains is indifferent to, is never more than a secondary benefit: "The *palissade*," he says, "stands in relation to the limits of the real, as a defensive reaction with regard to the real."[11] Retrospectively, all the objects produced by Hains, at whatever moment in his history, have their place in his world of verbal and logical coincidences, and it will no doubt seem rather arbitrary to attempt to divide up a body of work whose strength lies, in principle, precisely in the fact that it forms an indivisible whole. But the distinction remains valid, if only as a working hypothesis, and no one could deny that Hains's topicality at the present time owes more to what he has inherited from the marginal tradition of the *Hydropathes* and *Zwanseurs*[12] than to the paradoxical pictoriality of the "found collages" that are his sheet-metal pieces or torn posters.[13]

Not only can we put a very precise date on the emergence of the works in the second category, which can be referred to as blasons ("blazons," the term that respects the artist's own facing page: *Néo-dada emballé ou l'art de se tailler en palissade* at the Musée d'art Moderne de la ville de Paris, 4 March 1963. Photo: Harry Shunk, New York.

logic when he said that he would readily define his work as a "new heraldics"[14] [in French, blasonner means both to "represent something by means of a coded system" and to "mock, gibe at"]), but we can also isolate their distinguishing features. Two examples will suffice: the first *Palissade*, shown at the *Biennale de Paris* in 1959, and the *Néo-Dada emballé* [Packed horse], presented at the *Comparaisons* art show in 1963.

The chain of associations around the *word* palissade was found by Hains, but the decision to bring this out by exhibiting the palissade (fence) *object* can be attributed much more to his entourage. It was a choice to which he acquiesced but that he never really made. François Dufrêne recalls that in the very early fifties, conversations with Hains "were often organized around wordplay. His thinking was analogical.... His philosophical considerations were always linked to the present moment, to some memory, to his aunt, to his cousin."[15] "Hains had been talking about palissades for a good many years. He first filmed them in 1950. It was an idea that did not absolutely need to be made concrete. But it was a shame not to do it, and I told Hains that if he wasn't careful, someone might steal his idea. Anyway, one day, I saw workmen handling these magnificent planks a few steps from his place. I bought them and ... exhibited them in the framework of this *Lacéré anonyme* [Anonymous tear] a few months before the Biennale de Paris in 1959, as the 'first' palissade. Of course, this was just to get Hains to make his own."[16]

Around this palissade there crystallized a critical discourse that took up Hains's own discourse, but without really engaging the artist: An object that he did *not choose to show* became the instrument of a narrative that he *preferred not to write*. Thus, the famous *Palissade à Palewski*[17] (a fence made of skis,[18] as proposed to the director of the Galerie Rive Droite, Jean Larcade,[19] in 1965) only came into existence twenty-two days after its conception, at the initiative of Éric Fabre.[20] But it had an existence even before it was made, so much so that one journalist, so they say, praised it in his review of the exhibition at Larcade's gallery!

The oracular quality of Hains's passivity was spotted by one of the critics at the 1959 Biennale, Guy Lemborelle: "In the Informels room, Raymond Hains offers the triumph of laziness in the service of beauty. His palissade of torn posters stands in the room like a triumphant vestige of everything that has been and will never be."[21] As for Claude Rivière, in *Combat*, she was one of the first to spot the graft involved in Hains's find: "The palissade at the Biennale[22] is not a *réalité nouvelle*, not even a new reality.... It is a reject from the *Salon des Réalités Nouvelles* of 1949. While some newspapers, seeing Tinguely's machine, recalled that Roland Dorgelès had got a donkey's tail to paint a canvas. With a smile, Hains says, 'Posters are to collage what the donkey is to *frottage*. It is also the encounter of Mohican glue with the last of the *Abencerages* (Chateaubriand's novel). The lacerator's knife, like Yves—the Monochrome—Klein's *Roulor*,[23] is a courteous challenge to the paladins of the entirely handmade.' Dufrêne also says that 'the gesture is to Mathieu what the golden is to the mean.' Hains tops this with, 'What Mathieu is to the Carolingians, we are to the Good-for-Nothing Kings,' and that is why Dufrêne, with his *Décor de l'envers*, is more the Dagobert of France torn apart [*déchirée*]. And so the die is cast."[24]

The *Palissade*, the first *objet-blason*, enlists the artist's entourage in the creative decision and the art critic in the public revelation of the language in which this decision is rooted. But this principle of abandonment, or of the generalized delegation of decisions, could point to a risk of dependency. Indeed, some of the people around Hains were already issuing warnings. During a debate at the Galerie Braun, Claude Rivière apostrophized Hains and reproached him for his palissades, which, he said, led to a dead end.[25] Charles Estienne advised him to avoid "the temptation of spending your whole life exhibiting palissades."[26] One function of Hains's second *objet-blason*, the *Néo-Dada emballé* [Packed horse], was to manifest his independence.

This *Néo-Dada* was essentially a bit of a two-step with critics. We need to recall the circumstances in which it emerged. From May 17 to June 10, 1961, the Galerie J, at 8, rue Montfaucon, in Paris's sixth arrondissement, put on an exhibition called "À 40° au-dessus de Dada," uniting most of the signatories (with the exception of Raysse) to the declaration that had constituted Nouveau Réalisme the year before, plus César. It was organized by Pierre Restany, whose wife, Jeanine, owned the gallery (hence the *J*). It was he who chose the title and the artists, and appeared on the invitation, brandishing a dueling pistol.

The title met two imperatives: On one hand, it aimed to include artists participating in an international movement, whose two main figures, Johns and Rauschenberg, were commonly considered as "neo-dada"; on the other, it summed up Restany's own position, his vision of Nouveau Réalisme as taking over from dada, with the same premises and tactics but a more constructive spirit (hence, the metaphorical "40° above"): "The anti-art gesture of Marcel

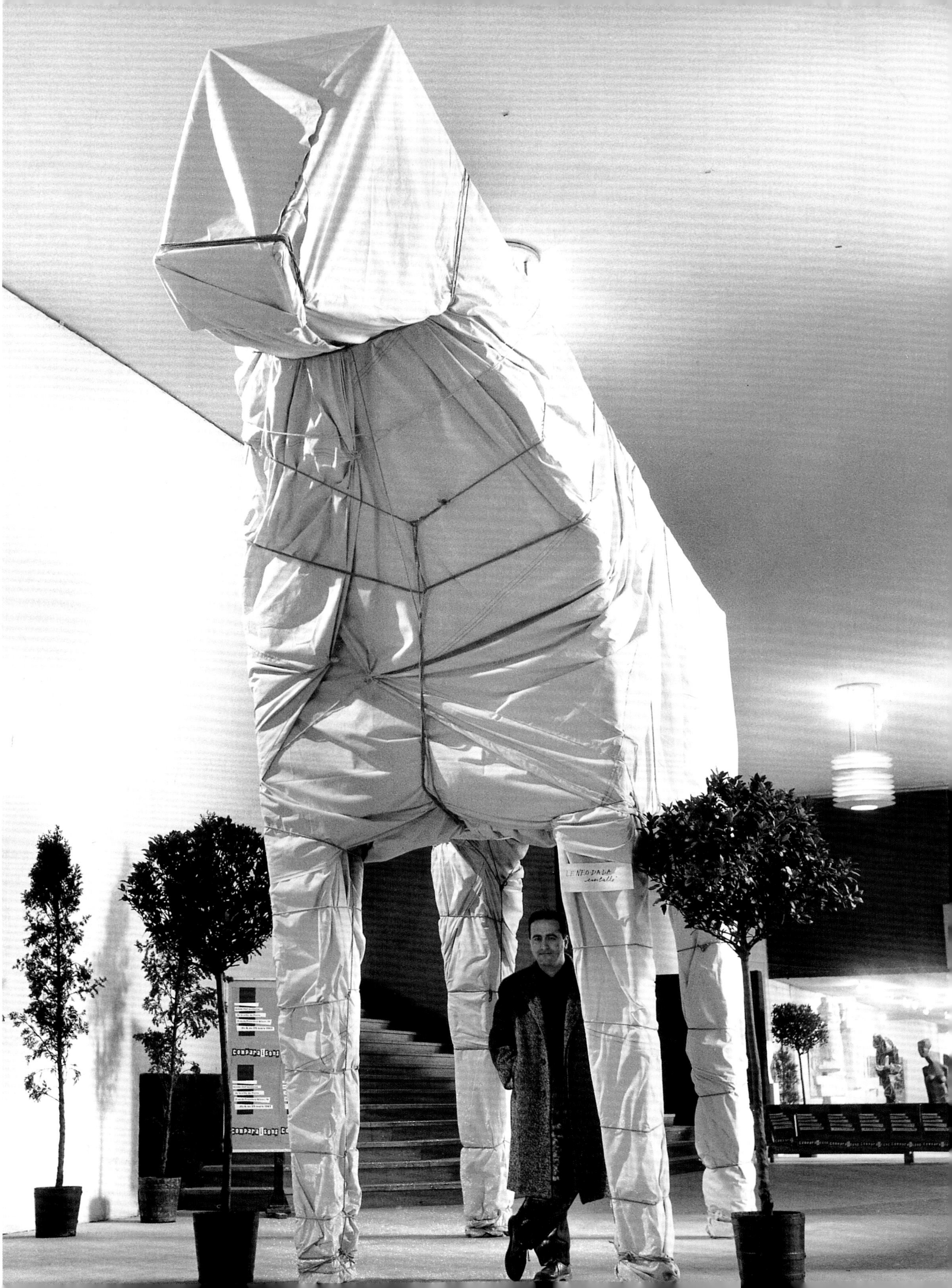
LE NEO DADA

Duchamp is infused with positivity. The dada spirit becomes identified with a way of appropriating the external reality of the modern world. The readymade is no longer the ultimate in negativity or polemics but the basic element of a new expressive repertoire."[27]

The artists took a different view. Klein, who was in New York when the show was on, wrote a letter to Restany[28] making this perfectly clear. His definition of *Réalisme d'aujourd'hui* was worlds away from the exhibition's, whose neo-dadaism also appeared to be a statement of allegiance to Leo Castelli, Johns's and Rauschenberg's dealer, with whom Klein's relations were far from smooth. Returning to France on October 8, 1961, he gathered a number of fellow artists—including Hains, naturally enough—and sympathetic critics whose approach was nonetheless different from Restany's: Alain Jouffroy, Pierre Descargues, and the poet John Ashberry. At the end of the day, which Hains described as the "day of neutral observers," Klein, Hains, and Raysse declared from the brasserie La Coupole that Nouveau Réalisme no longer existed, thus symbolically settling what Hains, again, called the "quarrel of investitures."

Still, for Hains this response did not go far enough. He was preparing his own. It would take the form of the *Néo-Dada emballé* two years later. This, then, was an eminently reactive work, a return shot, so to speak, and unintelligible for anyone who had not seen the previous round, the exhibition "À 40° au-dessus de Dada." The idea came to him after seeing *Helen of Troy*,[29] the epic movie directed by Robert Wise, in which we see the Spartans building the famous horse. The metaphor caught his fancy and he decided to make his own Trojan horse for critics out of planks from palissades covered—why not?—with torn posters. Then, thinking of Christo and his packed pieces (*emballages*), he had the idea of a packed horse, which would take on "a meaning that was both funnier and more conceptual."[30]

There are three versions of the *Néo-Dada*. A model by Christo, a photomontage by the American photographer Harry Shunk based on Christo's model, and the definitive construction shown at the *Comparaisons* salon by Gérard Matisse,[31] the grandson of Henri Matisse. Originally, it was Christo who was going to make the construction: The model was built using a toy filched from his own son, and Shunk's montage was intended to give an idea of how it would look in real space, once fully enlarged; Jeanine Restany had assembled the necessary bits of scaffolding.[32] But Christo was unable to complete the project, because of his frequent travels, and it came down to Gérard Matisse, with the help, among others, of Gérard Deschamps, to act as the providential engineer in realizing the object on a monumental scale.[33] Consequently, the three versions were all quite different. Evident in the model, the "Christo style" predictably got lost in the process of enlargement.

It may be worthwhile trying to break down the associative mechanism whereby this object, placed in the entry of the Musée d'Art Moderne, was able to function as a response to Pierre Restany (one thinks of the scholars of Balnibarbi, in *Gulliver's Travels*,[34] who converse not with words but with objects, which they carry around in bundles on their backs, and then lay out on the table between them). I offer a highly simplified table to the right.

The *Néo-Dada emballé* is an open work, of which a diagram can convey only the initial effects; the chain reaction of associated meanings is (almost) endless and evokes a whole world. A gardening term, "to prune hedges *en palissade*," is visually evoked by the presence of six potted plants around the packed construction, and links the piece to the first *objets-blasons*, the *Palissades*, and would serve as a hook for other, later associations, some of them extraordinarily convoluted: for instance, the Troy of the *Iliad* is assimilated to *Troyes*[35] in Champagne, which is geographically close to Romilly, whose homonym, *Jacqueline de Romilly*, is a famous French Hellenist, thus making the parallel meaningful. *Romilly* was also the name of the first tank to enter Paris at the Liberation. It was commanded by Guillebon, a companion of General Leclerc and father of Jeanne-Claude Christo, the wife of the inventor of *emballage* as an artistic practice. The type and number of references implied by an object of this kind is what sets Hains's wordplay apart from that of the *Incohérents*—which, in contrast, the artists of *Présence Panchounette* simply duplicated (one thinks of the very amusing *Trompette sous un crabe* [literally "trumpet under a crab," but evoking "tempête sous un crâne"—a "storm in the skull"]). While they both work in exactly the same way, the puns of the Incohérents make us laugh, or *only* make us laugh, whereas Hains's puns are rarely, outrightly funny but open up new worlds; they are, to borrow Nelson Goodman's formula, "ways of worldmaking." There is no better way of describing the circulation of meaning in Hains's work than the—admittedly anachronous—metaphor of the hypertext link. Each element in the artist's world is, in a sense, underlined, sketching out an irreducible and fascinating virtual arborescence.[36]

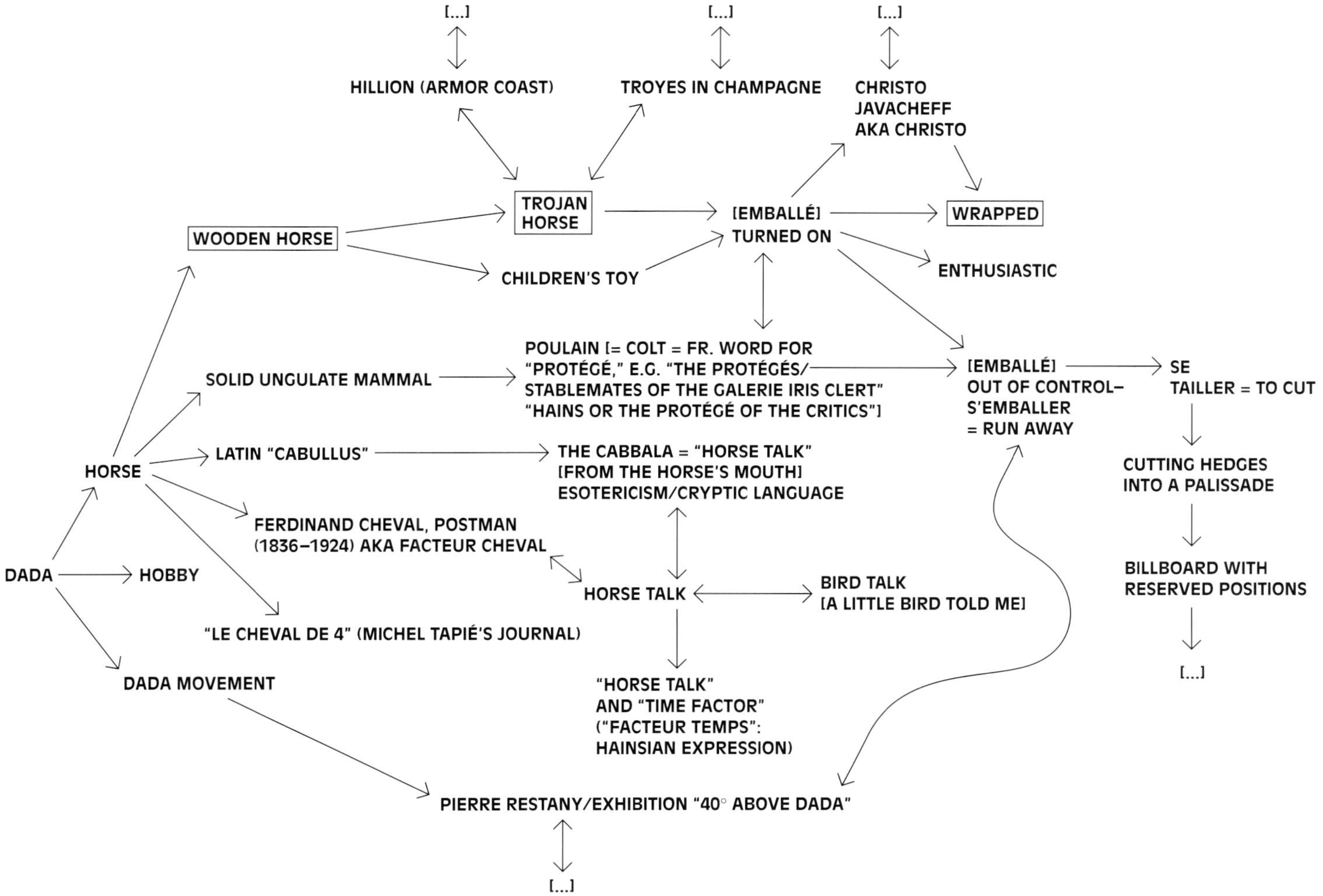
[...]
[...]
[...]
HILLION (ARMOR COAST)
TROYES IN CHAMPAGNE
CHRISTO
JAVACHEFF
AKA CHRISTO
TROJAN
HORSE
[EMBALLÉ]
TURNED ON
WRAPPED
WOODEN HORSE
CHILDREN'S TOY
ENTHUSIASTIC
POULAIN [= COLT = FR. WORD FOR
"PROTÉGÉ," E.G. "THE PROTÉGÉS/
STABLEMATES OF THE GALERIE IRIS CLERT"
"HAINS OR THE PROTÉGÉ OF THE CRITICS"]
SOLID UNGULATE MAMMAL
[EMBALLÉ]
OUT OF CONTROL–
S'EMBALLER
= RUN AWAY
SE
TAILLER = TO CUT
LATIN "CABULLUS"
THE CABBALA = "HORSE TALK"
[FROM THE HORSE'S MOUTH]
ESOTERICISM/CRYPTIC LANGUAGE
HORSE
CUTTING HEDGES
INTO A PALISSADE
FERDINAND CHEVAL, POSTMAN
(1836–1924) AKA FACTEUR CHEVAL
BILLBOARD WITH
RESERVED POSITIONS
DADA
HOBBY
HORSE TALK
BIRD TALK
[A LITTLE BIRD TOLD ME]
"LE CHEVAL DE 4" (MICHEL TAPIÉ'S JOURNAL)
[...]
DADA MOVEMENT
"HORSE TALK"
AND "TIME FACTOR"
("FACTEUR TEMPS":
HAINSIAN EXPRESSION)
PIERRE RESTANY/EXHIBITION "40° ABOVE DADA"
[...]

The *Néo-Dada emballé* is simultaneously an allegory of rebellion, a machine of war directed against an attempt at recuperation, and a demonstration of intelligence. Faced with a perceived attempt at appropriation by Restany, it reestablishes the preeminence of the artist. Hains readily presents himself as the "sigisbée" or beau of criticism, deliberately employing an old-fashioned name for the obliging and self-interested flatterer of a pretty woman. For if he defers to criticism, leaving it free to speak and, often, to decide whether or not to make a work in his name, he does so within a dialectic of master and slave that leaves the critic no chance of emerging untouched.

It is hard not to think that, ultimately, it is Hains who actively chooses his critics, while leaving them the illusion that they are free. He could not pass up the opportunity to substitute an *Otto Hahn*[37] for Restany's *Dada*. The associations evoked by the name Hahn corroborate the incoherent genea logy that we could justifiably attribute to the *Néo-Dada*: Otto Hahn = "auto-âne" [auto-donkey], which, like Tinguely's painting machine, as cited by Claude Rivière in *Combat*,[38] evokes the "âne Boronali," which was central to the hoax set up by Roland Dorgelès, very much in the spirit of the *Salon des Incohérents*. (My own surname, Bodet, a homophone of *baudet*, ass, was my gateway to Hainsian wordplay, and the object of all the usual classroom joshing.)

Above all, though, they allow Hains to demonstrate his system's effectiveness: In everyday French, the *coq-à-l'âne* [cock to donkey] is an expression for an abrupt conversational or discursive non sequitur. But while in ordinary discourse there is no logical relation, or relation of contiguity, between the cock and the *ass*, in Hains-speak âne *is* Hahn *is* coq [*Hahn* being the German for cock], a fact borne out by the French brand of hair lotion, Pétrole Hahn, whose label sports a cock.[39]

Donc [then, therefore] is the Hainsian conjunction *par excellence*, in that it makes it possible to transform a relation of proximity (in language, homophony, homonymy, assonance, and synonymy) into a relation of cause and effect. It sets in motion the demon of analogy, the keystone of what, speaking of the artist, Camille Bryen has described as a "verbal autism, which is at once benevolent and millenarian."[40]

For the dinner given for the vernissage of Hains's 1976 exhibition "La Faim du CNAC" (the event which marked the conclusion of the Centre National d'Art Contemporain's program before its fusion with the Musée National d'Art Moderne at the soon-to-be-opened Centre Georges Pompidou [*faim*, hunger, is a homophone of *fin*, end]), Daniel Spoerri wrote a menu featuring some "Notes pour le menu culturel homophone" [Notes for the cultural homophone menu], in which he took a friendly swipe at this particular linguistic tic: Each one is introduced by a donc and offers a transcription of some Hainsian associations. Note forty-eight concerns the "Garniture pommes de terres Fernandez emballées": *"Donc,* Christo again—see thirty-seven—*donc* the *Néo-Dada emballé*, as Hains said, but for me the finest example of megalomaniac Dadaism, *donc* also my *Conserves de magie à la noix:* not to mention the bones, teeth, hair, and nails, which served as pretexts for so many artists in all those centuries of Christian culture for surrounding themselves with packages [*emballages*] which are now exhibited as masterpieces. See fifty-one."

Note ninety-six explains "La palissade": "*Donc* the recipe for a cake in the *Encyclopédie Clartés* exhibited at the *Comparaisons* salon by Hains in May 1960, *donc La Palissade des emplacements réservés'* [Fence for reserved spaces], exhibited by Hains at the first Biennale de Paris, in 1959, *donc* the cake given out at the 'Festival du Nouveau Réalisme,' in Nice, on July 13, 1961, *donc* the cake of the 'Mille anni, Rrose Sélavy, Le Nocci' *Palissade* in my 'Ultima Cena, banquetto funebro del Nuovo Realismo' on November 27, 1970, an exhibition for the tenth anniversary of Nouveau Réalisme, *donc* in terms of architecture and fortification, a passive obstacle. See ninety-five."[41]

We may wonder if the *Palissade*, with its centripetal effect on critical discourse, and the *Néo-Dada emballé*, which puts that discourse back in its place, are not exactly programmatic of Hains's position and of the extraordinary love-hate relation with representatives of the art world—who have no choice but to submit—brought about by his sovereign position as an *inaction painter*. It would hardly be to betray a state secret to evoke the passionate atmosphere that usually surrounds his exhibitions. "To dare to exhibit Raymond Hains," writes Otto Hahn, "you need to be something of a hero. Much more than any other contemporary artist, he deserves the title of 'great disturber.' For years, he will accumulate documents and elaborate projects for hypothetical exhibitions, but, when the moment actually comes, Hains complicates his concept and, the day before the opening, starts on a new idea that cancels the earlier ones. Everytime, when the exhibition curator or gallery director assembles pieces or makes works in accordance with notes taken during their discussions with Hains, they do so against his will."[42]

Hains's exhibitions are necessarily incomplete illustrations of his scattered universe, but the responsibility for fixing this universe in an imperfect state ultimately rests

 Dada emballé of Christo, 1963, Private collection. Used as the maquette for *Néo-dada emballé ou l'art de se tailler en palissade*, by Raymond Hains. Photo: Harry Shunk, New York.

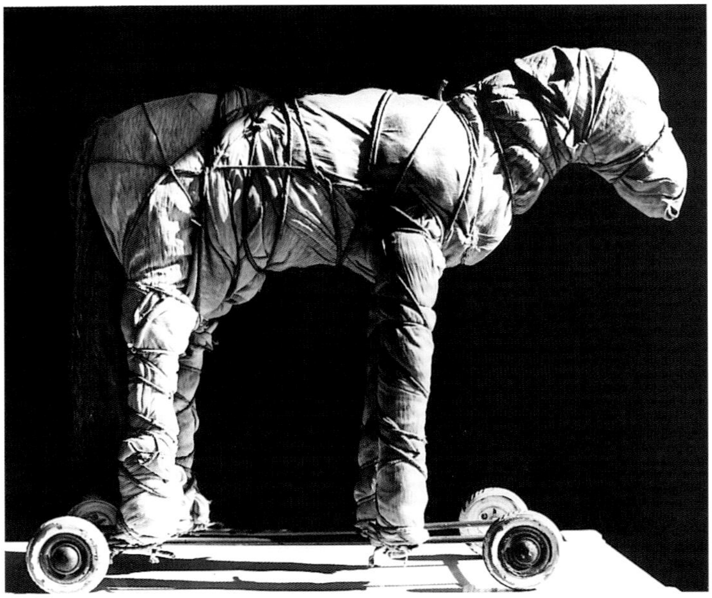

not on the artist but on the person who has used his discourse in order to bring forth a form: the critic (or the curator, who is often the same person). The theoretical interchangeability of the roles of artist and critic (or of curator, exegete, manager) is a constant in Hains's statements: "I think that art critics are artists who exhibit their point of view; they are artists, just like the others."[43] In 1964 and 1965, this view was even the pretext for two exhibitions at the Galleria del Leone, Venice, and at Iris Clert, in Paris, in which he presented giant matchboxes bearing the signatures SAFFA and SEITA (respectively, the Italian and French national tobacco authorities). Hains, here, was the "manager" of these two fictional artists: "What I was trying to do was reprise Correggio's words, *'Anche io sono pittore'* but this time saying, 'And I too am a critic.'[44] In fact, the actual making of these boxes was, to a large extent, delegated: "You should have seen us all at the gallery," recalls Iris Clert, "rubbing, painting, and finishing off the master's work until, satisfied by the result, he deigned to add his signature."[45]

But this fiction of the mutual permeability of roles is merely one more demonstration of authority. Whatever may happen, the person who finishes off the piece is, ultimately, in the wrong. When Marc Dachy asked him what, for him, an ideal exhibition would be like, Hains replied: "I don't know, I am happy to do exhibitions as I am at the moment, I think that's fine. I simply wanted to say that these exhibitions are not finished," thus reintegrating the idea of a constantly deferred closure, which was already contained in the title of the film he made with Villeglé (*Pénélope...*).[46]

Raymond Hains could claim the fine ambition expressed by Malevich, who wanted to "reduce calumny to nothing and make laziness not the mother of all vices but the mother of perfection."[47] His oddball logic makes him the dandy of a very particular genre whose exuberant prolixity is no easier to grasp than the distant silence of two other twentieth-century dandies, Duchamp and Warhol. In a way, it offers us even less of a handle, and the fact that this artist, who, as Otto Hahn puts it, is "viscerally opposed to any kind of productive activity,"[48] should now stand at the head of a gigantic body of work is truly prodigious, and the sign of an absolute mastery of paradox.

AUTHOR'S NOTE

I wish to extend special thanks to Christian Schlatter for his advice, and my gratitude to Didier Semin for his patience and precious suggestions throughout the process of writing and revising the text.

ENDNOTES

1. André Breton, *Nadja*, in *Oeuvres Complètes*, vol. 1 (Paris: Gallimard, Bibliothèque de la Pléiade, 1988), 744–46.
2. *Raymond Hains: La chasse au CNAC* (Paris: Centre National d'Art Contemporain, 1976), 232–35.
3. *Les Nouveaux Réalistes*, 16 mm, color, sound, 56 min., dir. Adrien Maben, commentary Otto Hahn, 1976.
4. He later admitted that this elusiveness was, to some extent, premeditated, or, at least, calculating: "It took me fifteen years to build up my persona, and I have no intention of taking apart my song for five minutes of film"; *Hains, La chasse au CNAC*, 234–35. The only person who captured anything was the soundman, who found Hains at his loquacious best until four in the morning.
5. *Raymond Hains, J'ai la mémoire qui planche*, ed. P. Leguillon, Musée National d'Art Moderne (Paris: Éd. du Centre Pompidou, 2001).
6. Raymond Hains, Jacques de la Villeglé, *Pénélope*, 16 mm color, silent, 14 min., shot 1950–54, ed. Jean-Michel Bouhours, 1981.
7. Georges-François Mareschal, Marquis de Bièvre (1747–89), the author of *Vercingentorixe* (1770), a burlesque tragedy chock-full of puns (Paris: Jean-Jacques Pauvert, 1964). One of Hains's favorite stories about the Marquis de Bièvre concerns six yews (ifs) that he planted on his estate, in front of which he was in the habit of pushing home his advantage with young women: It was, he said, the "l'instant des six ifs" (= "l'instant décisif," the decisive moment). Once he had cleared up the "misunderstanding," he invited them to go and drink milk in his dairy, where they saw a post surmounted by a "large placard with the letter *I* written on it in black carbon"; Duchesse d'Abrantès, *Histoire des salons de Paris*, vol. 2 (Paris: 1838), 340 sq. "One day, when I was with friends listening to Isidore Isou on the radio talking about Lettrism and the letter *I*, one of them, who was leafing through an issue of *L'Oeil*, found a print showing a saint in ecstasy before the letter *I*. That was when I realized that everything was about the letter I: the 'I.C.' of the Christians, the 'yod' of the cabala, the phallus of psychoanalysis..."; interview with the artist, 27 May 1985.
8. Catherine Charpin, *Les Arts incohérents (1882–93)*, preface by F. Caradec (Paris: Syros Alternatives, 1990).
9. Pieter Brueghel, *The Flemish Proverbs*, 1559, 117 x 163 cm (Berlin, Staatliche Museen). These games used to be extremely popular. We know of at least seventeen period replicas of this painting.
10. "La France déchirée," solo show by Raymond Hains, Galerie J, Paris, 1961.
11. Interview with the artist, 6 January 1986: This comment came after his reading of Anna Freud and does not rule out the allusion to Bibi Fricotin (Gaston Callaud, *Bibi Fricotin au Pôle Nord*, no. 8 [Paris: Société Parisienne d'Édition, 1936]). Bibi Fricotin knocks together a racecourse for penguins using boards from a palissade so as to entertain his traveling companions. "Bibi Fricotin could have been where I first saw *palissades*"; quoted in *Hains, J'ai la mémoire qui planche*, 2.
12. Charpin, *Les Arts incohérents*.
13. "I am not a creator, I don't show posters but inspirations"; interview with the artist, 5 August 1985.
14. "Buren or Mosset are the current representatives, their stripes and the *O* are their blazons"; interview with the artist, 21 January 1987. This comment was prompted by a visit to the exhibition "Héraldique et blason: du Moyen Âge au T.G.V.," at Dijon, in 1986.
15. Interview with François Dufrêne by Daniel Abadie, in *Hains: La chasse au CNAC*, 47.
16. Ibid., 48. "Lacéré anonyme," the exhibition by Hains, Dufrêne, and Villeglé, organ-

ized by François Dufrêne at the home of Ginette and François Dufrêne, in June 1959.

17. Hains had long been an admirer of Gaston Palewski's writings and actions to promote the preservation of Venice.

18. Derived from "wooden *palissades* in pâlâça wood, at Palissot or Palissy," in response to "palissade en palissandre pour les *Cendres de Sade*" (rosewood palissade for Sade's ashes) or "palissade polissonne pour personne seule et maussade" (saucy palissade for solitary and glum person) offered to Hains by François Dufrêne in 1959). See "L'Optique moderne de Daniel Spoerri," facing "Inutiles Notules," by François Dufrêne, in *Daniel Spoerri* (Paris: Centre National d'Art Contemporain, 1972), 44.

19. Raymond Hains was planning to borrow the equipment from Larcade Sports on rue de Rennes (Paris): "I was enticed by names ending in 'ski': Alechinsky, Palewski, Klossowski, Madame Hanska, General de Hanski ... because skis are not ugly, and in front of the shop window on the rue de Rennes, I heard something like the call of Alechinsky" (Appel Alechinsky—names of two artists in Cobra)"; interview with the artist, 19 December 1985.

20. Under the title "La foire aux skis" [Ski Fair], at "1, 2, 2 1/2, 3, Partez!," a group show at the Galerie de Paris in March 1988.

21. Guy Lemborelle, "La Biennale de Paris," *Genèse* (15 October 1959).

22. Raymond Hains, *La Palissade des emplacements réservés*, Salle des Informels, Biennale de Paris, 1959. The work disappeared when the exhibition was being taken down.

23. The brand of the paint roller used by Yves Klein.

24. Claude Rivière, "Biennale de Paris : Du monde pictural à la palissade," *Combat* (5 October 1959).

25. Raymond Hains retorted: "They do not lead to an impasse but to La Palice!"; interview with the artist, 17 December 1984. And, as he also said: "For me, going to La Palice is going hunting for misunderstandings"; interview with the artist, 18 March 1985.

26. "As Charles Estienne said to me the day after the first Biennale de Paris: '*Palissades* are fine, but you don't mean to go exhibiting palissades all your life. What is interesting is to make an ideal palace, like the postman Cheval, an ideal palace through time and space'"; *Raymond Hains, les 3 Cartier, du Grand Louvre aux 3 Cartier* (Paris: Fondation Cartier pour l'Art Contemporain, 1994), 126.

27. Pierre Restany, preface to the exhibition catalog *À 40° au-dessus de Dada* (Paris: Galerie J, May 1961). The exhibition featured Arman, César, Dufrêne, Hains, Klein, Rotella, Spoerri, Tinguely, and Villeglé.

28. "My dear Pierre, I have just seen the catalogue-cum-manifesto of the 'Nouveaux Réalités' exhibition. It is very fine and the text is brilliant, as always, but I really do not agree with '40° au-dessus de Dada.' But, I mean, really not!

"Please, don't be angry with me for being frank with you, after all, we have been friends for too long to fake politeness. Moreover, I see the list of the N.R. (Nouveaux Réalistes) has been extended again, as before, with all those guys, who are all very well, but whom we decided not to include when the movement started.

"As you know, my dear Pierre, I was the one who started this idea with you.

"I suggested 'Réalisme' or 'Réalistes d'aujourd'hui.' You wanted 'Nouveau Réalisme.' Okay, but not okay for 'À 40° au-dessus de Dada.'

"I am therefore leaving the group and ask you to respect my resignation and to solemnly remove from the exhibition the work of mine that is probably hanging there.

"Once again, I ask you not to be angry with me. Please don't hold it against me.

I have fought too hard for a long, long time for my spiritual, emotional, and realist position to allow myself to be affiliated in any way to Dada, either closely or remotely, be it 40° above or below!" Private collection; quoted in part by Catherine Millet, *Yves Klein* (Paris: Artpress/Flammarion, 1983), 26.

29. *Helen of Troy*, starring Stanley Baker, Rossana Podesta, Jacques Sernas, Cedric Hardwicke, and Brigitte Bardot, 1955.

30. Interview with the artist, 21 January 1985.

31. Whether by Hainsian coincidence or objective chance (you could argue that it's the same thing), Gérard Matisse is now the owner of a stud farm in Savoy.

32. Model for the *Néo-Dada emballé ou l'art de se tailler en palissade*, by Raymond Hains, made by Christo under the title *Dada emballé*, 1963, toy, fabric, rope, 43 x 51 x 16 feet; private collection.

33. After making the 1:10 scale model in balsa wood, it took Gérard Matisse eight days and a few sleepless nights to produce the construction. In the end, given the technical difficulties and the worries of the director of the art fair, they gave up the idea that they had entertained for a while of mounting the horse on wheels and having it hauled in by the Grande Masse from the Beaux-Arts. During its construction, when the object tottered over and smashed a window in the museum, the damage was amusingly attributed to the animal's untimely kicking; interview with Gérard Matisse, 8 October 2001.

34. In order to perfect the language of Balnibarbi, a professor at the School of Languages proposes a scheme "for entirely abolishing all Words whatsoever; and this was urged as a great Advantage in Point of Health as well as Brevity. For it is plain, that every Word we speak is in some Degree a Diminution of our Lungs by Corrosion, and consequently contributes to the shortening of our Lives. An Expedient was therefore offered, that since Words are only Names for Things, it would be more convenient for all Men to carry about them, such Things as were necessary to express the particular Business they are to discourse on.... However, many of the most Learned and Wise adhere to the New Scheme of expressing themselves by Things, which hath only this Inconvenience attending it, that if a Man's Business be very great, and of various kinds, he must be obliged in Proportion to carry a greater bundle of Things upon his Back, unless he can afford one or two strong Servants to attend him. I have often beheld two of those Sages almost sinking under the Weight of their Packs, like Pedlars among us; who, when they met in the Streets, would lay down their Loads, open their Sacks, and hold Conversation for an Hour together; then put up their Implements, help each other to resume their Burthens, and take their Leave.

"But for short Conversations a Man may carry Implements in his Pockets and under his Arms, enough to supply him, and in his House he cannot be at a loss: Therefore the Room where Company meet who practice this Art, is full of all Things ready at Hand, requisite to furnish Matter for this kind of artificial Converse"; Jonathan Swift, *Gulliver's Travels*, Part 3, in J. Swift, *Gulliver's Travels and Other Writings* (Oxford: Oxford University Press, 1976), 150–51.

35. "Before going to Troyes I would have said: Cassandre, therefore Savignac, but I would not yet have said Ilion therefore Yffiniac"; interview with the artist, 27 May 1985. Now, Ilion is Troie in Troade and Hillion, a village in the bay of Saint-Brieuc, Hains's birthplace, is close to Yffiniac: "By making *equations*, I am trying to make anti-atomic discoveries and, through a network of disarming coincidences, to drive the scientists of the arms industry mad. My basic thinking is that I believe in the equations of life"; interview with the artist, 22 May 1983.

36. In this regard, Raymond Hains's latest works, the *Macintoshages*, which came out of his collaboration with the FRAC Champagne-Ardenne in 1998, show how the associative procedures governing computers are compatible with the artist's own thought processes. Starting from the idea of a "CD-ROM-CD-REM," (Rem brings to mind *Rémois*, the name of an inhabitant of Reims, and Rem, a make of cookie.) Hains, the exhibition curators, and their photographer and computer programmer, Georges Dupin, ended up with photographic images based on "screen grabs" ["*capture d'écran*"] showing several windows simultaneously open, including the apple and menu bars. No doubt, Hains found the expression "*capture d'écran*" pleasing in itself. The companionship between Hains and his photographer plays an important role in this preparatory phase. Émeric Dubois, Daniel Pype, and Joël Audebert were the first *interpreters* of the *images cryptées*; Liliane Vincy and Éric Fabre were the first to commission them—Liliane Vincy, in 1976, with the exhibition "L'Art à Vinci" at the Galerie Lara Vincy, Éric Fabre, starting in 1982, and, notably, with the 1983 exhibition "*Monochrome dans le métro*" (combined with the exhibition of Flaminio Gaggioni's first bar-code pieces).

37. Shortly after he read an article in *Sciences et Avenir* about the German ore tanker Otto Hahn (named after the German scientist who discovered nuclear fission and equipped with a nuclear reactor using boiling water), Hains was at the Café de Flore when he was introduced by Erik Dietman to the critic Otto Hahn, whose article "Pop Art and Happenings" he had read in *Les Temps modernes* (January 1964). This meeting was to inspire numerous declarations: "Otto Hahn is the eponym of the critic. I am myself an *auto-âne* or an *auto-cock*—*Hahn* is cock in German—and I can do my own auto-analysis just as Freud did his, or my own Otto-critique thanks to Otto Hahn. I am hunting for the truths of La Palice, which are not silly truisms but profound truths. If I go to La Palice, a land of Truths, and to Cambrai, a land of *Bêtises* (literally "nonsense" or "mischief," a *bêtise de Cambrai* is a hard mint candy), it is to ask myself what truth, what idiocy or mischief Critics are going to find to write about the Roulor or the torn posters in relation to painting. I am anachronous, or a professional an-artist: Instead of painting a picture with a mythological theme—which would be an anachronism—I prefer to keep a precise chronicle of my adventures. All my inspirations, I owe them to the people I meet, which explains the importance of my notes and cards"; interview with the artist, 10 May 1986. "The real oil [*pétrole*, as in Pétrole Hahn] is in the names"; interview with the artist, 6 June 1985.

38. Rivière, "Biennale de Paris."

39. In 1966, Olivier Mosset attempted to transcribe all this: "*Seita* and *Saffa* are the two twins of space imagined by Hains and are part of his critical cosmology in the form of a spider's web/riddle.... Seita is itself the creator of the matchbox (*mise en boîte*) illustrated by the La Fontaine fable (Racine Boileau de La Fontaine): the donkey [*âne*] in a lion's skin. The donkey, Christ signifies donkey, said Artaud, therefore Otto Hahn, therefore Pétrole Hahn, therefore the cock, therefore the *coq à l'âne*, therefore the foal, therefore the Trojan horse, therefore the néodada, therefore Hains the protégé [*poulain*] of the critic (Hahn), brings his own stone ([= *pierre*] Restany) to the criticism of this society of wild men (lions) and ravagers (torn posters, the body of the Nemean lion)"; from "Seita & Saffa et Raymond Hains," *Le Petit Colosse de Simi*, no. 1 (1966), 24–25. On the back of the Pétrole Hahn illustration shown here, the artist has written, "We are no longer looking for a *pétrolier* (petroleum) agreement with Xour or Panthène. When it is a matter of celebrating the critique of the express and the scientist who discovered nuclear fission! [signed] Raymond the abstract, *auto-âne*."

40. Interview with Camille Bryen, by Daniel Abadie, in *Hains: La chasse au CNAC*, 152.

41. *Donc Daniel Spoerri*, "Menu pour le Dîner de la Société Homonyme," *La Faim*

du CNAC, le 2 juin, 1976: Notes pour le menu culturel homophone, en hommage refusé au sigisbée de la critique, by Daniel Spoerri, assisted by Daniel Abadie and Nathalie Menasseyre (Paris: Centre National d'Art Contemporain, June 1976).

42. Otto Hahn, "Raymond Hains," *Beaux-Arts Magazine*, no. 34, (April 1986), 60–63.

43. Raymond Hains, Marc Dachy, *Langue de Cheval et Facteur temps, entretien au café du Palais, Reims, le 8 avril, 1998, dans l'après-midi* (Arles/Reims: Actes Sud/FRAC Champagne-Ardenne, 1998), 37.

44. Interview with the artist, 18 March 1985.

45. Iris Clert, *Iris.Time* (*L'Artventure*), (Paris: Denoël, 1978), 306.

46. "There is what is manifest and what is hidden: There is what can be seen in an exhibition and there are the facts that even I don't know and that one of these days we are going to discover"; interview with the artist, 27 May 1985. "What interests me is giving an answer in advance, in my own way, to a certain number of questions that no one asks"; Hahn, "Raymond Hains," 63).

47. From Kazimir Malevich, *La Paresse comme vérité effective de l'homme*, trans. R. Gayraud (Paris: Allia, 1999), 40.

48. Hahn, "Raymond Hains," 60.

AUTHOR

Aude Bodet has an advanced degree from the École du Louvre and a doctorate in art history from Paris IV-Sorbonne. From 1987 to 2000, she was adviser in visual arts to the DRAC Île-de-France (Ministère de la Culture et de la Communication).

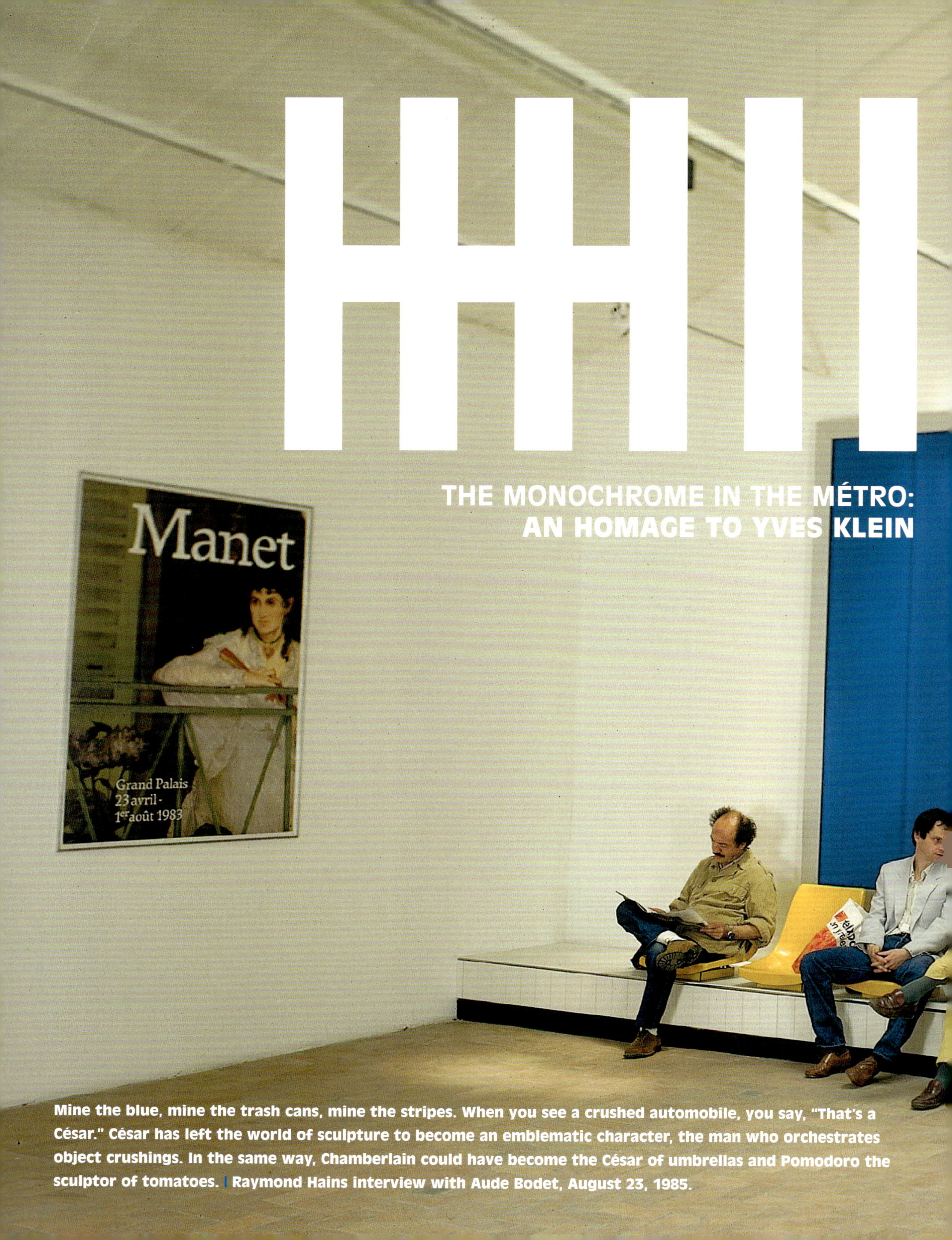

THE MONOCHROME IN THE MÉTRO: AN HOMAGE TO YVES KLEIN

Mine the blue, mine the trash cans, mine the stripes. When you see a crushed automobile, you say, "That's a César." César has left the world of sculpture to become an emblematic character, the man who orchestrates object crushings. In the same way, Chamberlain could have become the César of umbrellas and Pomodoro the sculptor of tomatoes. | Raymond Hains interview with Aude Bodet, August 23, 1985.

Le Monochrome dans le métro [Monochrome in the Métro], 1983/2001. Collection Éric Fabre, Brussels.

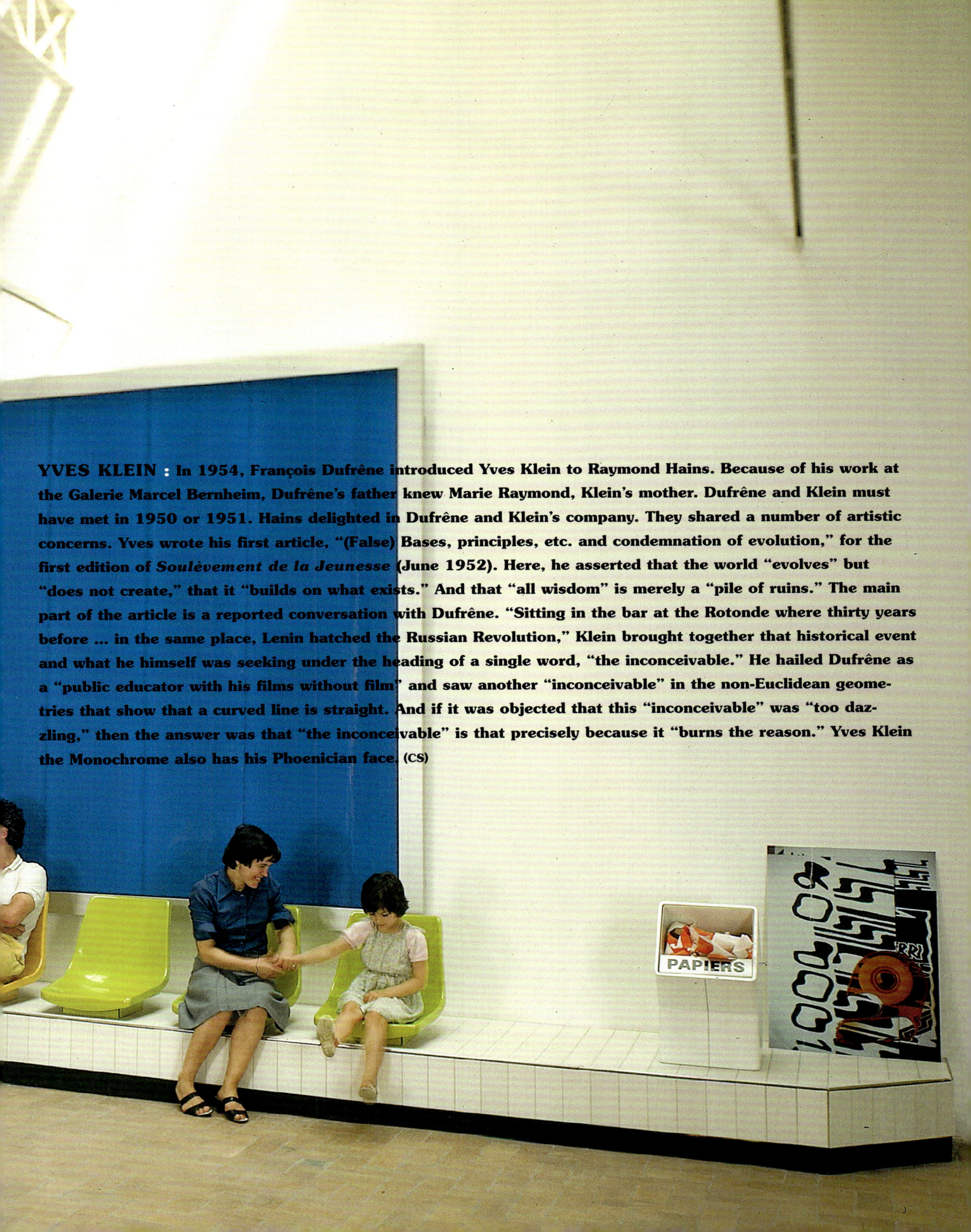

YVES KLEIN : In 1954, François Dufrêne introduced Yves Klein to Raymond Hains. Because of his work at the Galerie Marcel Bernheim, Dufrêne's father knew Marie Raymond, Klein's mother. Dufrêne and Klein must have met in 1950 or 1951. Hains delighted in Dufrêne and Klein's company. They shared a number of artistic concerns. Yves wrote his first article, "(False) Bases, principles, etc. and condemnation of evolution," for the first edition of *Soulèvement de la Jeunesse* (June 1952). Here, he asserted that the world "evolves" but "does not create," that it "builds on what exists." And that "all wisdom" is merely a "pile of ruins." The main part of the article is a reported conversation with Dufrêne. "Sitting in the bar at the Rotonde where thirty years before ... in the same place, Lenin hatched the Russian Revolution," Klein brought together that historical event and what he himself was seeking under the heading of a single word, "the inconceivable." He hailed Dufrêne as a "public educator with his films without film" and saw another "inconceivable" in the non-Euclidean geometries that show that a curved line is straight. And if it was objected that this "inconceivable" was "too dazzling," then the answer was that "the inconceivable" is that precisely because it "burns the reason." Yves Klein the Monochrome also has his Phoenician face. (CS)

 Yves aux azulejos, 2000. Courtesy Galerie Daniel Templon, Paris.

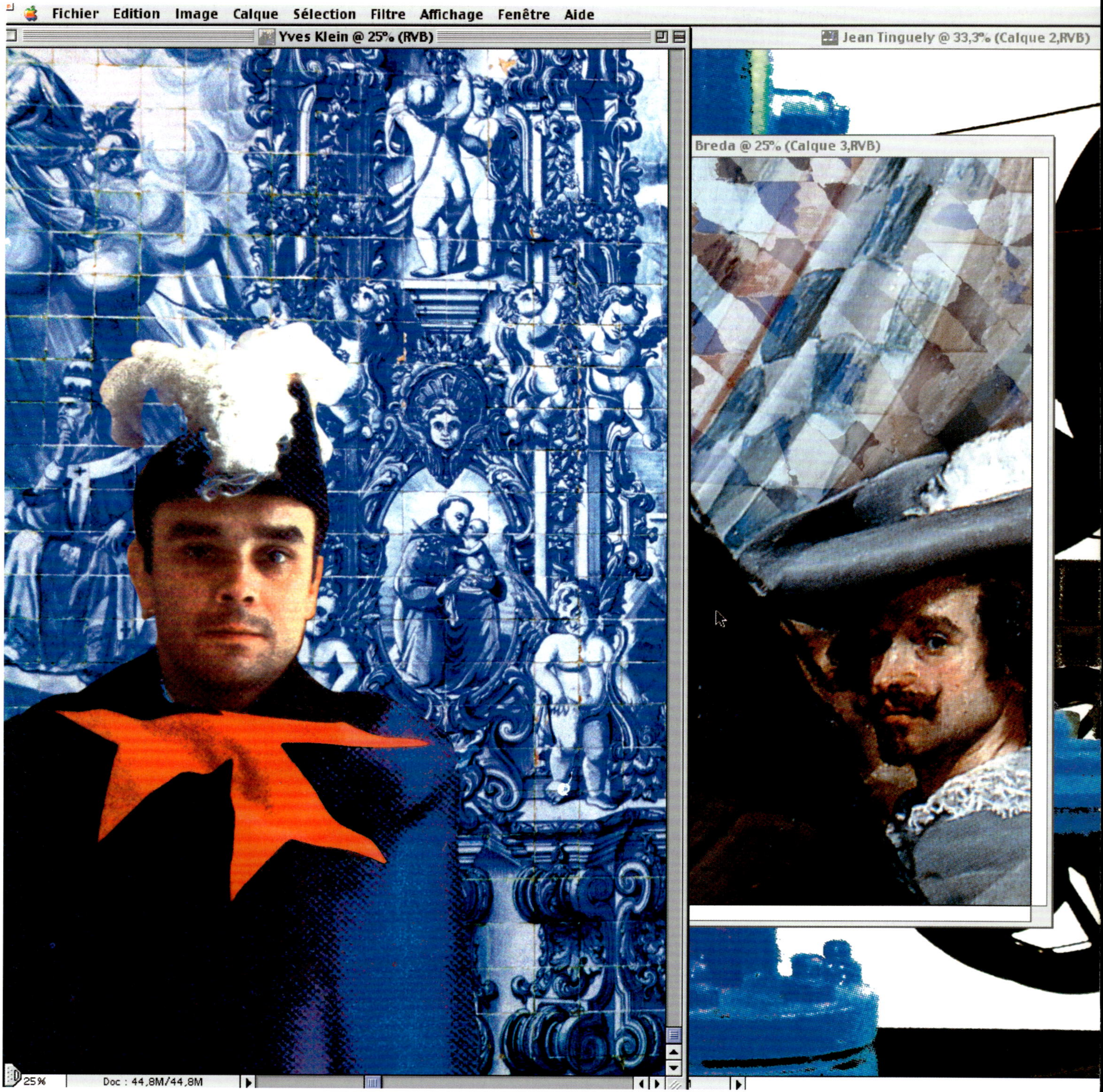

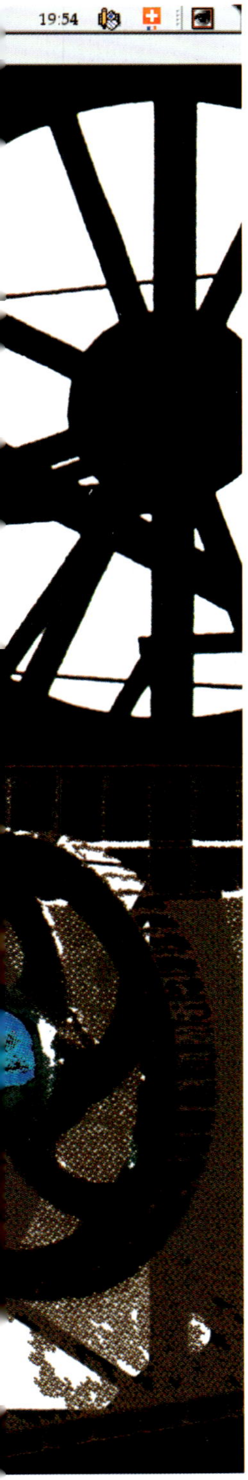

ÉRIC FABRE : The French collector and gallerist (Galerie Éric Fabre, 1974–81, and from 1984, Galerie de Paris) Éric Fabre put on four solo shows of Hains's work, and featured his contributions in two group shows. These manifested his "new manners." Each time, new pieces were produced, linked to current events. In 1983, he exhibited *Le Monochrome dans le metro*, a partial reconstitution of a French subway station with, above the seating, an advertising billboard filled with blue paper, in an allusion to Yves Klein, blotting out the old advertisement. Then, there was a poster for the Manet exhibition at the Grand Palais, and an enameled sheet of metal with the logo of a packet of twenty-four LU Petit Beurre cookies and their identifying code deformed by the ribbed glass. Flaminio Gaggioni, Hains's guest artist, exhibited his bar codes. In 1989 (Foire Internationale d'Art Contemporain, Galerie de Paris booth), he presented his *Le Piédestal du Louis XIV*, alluding to the construction work on the Grand Louvre. In 1992, "Raymond Hains, la nouvelle architecture du Grand Louvre," with a drawing by the architect Jean Nouvel and a maquette of the Louvre's Pavillon Richelieu wing by Philippe Le Heuzey, identical to the one he made for the Établissement Public du Grand Louvre. "And why not some Jean Nouvel, clashing metal, a shining château on the roofs of the Louvre?" commented Hains. (CS)

PERSONIFIED ABSTRACTIONS : Raymond Hains took this lexical item, pertaining to Indo-European mythology, from Georges Dumézil in 1948. Dumézil contrasted personified abstractions and sovereign divinities. By transposing the idea into the artistic sphere, Hains was suggesting a critique of art and artists: "What interests me in Nouveau Réalisme are the personified abstractions. One comes up against the question of the artist's relation to his name and his work. Like Klein, Fontana, and Buren, do not all artists become characters who are emblematic of their work? I myself am a personified abstraction." But, at the same time, Hains was constantly finding "new ways" of avoiding the spells of repetition. About Jean Tinguely: "Like Tinguely, I build machines, but Jean's are joke and trick machines, mine are word-traps, portmanteau words, words in valises, and, sometimes, too, *bons mots*." About Yves Klein: "People always say that Arman was the Nouveau Réaliste who did 'fullness' the way Yves did 'emptiness.' But Yves, who was a knight of the Order of Saint Sebastian, whose blazon is of a single tincture (*plein*), became, when in this order, 'Yves the Monochrome.' In the Middle Ages, did they not give the knight who had yet to accomplish an exploit a *plein*, that is, monochrome blazon?" (CS)

this page: *La Déclaration constitutive du Nouveau Réalisme* [Constitutional Declaration of the New Realists], October 27, 1960. Collection Musée d'art moderne de la Ville de Paris.
facing page, top left and right: *Les Nouveaux Réalistes* [The New Realists], 1960/1990. Collection Réunion des Musée Nationaux/Musée National d'art Moderne, Centre Pompidou, Paris.
bottom, and next page: *Hépérile éclaté* [Shattered *Hépérile*], with Jacques Villeglé, Librairie Lutétia, Paris, 1953. Documentation Musée National d'art Moderne, Centre Pompidou, Paris.

NEW REALISM

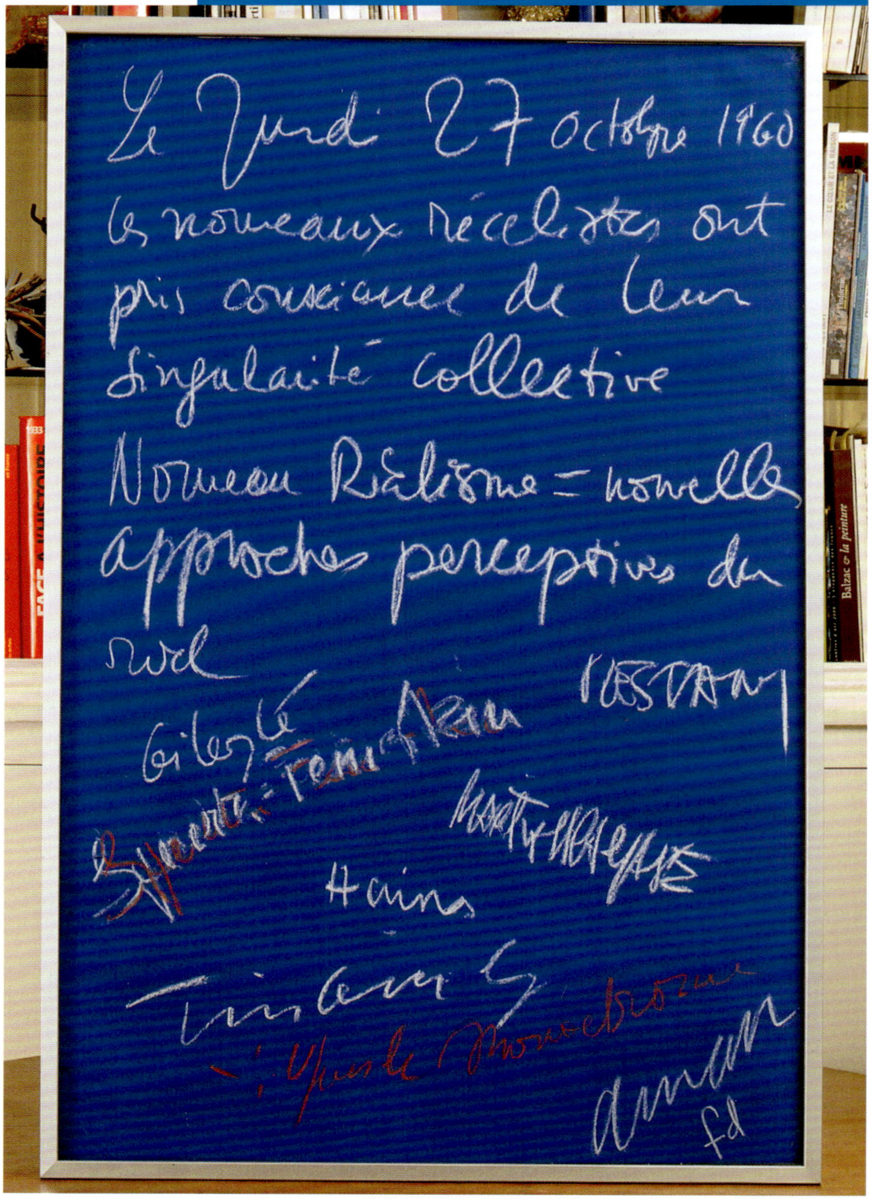

New Realism is not a group of artists but a kind of brotherhood. A group of little Caesars who divide up the world the way you cut a cake. Yves Klein takes the color blue, César the crushed cars, Arman the trash cans, Villeglé, Rotella, and me the torn posters, Christo the wrappings. With the Nouveaux Réalistes, we are leaving the world of painting for the world of truth. Artists are leaving the creation of art to become abstractions personified. | Raymond Hains, from Otto Hahn, "Raymond Hains," BEAUX-ARTS MAGAZINE, **April 1986.**

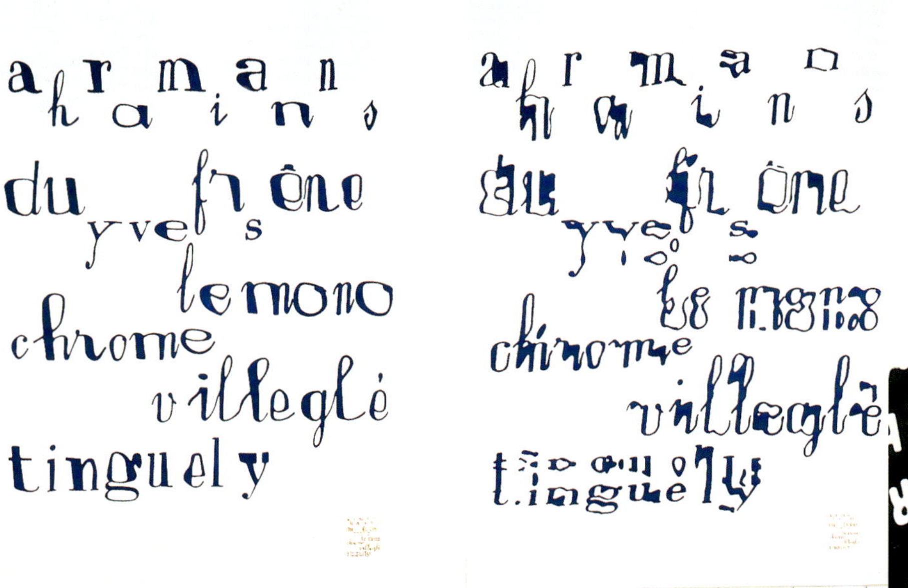

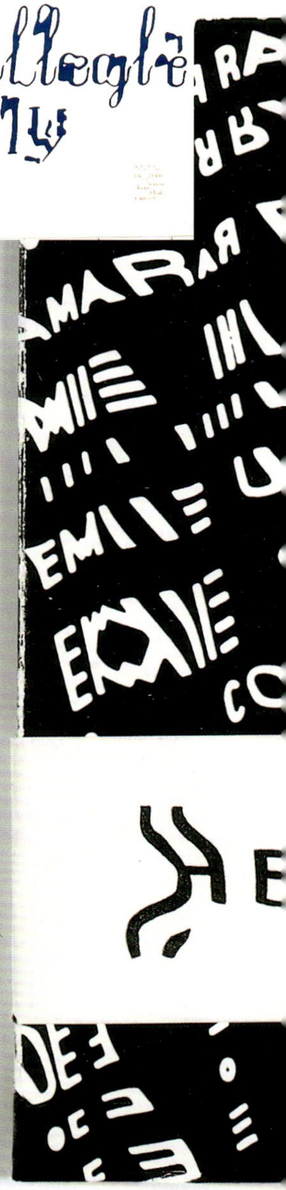

PIERRE RESTANY : Hains first used the term "other reality" in 1952. After Villeglé's *Des réalités collectives* in 1958, the art critic Pierre Restany wrote the first Nouveau Réaliste manifesto for the group exhibition by Arman, Dufrêne, Hains, Yves le Monochrome, Tinguely, and Villeglé at the Galleria Apollinaire, Milan, on April 16, 1960. On October 27, the founding statement of Nouveau Réalisme was signed at Klein's apartment by Arman, Dufrêne, Hains, Klein, Raysse, Restany, Spoerri, Tinguely, and Villeglé. This "new realism based on pure sensibility" was not always wholeheartedly espoused by some of the artists grouped under this banner, who had all known each other for a good many years. Hains rejected the term: "There is no Nouveau Réalisme, there is only a Tinguely-type movement of which we are the *rotellas* [*rotella* in Italian meaning small wheel, and evoking the can of Rotella machine oil] and this movement, which is our glory machine [*Machine à Gloire* being the title of a short story by Villiers de l'Isle Adam], would become our shame machine if we failed to stick a nail in the tree of liberty." That said, as Hains admitted, "I like Restany a lot ... [he] ... put me on the train for Italy." (CS)

It was an encounter, and an encounter doesn't necessarily mean a group. When Churchill met Roosevelt and Stalin at Yalta, it didn't mean they were in the same group. So, we were artists who came to share the interdependence of the territory of the retina: I'll take blue, I'll take green, I'll take the posters...." I think that art critics are artists who exhibit their point of view, like any other artists. So are ministers of culture. That's why I think that an artist in France has to be the minister of his own culture. This is what I have learned from Nouveau Réalisme. | Raymond Hains interview with Marc Dachy, HORSE-LANGUAGE AND FACTOR TIME, FRAC Champagne-Ardenne/Actes Sud, Arles, 1998.

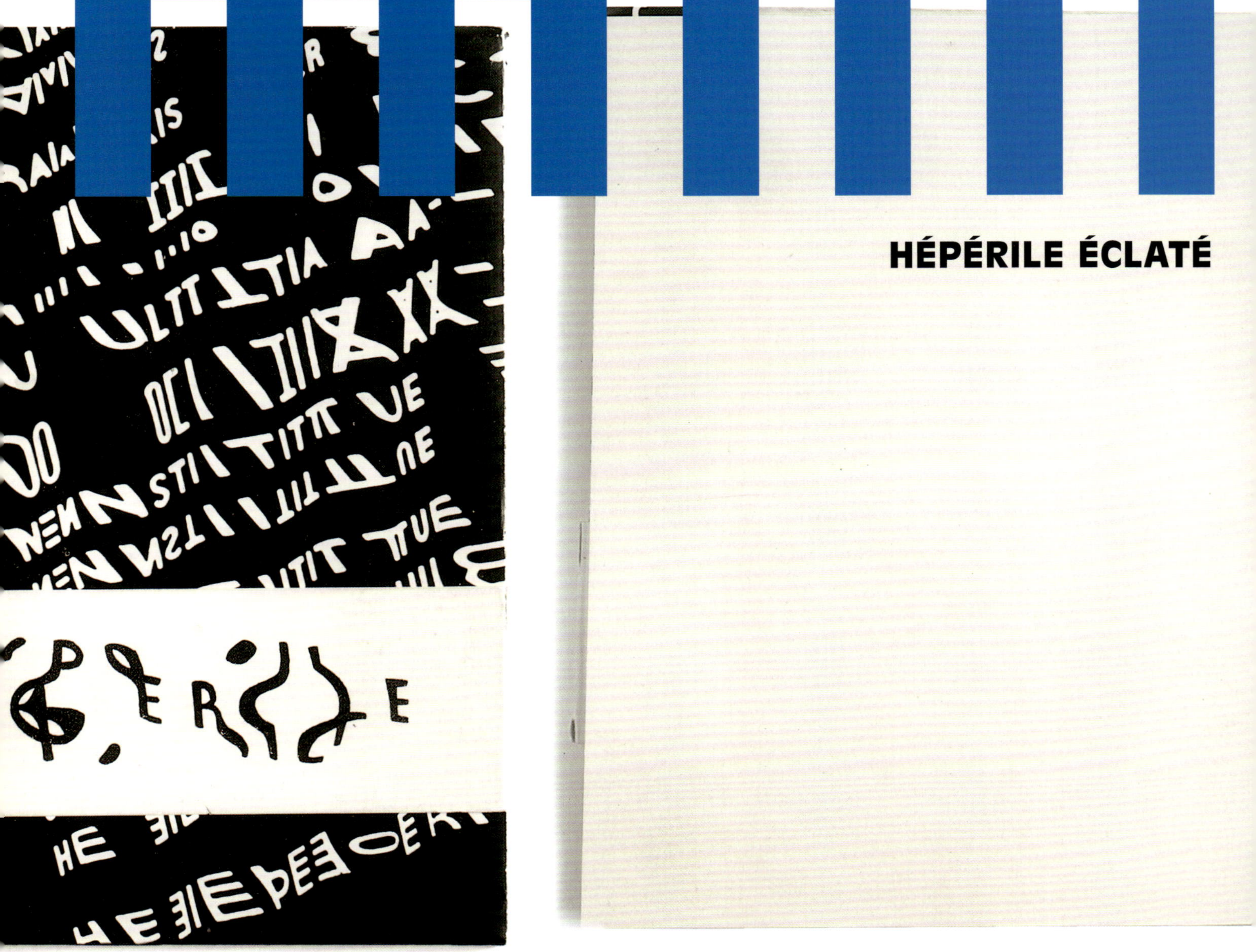

HÉPÉRILE ÉCLATÉ

81 *Hépérile éclaté* [Shattered *Hépérile*], with Jacques Villeglé, Librairie Lutétia, Paris, 1953. Documentation Musée National d'art Moderne, Centre Pompidou, Paris.

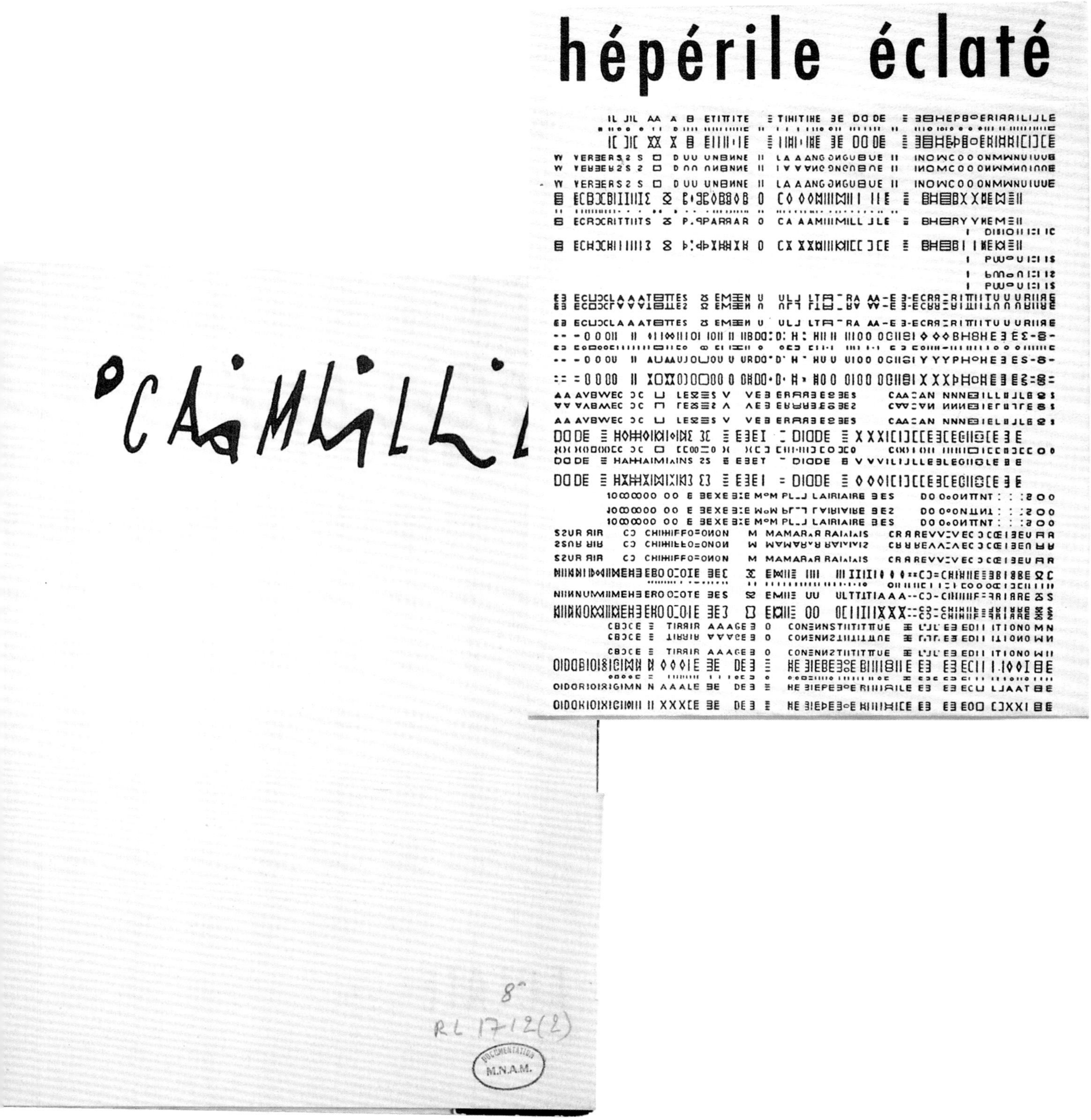

this page, left, top and bottom: *Lunettes en verre cannelé* [Eyeglasses with ribbed lenses], 1957. Collection Ginette Dufrêne, Paris.

this page and facing page: *Hépérile éclaté* [Shattered *Hépérile*], with Jacques Villeglé, Librairie Lutétia, Paris, 1953. Documentation Musée National d'art Moderne, Centre Pompidou, Paris.

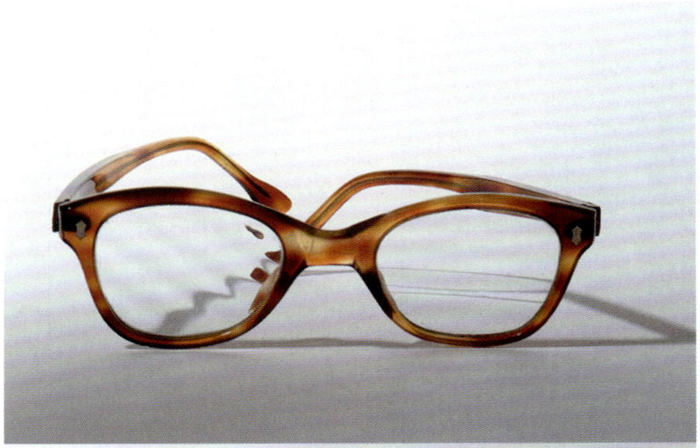

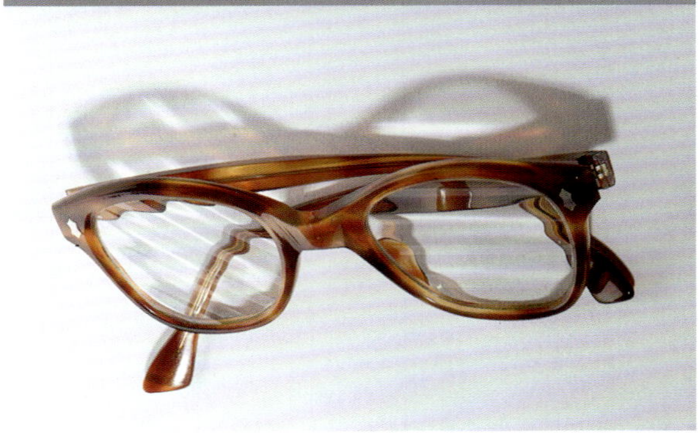

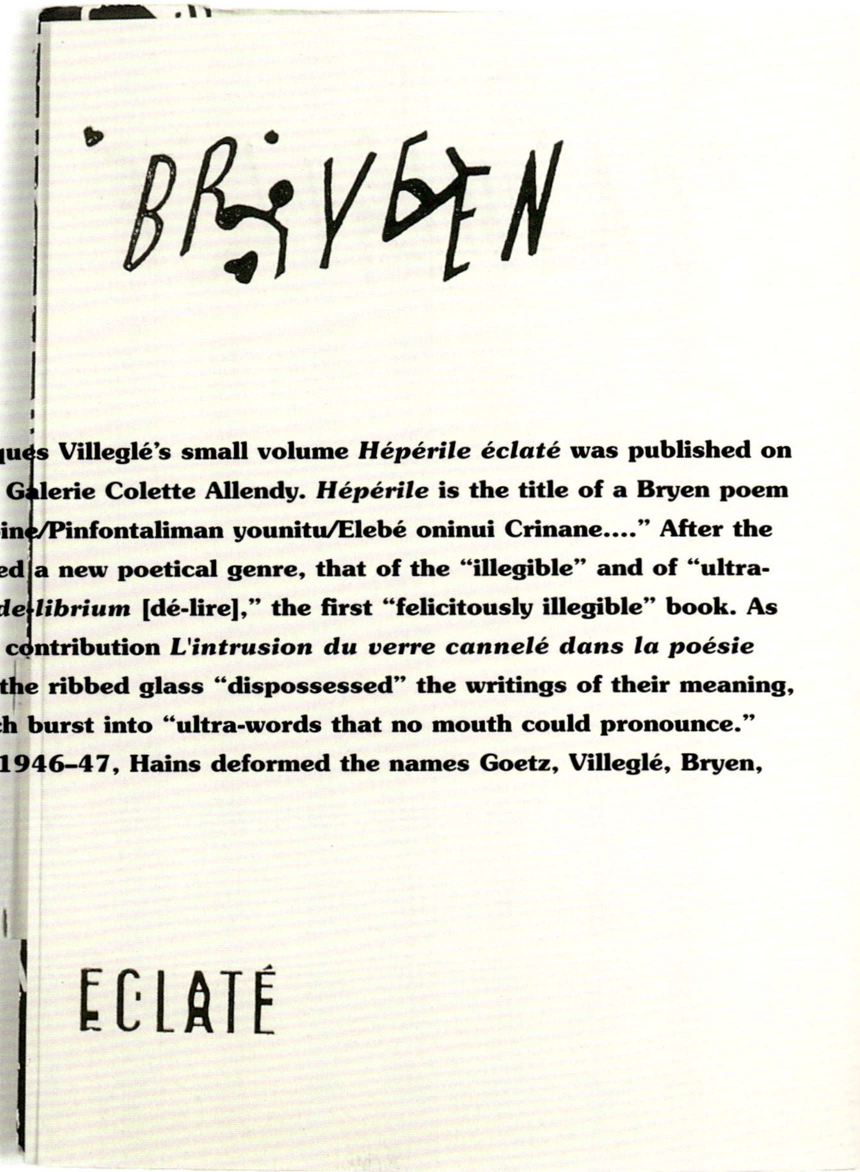

HÉPÉRILE ÉCLATÉ : Raymond Hains and Jacques Villeglé's small volume *Hépérile éclaté* was published on June 19, 1953, for Camille Bryen's exhibition at Galerie Colette Allendy. *Hépérile* is the title of a Bryen poem written in "unknown words": "Hépérile nidi nenoine/Pinfontaliman younitu/Elebé oninui Crinane...." After the intervention of his "fragmenters," Bryen pioneered a new poetical genre, that of the "illegible" and of "ultra-letters." *Hépérile éclaté* was the "first poetical *de-librium* [dé-lire]," the first "felicitously illegible" book. As for Hains and Villeglé, they entitled their textual contribution *L'intrusion du verre cannelé dans la poésie* (*Ribbed glass breaks into poetry*). The lines of the ribbed glass "dispossessed" the writings of their meaning, a procedure that, if continued, could make speech burst into "ultra-words that no mouth could pronounce." The splintering of *Hépérile* was not the first. In 1946–47, Hains deformed the names Goetz, Villeglé, Bryen, and Vitali. (CS)

HEPÉRILE ECLATÉ

hépérile éclaté

nous sommes saturés de communiqués, de lectures, d'humanisme.
vive le courant d'air de l'illisible, de l'inintelligible, de l'ouvert!
en écrivant hépérile en mots inconnus, je criais organiquement sans référence au vocabulaire — cette police des mots...
aujourd'hui, grâce à raymond hains et à jacques de la villeglé, les deux christophe colomb des «ultra-lettres», voici le premier livre heureusement illisible.
un américain invente une machine électronique destinée à rien.
moi-même fus l'inventeur d'objets inutiles.
hépérile éclaté, nouveau degré poétique, fait réapparaître le non-humain inexplicable à travers le machinisme dépassé.
le premier poème à dé-lire.

camille bryen

l'intrusion du verre cannelé

en voyant débarquer christophe colomb, les indigènes se dirent : « alors sommes-nous découverts, cette fois-ci ? ».
anecdote chère à camille bryen

nous n'avons pas découvert les ultra-lettres. nous nous découvrons plutôt en elles.
l'écriture n'a pas attendu notre intervention pour éclater.
il y a des ultra-lettres à l'état sauvage.
notre mérite — ou notre astuce — c'est d'avoir vu des ultra-lettres, là où nous étions habitués à voir des lettres déformées.
enfin nous nous servons de trames de verres cannelés qui dépossèdent les écrits de leur signification originelle. — par une démarche analogue, il est possible de faire éclater la parole en ultra-mots qu'aucune bouche humaine ne saurait dire.
le verre cannelé nous semble l'un des plus sûrs moyens de s'écarter de la légèreté poétique.
hépérile éclaté est un livre bouc-émissaire.

raymond hains
jacques de la villeglé

dans la poésie

this page, top: *Ach Alma Manetro*, with Jacques Villeglé. Collection Musée National d'art Moderne, Centre Pompidou, Paris.
this page, facing page, and following pages: *Hépérile éclaté* [Shattered *Hépérile*], with Jacques Villeglé, Librairie Lutétia, Paris, 1953. Documentation Musée National d'art Moderne, Centre Pompidou, Paris.

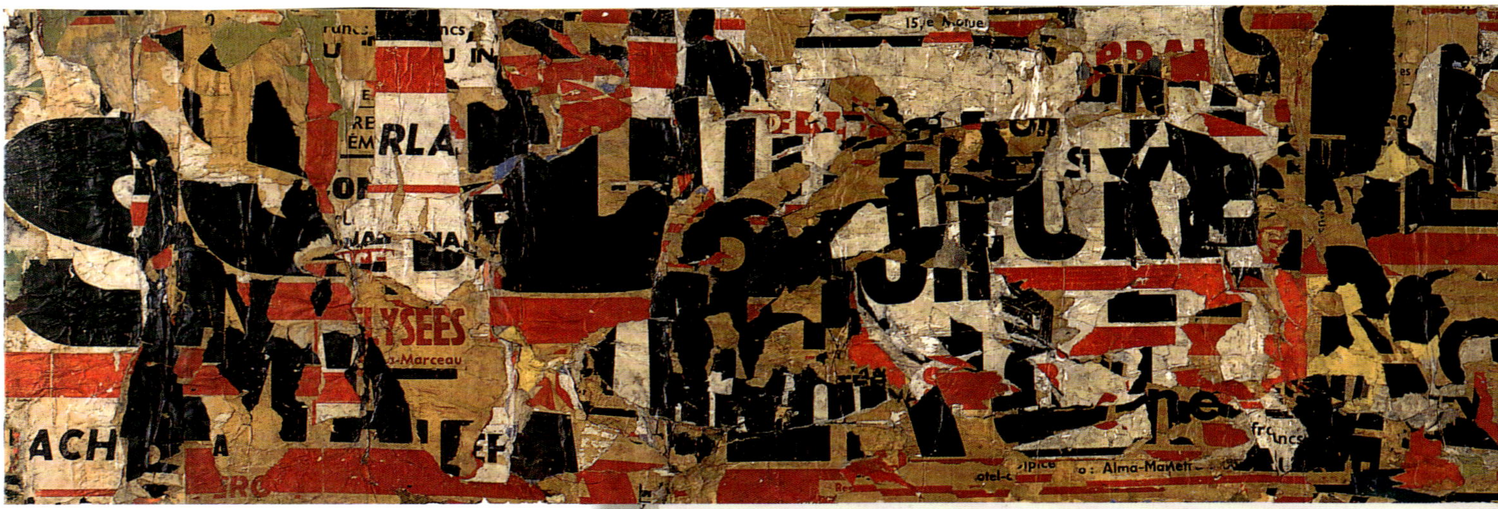

What I retained at the time from those events and my readings was the pleasure of hearing a language spoken, without seeking to understand its meanings or its logic.... When I was taking my first photos in 1946, I was thinking about a relation between these photos, and a preface that would be made of deformed letters. I met Camille Bryen at Colette Allendy's in 1948, around the time of my exhibition of "Hypnagogical Photographs." I had given him my name in deformed letters, as I had done with Villeglé, Goetz, and a few others. That was when Bryen invited me to deform his little poem HÉPÉRILE. **Bryen wanted to become a voluntarily illegible poet. In his preface to** HÉPÉRILE ECLATÉ, **he wrote: "Long life to the little breeze of the illegible, of the unintelligible, of the open!" | Raymond Hains interview with Christian Schlatter,** POETING AND PAINTRY, **Musées de Marseille, Réunion des Musées Nationaux, Paris, 1993.**

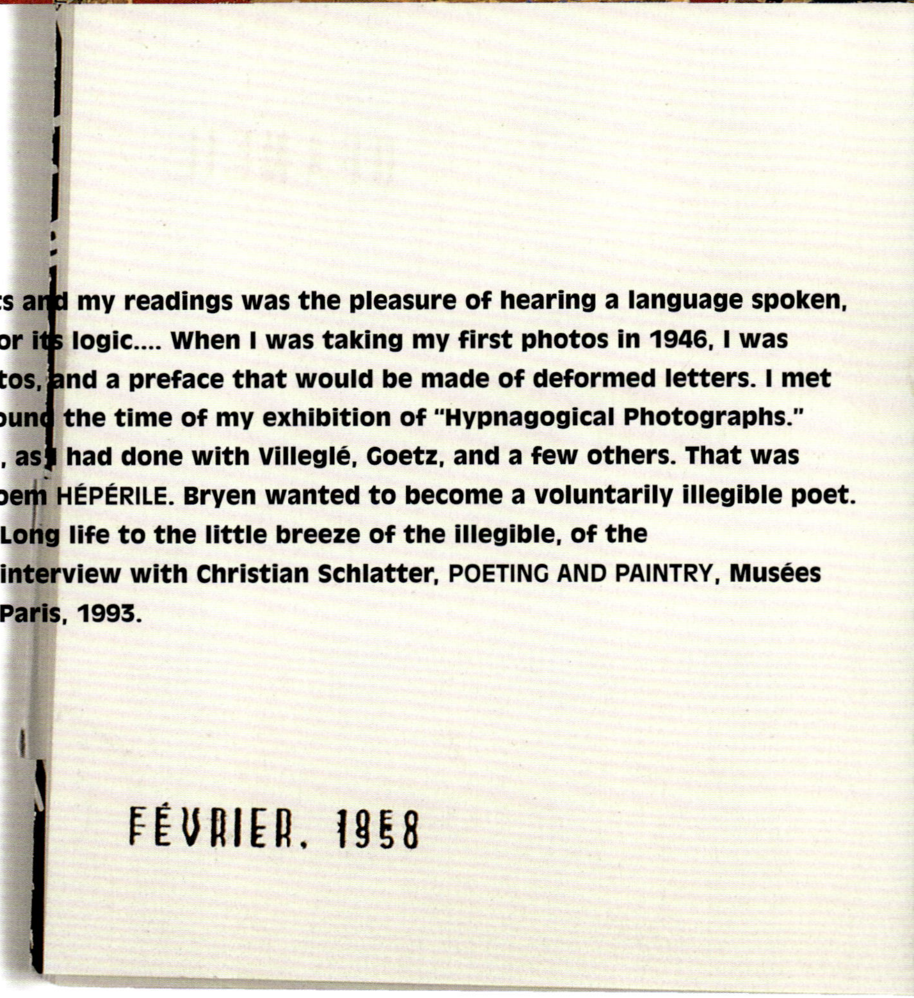

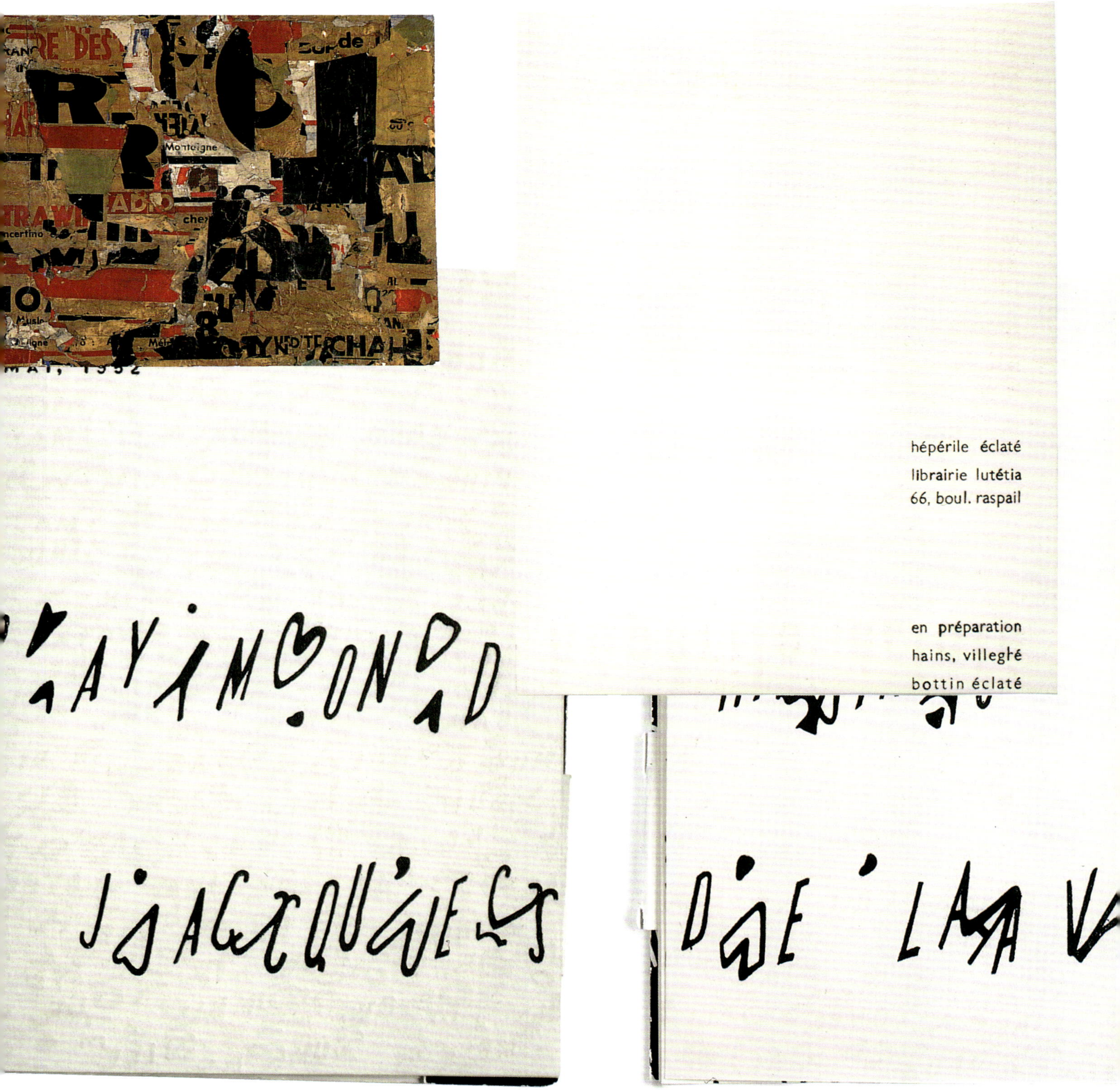
hépérile éclaté
librairie lutétia
66, boul. raspail
en préparation
hains, villeglé
bottin éclaté

BILE
HEPO ÉRI
INFO
PIN ONT ALIN MAN
FO
MA
ÉLE BE ONIN
ÉBE
BAN DVRC
MU NOLO SA DI
ABE FIL AVE
MB
ME UM BIL

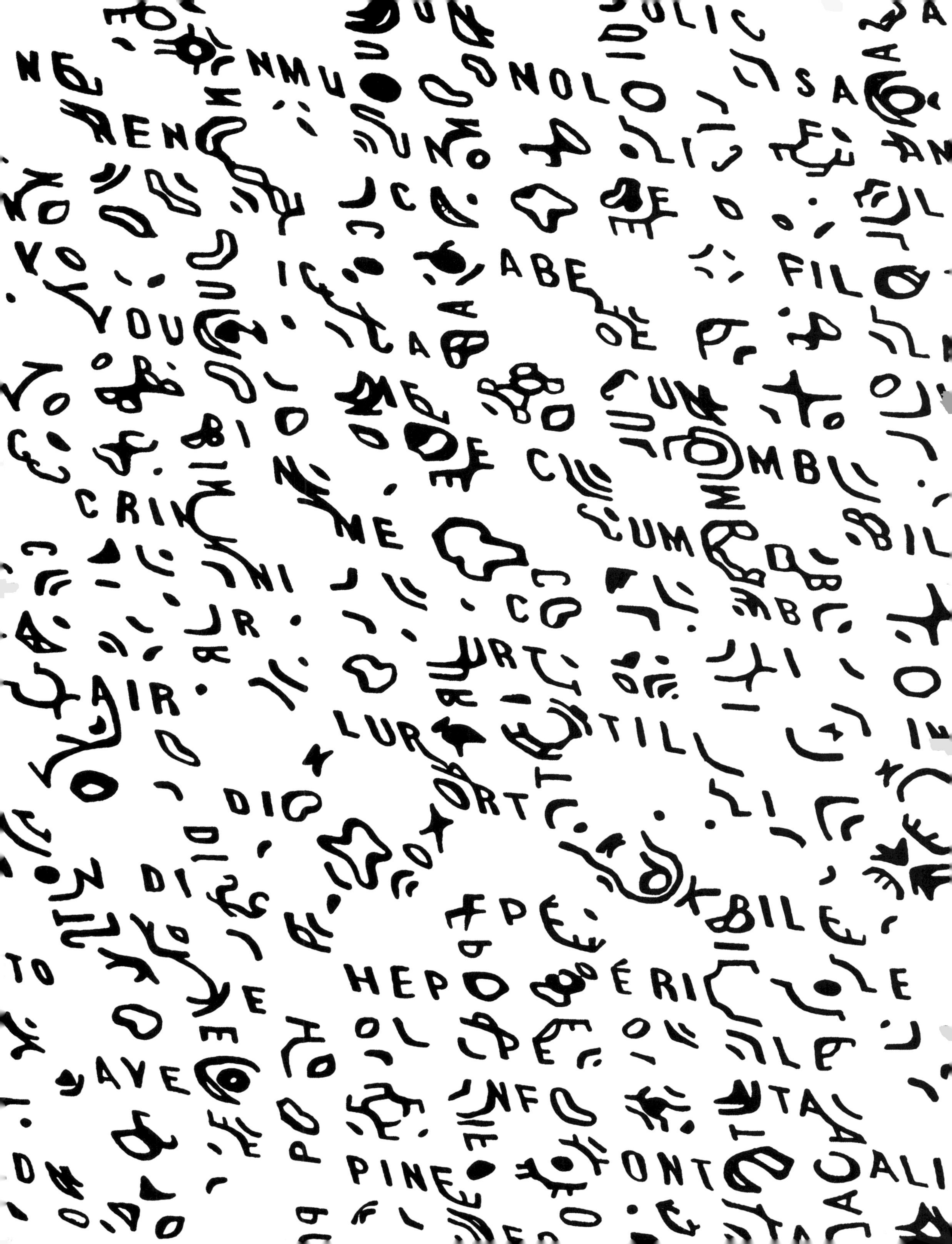

VOYAGE TO AMERICA

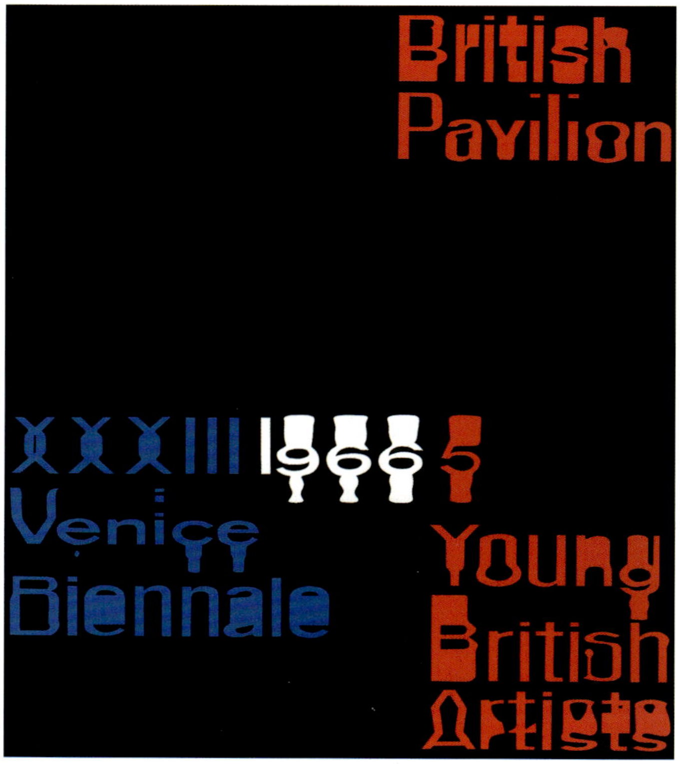

facing page: *La biennale éclatée* [Shattered biennale], 1968. Archives Raymond Hains, Paris.
this page: *Armorican Express*, 1987. Courtesy L'Atelier Soardi, Nice.

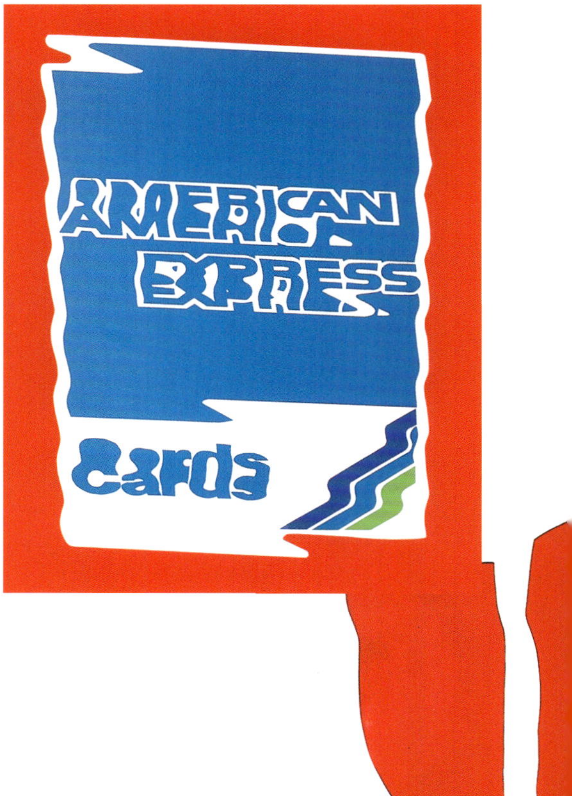

Although all four were part of the Nouveaux Réalistes movement, the "poster artists" [AFFICHISTES], Hains, Dufrêne, Villeglé, and the Italian Rotella, were all relatively unknown in New York at the beginning of the sixties. They were included, however, in the big exhibition at MoMA, "The Art of Assemblage," which extensively covered the use of the object in America and Europe. And 6, BD. POISSONNIÈRE, **featured in that show, was attributed to Villeglé alone. At the time, too, a number of American artists, such as William Getman, who appeared in the exhibition, seemed to be interested in torn posters. But these "bits of the environment presented as paintings," as William C. Seitz described them in the catalog, were only remotely in keeping with the American aesthetic. Posters on either side of the Atlantic were very different, and the pop artists' interest in them was hardly comparable, focusing as it did only on the image and not on destruction over time. | Alfred Pacquement, "De l'abstrait à l'objet. 1955–1960,"** PARIS NEW YORK, **Centre National d'Art et de Culture Georges Pompidou, Paris, 1977.**

Not all the Nouveaux Réalistes have seized the American opportunity. The Parisian poster artists and Deschamps have dreamed of New York but never set foot there. Rotella was artist in residence at Kansas City University in 1951–52, and made a record of his first phonetic poems there. He returned to New York fifteen years later, in December 1967, to attend a group show at Sydney Janis on the theme of Marilyn Monroe, featuring his famous décollage from 1963. He stayed there six months, through 1968, leaving memories of a refined erotomaniac around Chelsea. He was happy just to breathe the air of New York, like César in 1961, when he exhibited classical, welded metal pieces at Saidenberg a year after his crushed cars at the Salon de Mai (made in Paris on an AMERICAN press), and who simply came and went: "It's great, but you know, there's the language." | Pierre Restany, "Chelsea, 1960," PARIS NEW YORK, **Centre National d'Art et de Culture Georges Pompidou, Paris, 1977.**

 this page: *La biennale éclatée. USA* [Shattered biennale: USA], 1968. Collection Éric Fabre, Brussels.
facing page, following pages: *La biennale éclatée* [Shattered biennale], 1968. Archives Raymond Hains, Paris.

ARMORICAN EXPRESS : "Since I was born in Saint-Brieuc *de la cabbage patch*, I am an Armorican artist and not an American one." Behind this statement from Hains's classic repertoire, he is sending up French galleries that are more interested in American art than French art. But, at the same time, Hains notes that at big exhibitions abroad, his works are shown alongside pieces by Robert Rauschenberg or Jasper Johns, and are better promoted than in France.
Instead of "paying, go with the greenback and American Express," says Hains, but with his *Armorican Express*, in the colors of Plougastel folk costumes and Quimper earthenware. The work consists of a hypnagogic deformation of an American Express card. (CS)

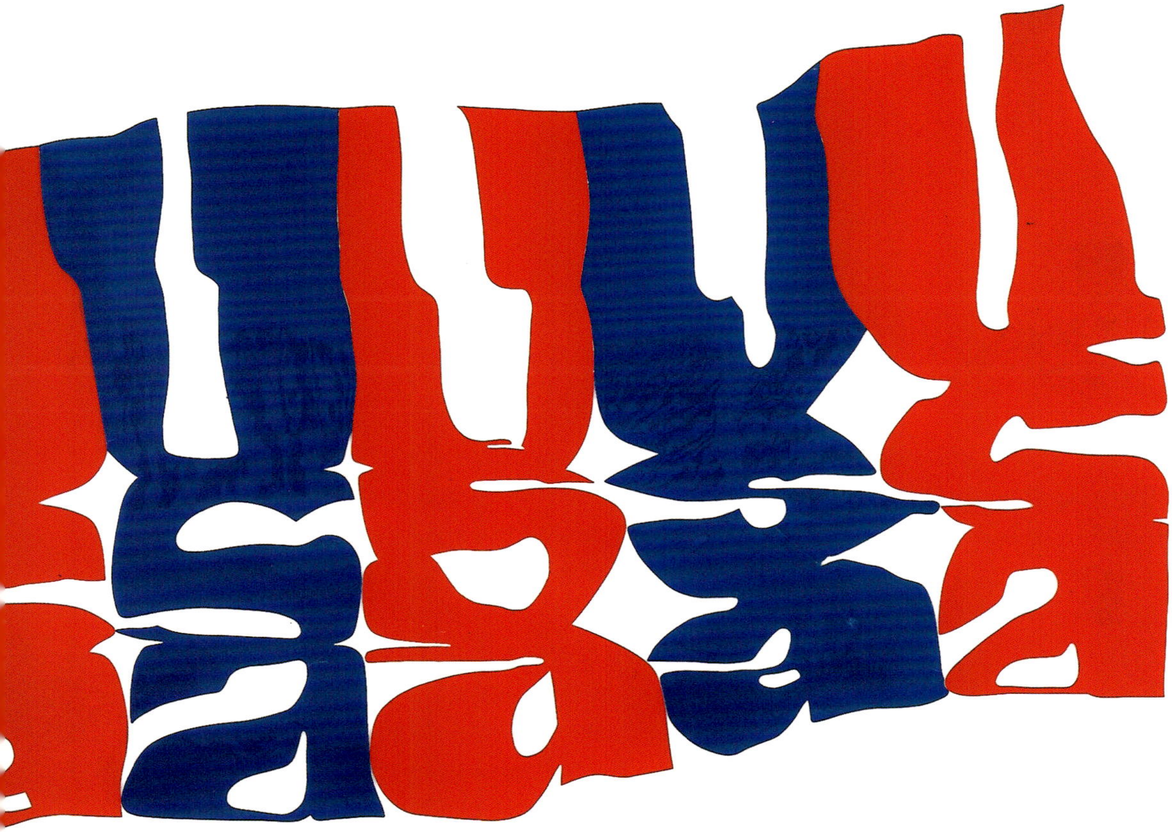

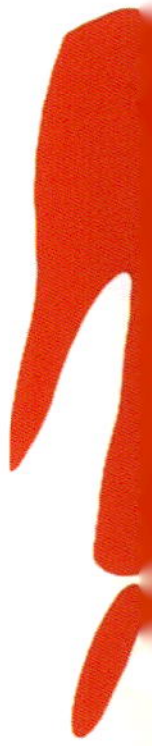

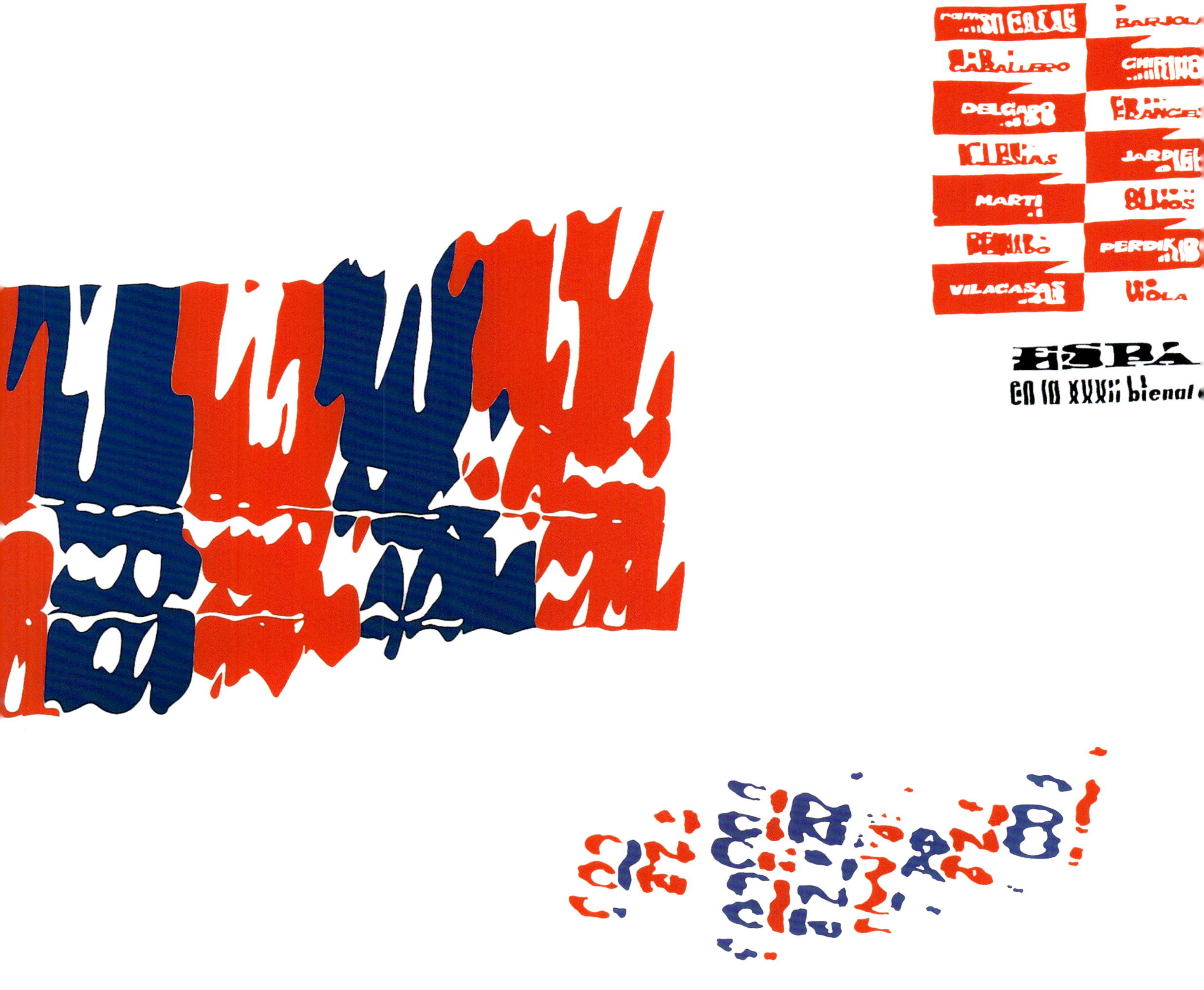
BARJOLA
CABALLERO
DELGADO
MARTI
PERDIK
VILACASAS
VIOLA
en la XXXII bienal

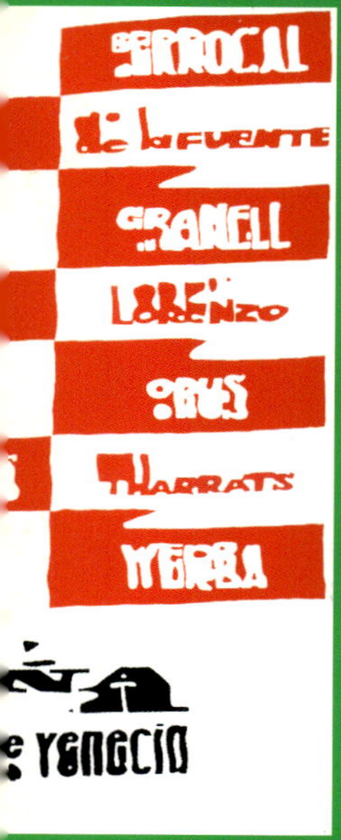

Let's say that I am an artist whose nature is CURIOSOLITIC. At the 1964 Venice Biennale, I thought I could deform the catalog of the U.S. exhibition, which looked a bit like an alcohol advertisement, and I wondered if Cin-Cin-Cinzano* could not become the catalog of the Chinese. In biennales, artists are the cultural propaganda instruments of their countries. I have no wish to have ways of seeing imposed upon me. I represent my own cultural heritage. | Raymond Hains interview with Michel Giroud, HORS LIMITES, L'ART ET LA VIE 1952–1994, Éditions du Centre Pompidou, Paris, 1994. | *Cin-Cin-Cinzano=a probable allusion to the famous ad campaign for the French vermouth Dubonnet ("du bon, du bon, Dubonnet"), whose three-part posters hung deep inside Paris metro tunnels, between stations, in the postwar years. The faded remains of some of them can still be seen.

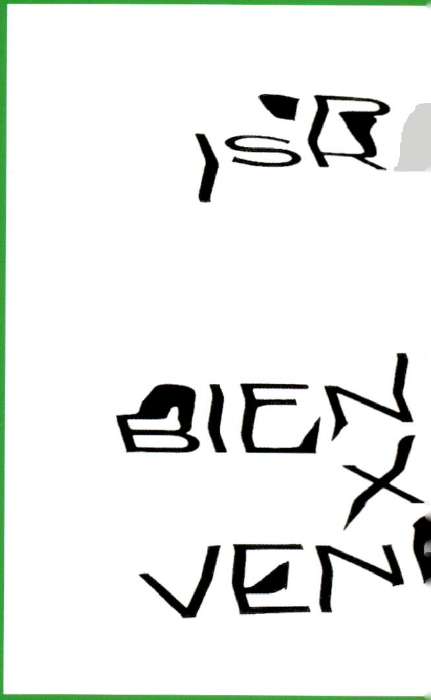

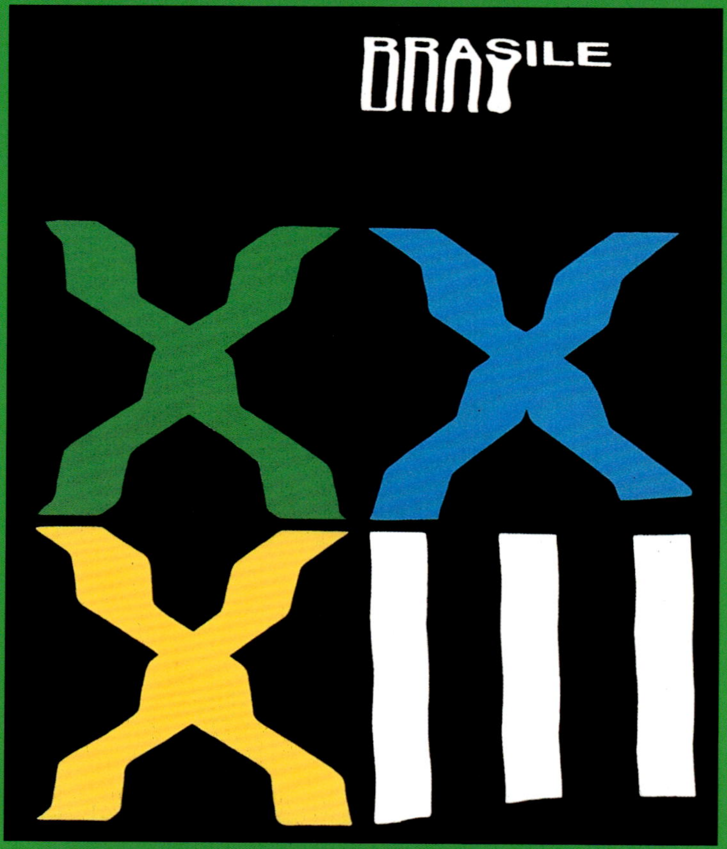

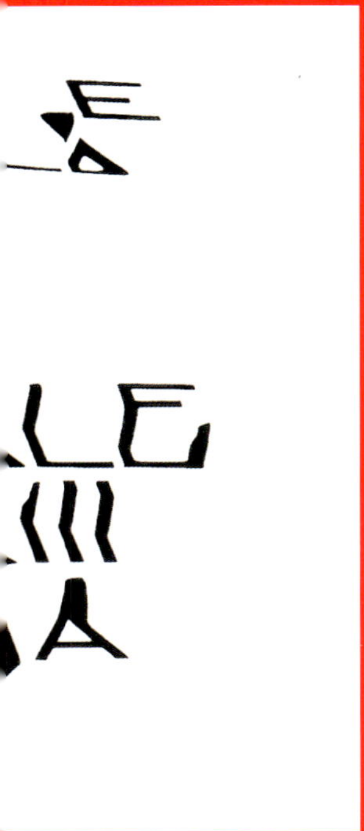

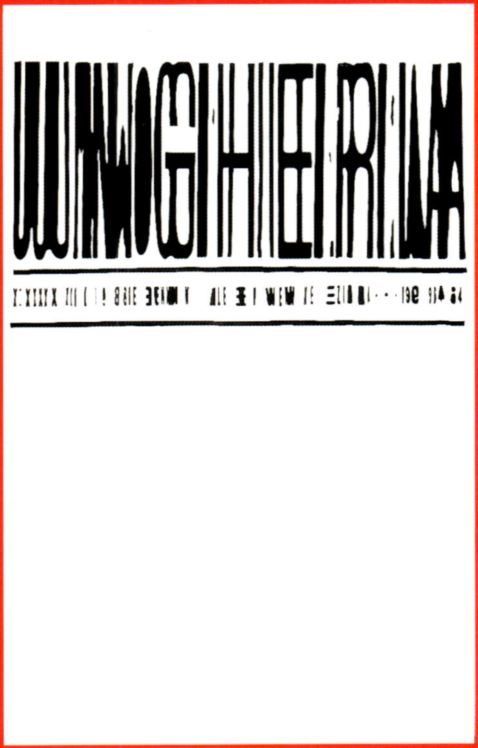

JAPON
BIENNALE INTERNATIONALE

 this page: *Les tuyauteries du centre*, 2000. Courtesy Galerie Daniel Templon, Paris.
facing page: *Castelli, Castellani*, 1998. Courtesy Galerie Daniel Templon, Paris.

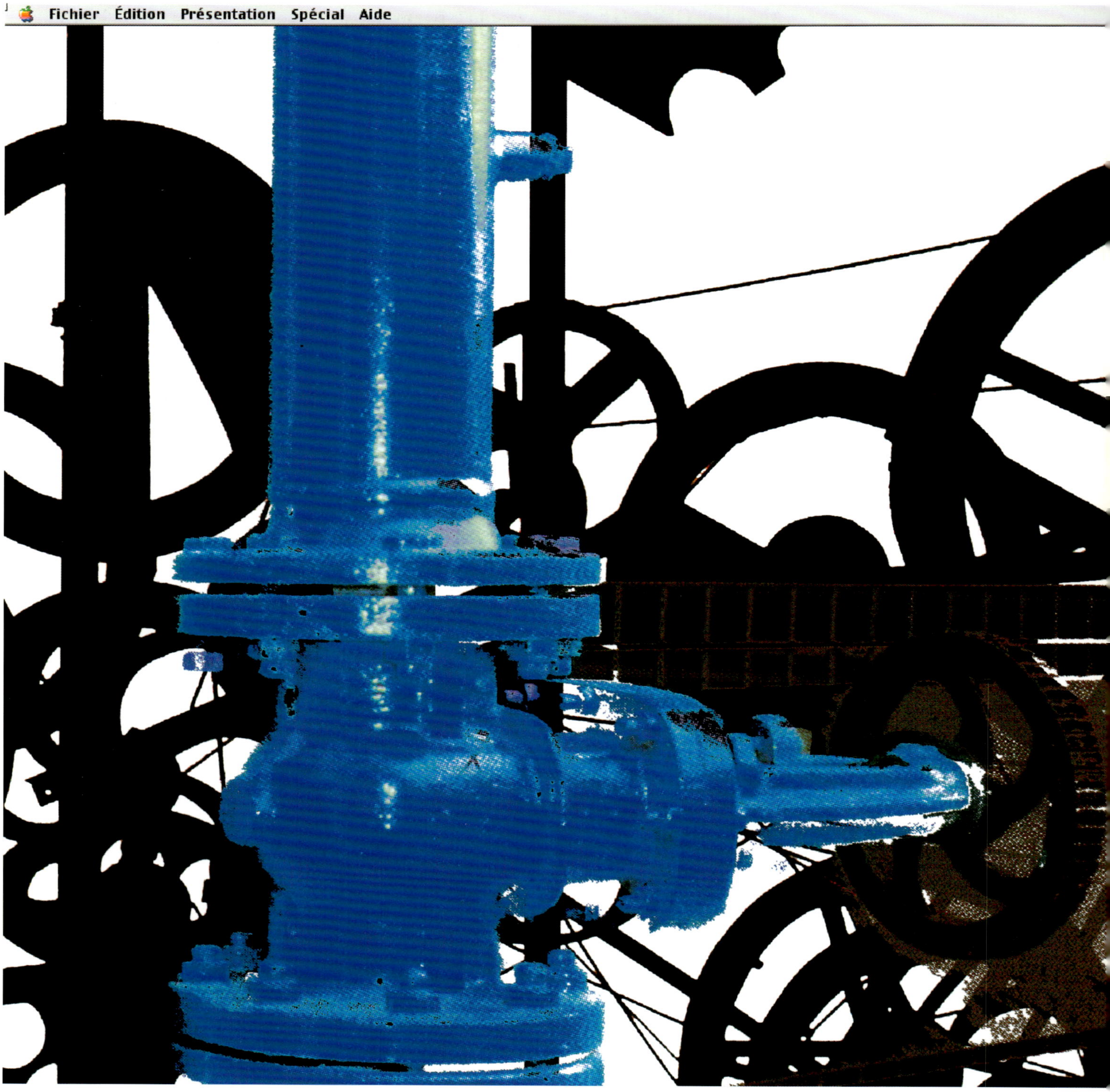

There is a work of art that I will always regret I never saw. When Jean Tinguely took the Queen Mary for New York, in January 1960, to make HOMAGE TO NEW YORK **at the Museum of Modern Art, he carried another idea in his bags: the construction in Central Park of a pavilion whose outer walls would be** PALISSADES **by Raymond Hains and whose inner walls monochromes by Yves Klein, with the free space being taken up by Tinguely's drawing machines.**
If Shchukin's Matisses had stayed in France, and if that pavilion had been built, today's art (and world) would be different. | Pontus Hulten, in RAYMOND HAINS ET LA PHOTOGRAPHIE, CNAC, **Paris, 1976.**

MACINTOSHAGE : **The term is a portmanteau word containing "machine," "Macintosh," "McLuhan," "Gutenberg Galaxy," "Mother MacMiche," and other associations. The *Macintoshage* is a method of combining and manipulating texts and images, without obscuring the visibility of the computer and its screen. It is a means of collaging and decollaging. The *Macintoshages* produced since 1997 function as an ensemble organized around *Yves Klein*, *Margaret of Austria*, *Raynaud's giant flowerpot*, and *Garry Davis*. Its reactivity makes it a tool for responding to current events. Its procedures turn images and texts into concatenations that remain constantly open onto "works in progress," "chains," "chaining points," and "enfoldings." It is a process of condensation, the work of displacement of words and images, synecdoche, metonymy and metaphor, linguistic work on tropes, dream work, the work of the unconscious in dreams, in the Freudian sense; Hains's hypnagogic work.** (CS)

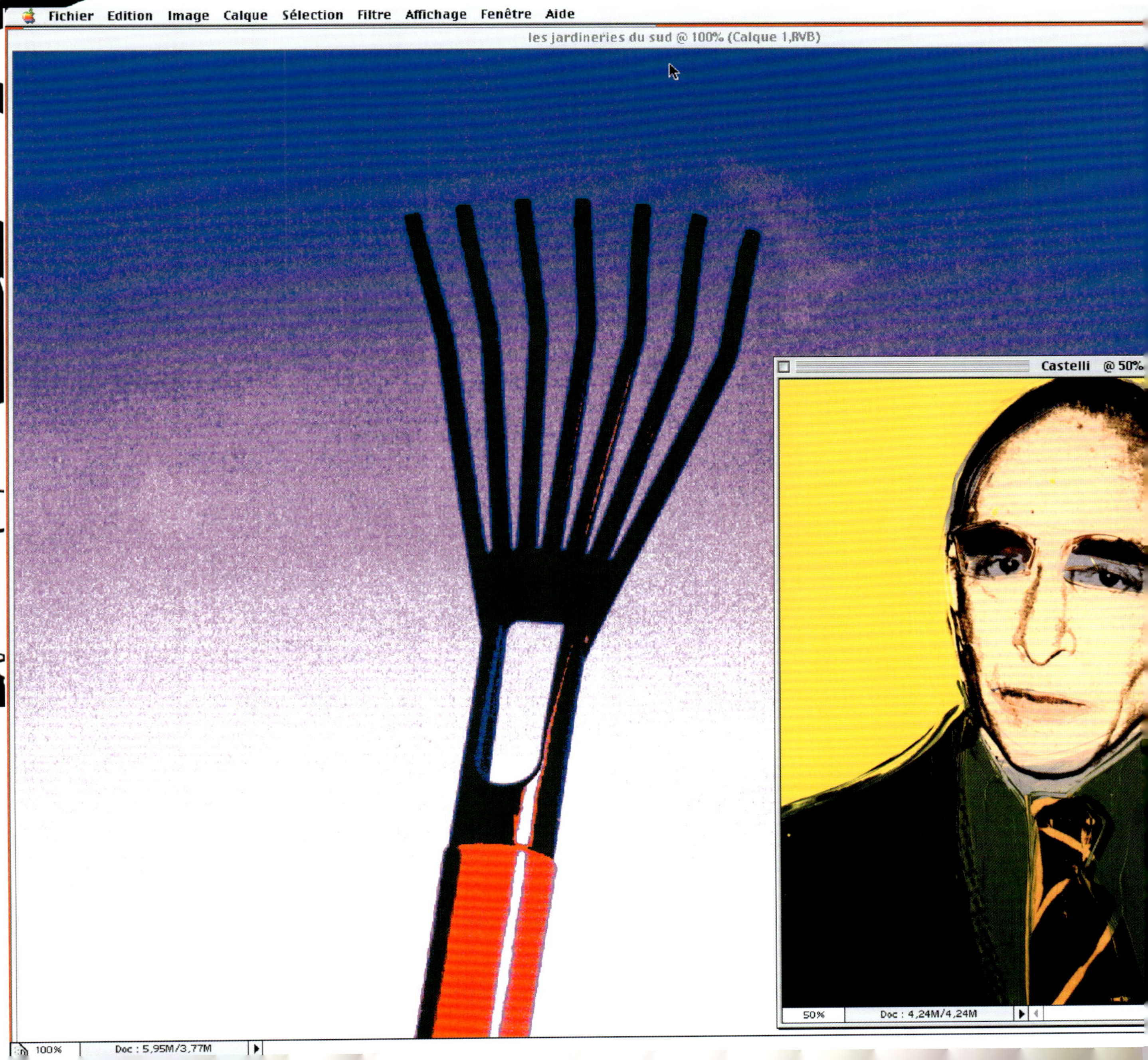

 this page: *Castelli, Castellani*, 1998. Courtesy Galerie Daniel Templon, Paris.
facing page, left and right: *Castelli, les jardineries du sud, Saint-Isidore*, 1998.
Archives Raymond Hains, Paris.

The reason why I did the "Castelli, les jardineries du sud" exhibition is that I feel both very close to the Americans and, yet, different. For instance, Rauschenberg, who has been linked to dada, did combine paintings, whereas I, because I am called Raymond, do combinatory art in the manner of Raymond Lully. I can understand very well why artists like Martial Raysse and Bernar Venet were fascinated by America. Personally, I felt the need to go to Italy and drink the wine of the Castellis. | Raymond Hains interview with Marc Bormand, March 26, 1999.

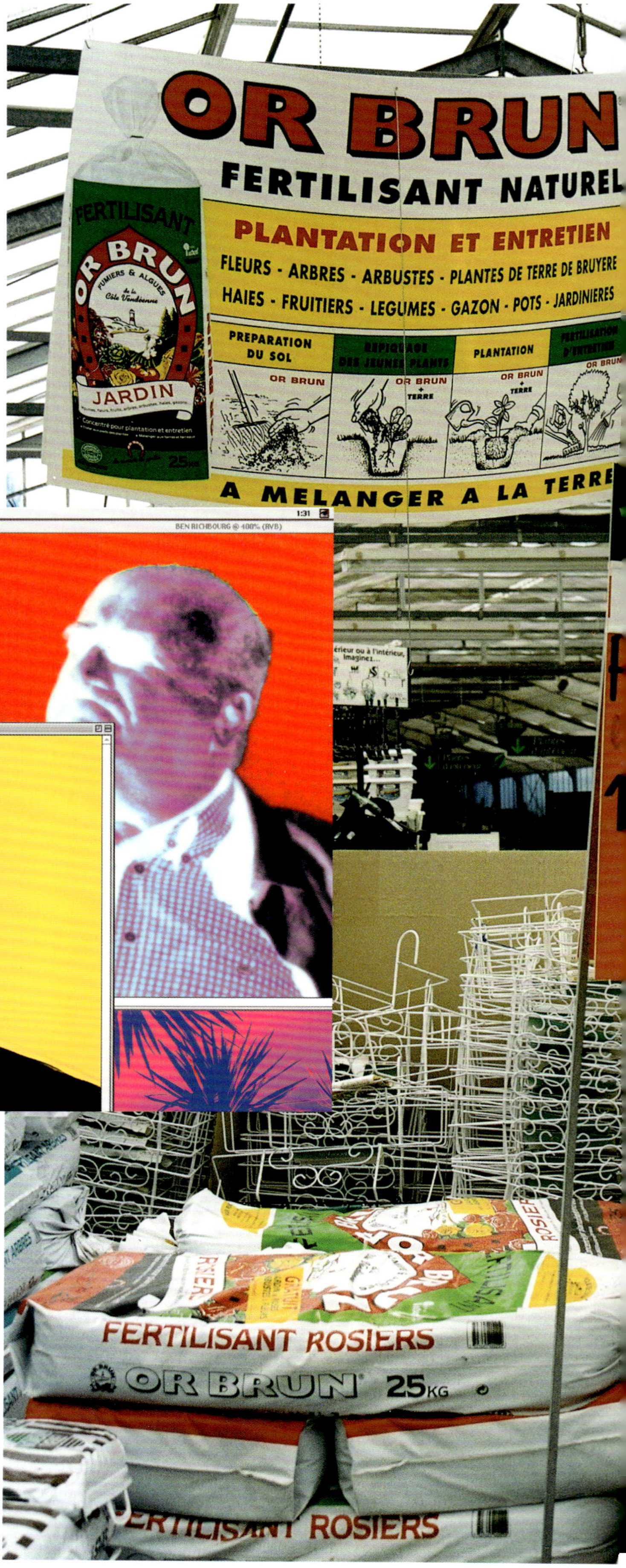

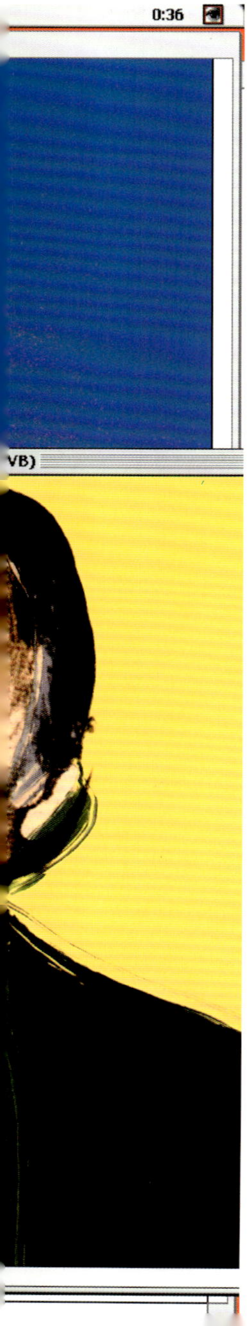

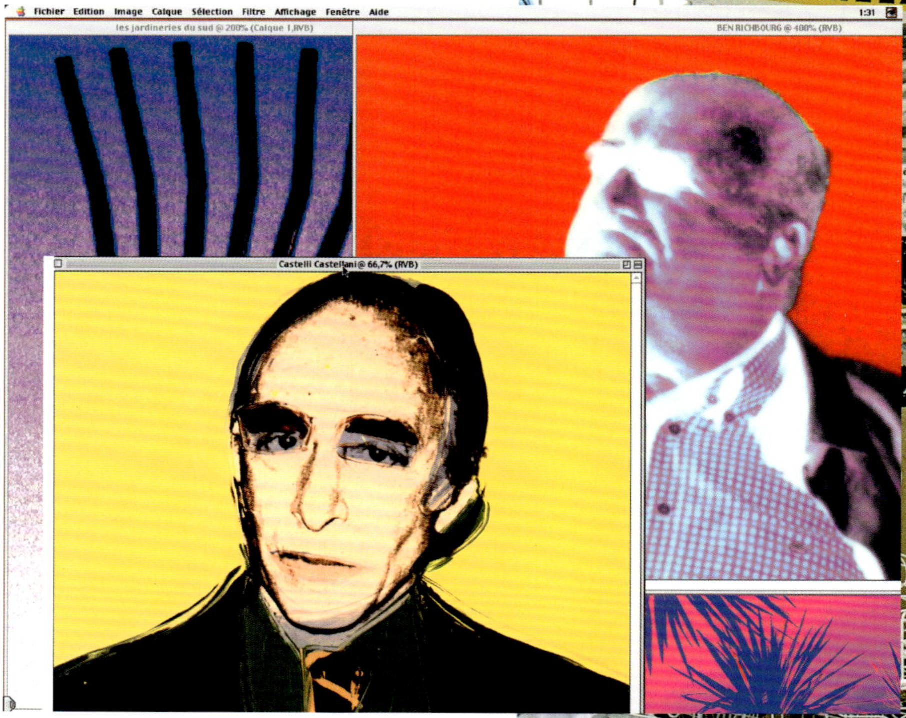

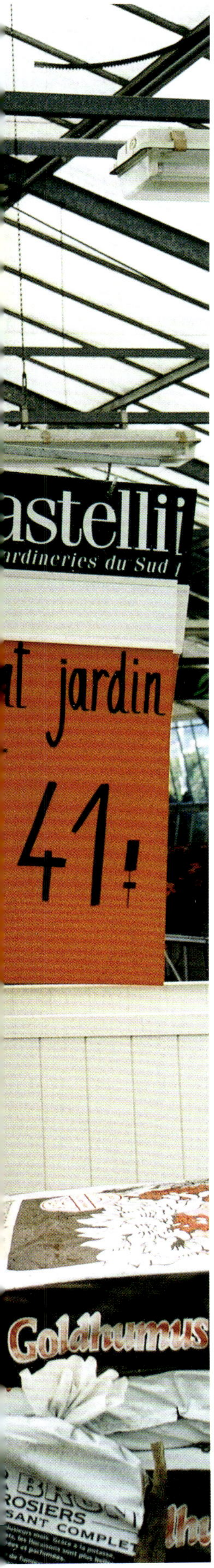
astelli
ardineries du Sud
t jardin
41
Goldhumus
ROSIERS
SANT COMPLET

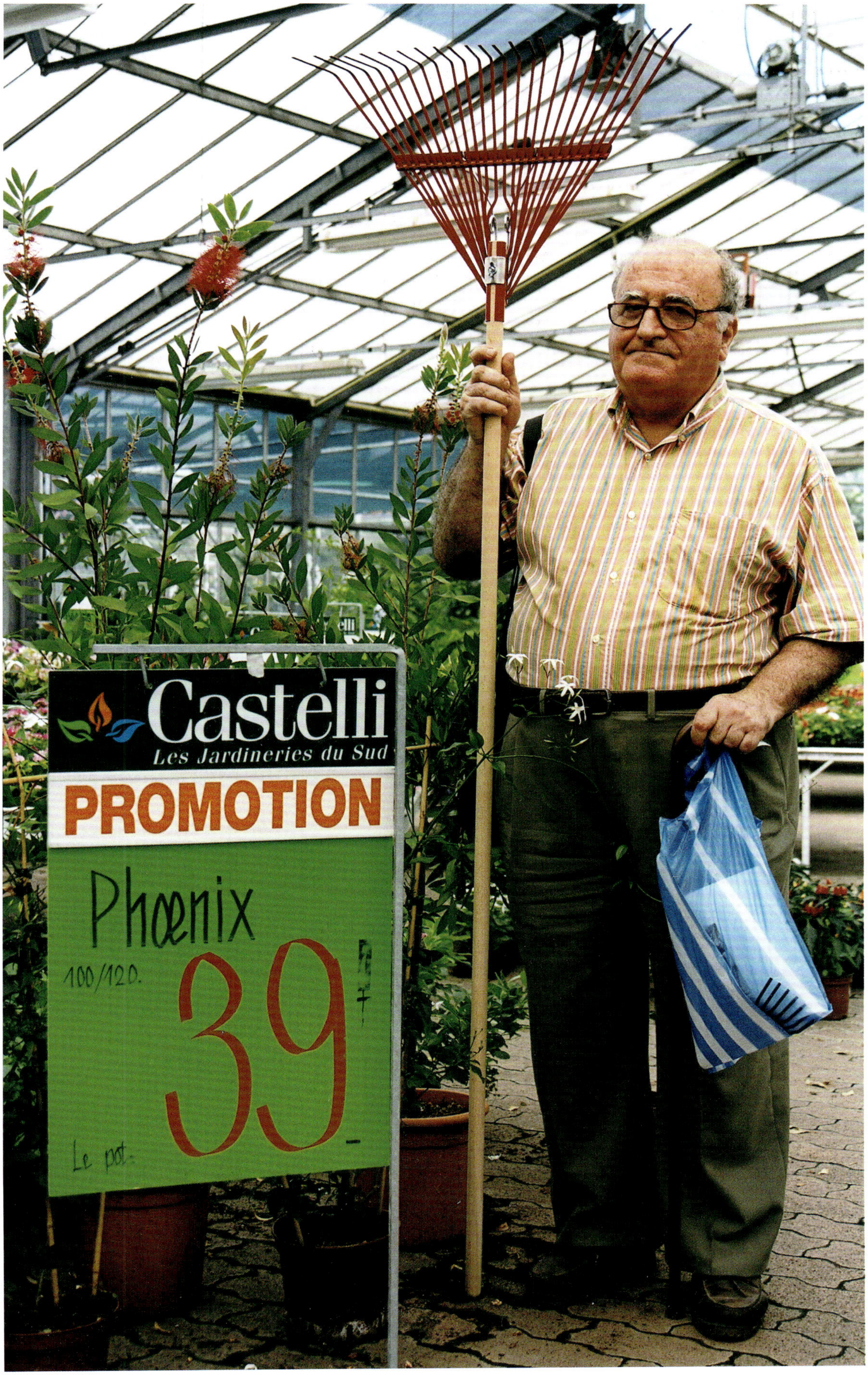
Castelli
Les Jardineries du Sud
PROMOTION
Phœnix
100/120.
39
Le pot.

EXHIBITION CHECKLIST
SELECTED EXHIBITION HISTORY
SELECTED BIBLIOGRAPHY

CATALOG OF THE EXHIBITION

All measurements are in centimeters; height precedes width precedes depth.

LIT-CLOS BRETON **[Breton cupboard bed], 1663**
190 x 127 x 175
Collection Musée de Bretagne, Rennes

Untitled, c. 1946
silver gelatin print
30 x 24
Collection Centre Georges Pompidou, Musée National d'Art Moderne/
Centre de Création Industrielle, Paris

Untitled (Figurine multiplée) [Figurine multiplied], n.d. (1946/55)
silver gelatin print
18 x 24
Courtesy Galerie Françoise Paviot, Paris

LA CHIMÈRE D'AREZZO **[The Chimera of Arezzo], 1947**
silver gelatin print
24 x 30
Collection Centre Georges Pompidou, Musée National d'Art Moderne/
Centre de Création Industrielle, Paris

LE CONQUÉRANT **[Conqueror], 1947**
silver gelatin print
23.5 x 30
Collection Centre Georges Pompidou, Musée National d'Art Moderne/
Centre de Création Industrielle, Paris

TRÉSOR DE GOLCONDE **[Treasure of Golconde], 1947**
silver gelatin print
30.5 x 24
Collection Centre Georges Pompidou, Musée National d'Art Moderne/
Centre de Création Industrielle, Paris. Gift of the artist, 1981

COMPOSITION AUX MIROIRS **[Composition of Mirrors], 1947/1989**
silver gelatin print
30.4 x 23.7
Collection Centre Georges Pompidou, Musée National d'Art Moderne/
Centre de Création Industrielle, Paris

LA JAVANAISE AUX DENTS BLANCHES **[Javanese woman with white teeth], c. 1948**
silver gelatin print
19.5 x 13.5
Collection Centre Georges Pompidou, Musée National d'Art Moderne/
Centre de Création Industrielle, Paris

LA MAIN MULTIPLIÉE PAR UN JEU DE MIROIRS
[The hand multiplied by mirrors], c. 1948
silver gelatin print
29.1 x 40.2
Courtesy The Buhl Collection, New York

HOMMAGE À BACH **[Homage to Bach], n.d. (1946/55)**
silver gelatin print
29.6 x 23.7
Courtesy Galerie Françoise Paviot, Paris

LA GRILLE **[The grate], 1948**
silver gelatin print
24.2 x 18.3
Courtesy Galerie Françoise Paviot, Paris

LES DEUX CROIX **[Two crosses], n.d. (1946/55)**
silver gelatin print
40.1 x 29.1
Courtesy Galerie Françoise Paviot, Paris

Untitled, 1950/1953
gouache and graphite on paper
10 drawings, 27 x 35 each
Collection FRAC Bretagne, Châteaugiron

LES PAROGLYPHES OU BAS-RELIEFS
[Paroglyphs or low reliefs], 1950
silver gelatin print
30.2 x 24.4
Courtesy Galerie Françoise Paviot, Paris

L'AFFICHE EN YIDDISH **[Poster in Yiddish], 1950**
torn posters
34 x 54
Collection Yehuda Neiman, Paris

BORNE KILOMÉTRIQUE CAHORS, PARIS, NEW YORK
[Milestone Cahors, Paris, New York], June 1950
metal
170 x 50 x 25
Collection Alain Prillard, Saint-Cirq-Lapopie

Untitled, c. 1950/1954
painted slips of paper, cut and glued to larger sheet
36 x 131.5
Collection Centre Georges Pompidou, Musée National d'Art Moderne/ Centre de Création Industrielle, Paris. Gift of the artist, 2001

Untitled, c. 1950/1954
painted slips of paper, cut and glued to larger sheet
73.5 x 110
Collection Centre Georges Pompidou, Musée National d'Art Moderne/ Centre de Création Industrielle, Paris. Gift of the artist, 2001

Untitled (Déformation) [Deformation], 1951
silver gelatin print
29 x 23
Courtesy Galerie Françoise Paviot, Paris

Jacques Villeglé
Untitled (l'Hypnagogoscope) [Hynagogoscope], 1952
china ink on paper
2 drawings, 33 x 20.8 each
Collection the artist

HÉPÉRILE ÉCLATÉ **[Shattered Hépérile]**
with Jacques Villeglé
Librairie Lutétia, Paris, 1953
Collection Christine Macel, Paris

HÉPÉRILE ÉCLATÉ. L'INTRUSION DU VERRE CANNELÉ DANS LA POÉSIE
[Shattered Hépérile: Ribbed glass intrudes into poetry]
with Jacques Villeglé and Camille Bryen, 1953
Leaflet announcing publication of Hépérile éclaté,
Librairie Lutétia, Paris, 1953
Collection Christine Macel, Paris

PÉNÉLOPE**, with Jacques Villeglé, 1954/1981**
11'30"
16 mm color film, endless loop
shot 1950–54, edited by Jean-Michel Bouhours, 1981
Collection Centre Georges Pompidou, Musée National d'Art Moderne, Paris

PAIX EN ALGÉRIE **[Peace in Algeria], 1956**
torn posters on linen
39 x 33.5
Collection Ginette Dufrêne, Paris

POUR BATTRE LA RÉACTION, POUR UNE POLITIQUE DE GAUCHE AVEC JACQUES **[To beat the forces of reaction, a left-wing policy with Jacques], 1956**
torn posters
48 x 61
Collection Éric Fabre, Brussels, Belgium

L'HUMANITÉ C'EST LA VÉRITÉ **[L'HUMANITÉ tells the truth]**
with Jacques Villeglé, 1957
torn posters on linen
110 x 74
Collection Ullmann, Paris

CET HOMME EST DANGEREUX **[This man is dangerous], 1957**
torn posters on linen
95 x 61
Collection Ginette Dufrêne, Michel Marcuzzi, Paris

Untitled, 1957
torn posters on linen
54 x 72
Collection Jean-Louis Milin

LUNETTES EN VERRE CANNELÉ **[Eyeglasses with ribbed lenses], 1957**
Collection Ginette Dufrêne, Paris

ALLEG, ALGER**, 1958**
torn posters
92 x 65
On loan from Ginette Dufrêne, Collection the artist

Untitled, 1959
torn posters on steel
44.5 x 201
Collection Christine and Gérard Cohen, Garches

PALISSADE À DE FUEGAS **[Billboard/fence in de Fuegas], 1959**
250 x 61.5 x 18
Collection Musée de l'Objet, Blois

ÉTUDE AUX ALLURES **[Study in appearances]**
with Jacques Villeglé, 1960
5'31"
16 mm color film, sound, music by Pierre Schaeffer
Collection INA, Bry-sur-Marne

Untitled, 1960
torn posters on linen
67 x 46
Collection Jean-Pierre Raynaud, La Garenne-Colombes

Untitled, 1960
torn posters on linen
46 x 86
Collection Jean-Pierre Raynaud, La Garenne-Colombes

LES NOUVEAUX RÉALISTES **[The New Realists], 1960/1990**
diptych, stencil painting on wood
245 x 354
Collection Centre Georges Pompidou, Musée National d'Art Moderne/
Centre de Création Industrielle, Paris

O.A.S. FUSILLEZ LES PLASTIQUEURS **[Shoot the bombers], c. 1961**
torn posters on linen
50 x 73
On loan from Ginette Dufrêne, Collection the artist

OUI À DE GAULLE **[Yes to de Gaulle], c. 1961**
torn posters
72 x 65
On loan from Ginette Dufrêne, Collection the artist

COMITÉ POUR LA PAIX EN ALGÉRIE **[Committee for peace in Algeria], 1961**
torn posters
73 x 68
Collection Éric Fabre, Brussels, Belgium

Untitled, 1961
torn posters on steel
100 x 100
Collection Jean-Pierre Raynaud, La Garenne-Colombes

Untitled, 1961
torn posters on steel
100 x 100
Collection Jean-Pierre Raynaud, La Garenne-Colombes

HAINS ET LES AFFICHES LACÉRÉES
[Hains and the torn posters], 1961
from En français dans le texte series
16 mm film black and white, sound, 2'
made by Yvan Jouhannot, production ORTF
Collection INA, Bry-sur-Marne

Untitled, 1962
torn posters on linen
68 x 66
Courtesy Galerie Lara Vincy, Paris

L'ENTREMETS "LA PALISSADE" **["La Palissade" dessert], 1964**
photograph on display unit
h 150
Collection the artist
Courtesy Cartier Foundation for Contemporary Art, Paris

SAFFA, **1964**
matchbook on painted wood on plywood
114 x 84
Collection Daniel Pérel, London, England
Courtesy Galerie Georges-Philippe and Nathalie Vallois

SEITA & SAFFA, COPYRIGHT BY RAYMOND HAINS. IRIS.TIME, **no. 21, October 12, 1965**
facsimile
2001
Documentation of Centre Georges Pompidou, Musée National d'Art Moderne, Paris

L'ÂNE VÊTU DE LA PEAU DE LION **[The donkey dressed in the lion skin], 1967**
paint on laminated plywood, varnish, paper
110 x 189.5 x 34
Collection Centre Georges Pompidou, Musée National d'Art Moderne/Centre de Création Industrielle, Paris

LA BIENNALE ÉCLATÉE. USA **[Shattered biennale: USA], 1968**
Plexiglas
150 x 240
Collection Éric Fabre, Brussels, Belgium

DISQUE BLEU POUR SAFFA **[Blue disc for SAFFA], 1970**
vinyl record and paper sleeve
18.5 x 18.5
Courtesy Galleria l'Elefante, Treviso, Italy

HOMMAGE À MONDRIAN ET À DE CHIRICO **[Homage to Mondrian and de Chirico], 1971**
matchbox, wood, cardboard
97 x 50.5 x 19
Collection Centre Georges Pompidou, Musée National d'Art Moderne/
Centre de Création Industrielle, Paris

RAYMOND HAINS, **1976**
from ZIGZAG **series**
16 mm color film, sound, 11'
made by Yves Kovacs, production Antenne 2
Collection INA, Bry-sur-Marne

LES NOUVEAUX RÉALISTES, **1976**
16 mm color film, sound, 5'6"
made by Adrian Maben, commentary Otto Hahn
production Michèle Arnaud, Reiner Moritz
Collection Adrian Maben, Paris

LE MONOCHROME DANS LE MÉTRO
[Monochrome in the Métro], 1983/2001
variable dimensions
Collection Éric Fabre, Brussels, Belgium

ARMORICAN EXPRESS, **1987**
serigraph on Forex, edition of 50
58 x 42
Courtesy L'Atelier Soardi, Nice

LES VÉRITÉS DE LA PALISSE **[Truisms of La Palisse], 1987**
photograph mounted on aluminum, mounted on frame
120 x 160, 112 x 160
Collection FRAC Champagne-Ardenne, Reims

LA FOIRE AUX SKIS **[Ski fair], 1988**
Rossignol skis
190 x 200
Collection National Contemporary Art Fund, Ministry of Culture and Communication, Paris

Interview with Éric Fabre and Christian Schlatter,
2 July 1992, excerpt, 2h58'
Christian Schlatter Archives, Paris

IRIS CLERT, LA MESSAGÈRE DES ARTS **[Iris Clert, messenger of the arts], 1997**
wood, straw, papier-mâché
h 340
Collection Éric Fabre, Brussels, Belgium

ETAGÈRES **[Shelves], 1998**
metal shelves
200 x 480 x 60
Collection FRAC Champagne-Ardenne, Reims

PETITE BIBLIOTHÈQUE DE RAYMOND HAINS **[Raymond Hains's little library]. Selection of Raymond Hains's favorite books,**
made by Christian Schlatter
Collection Christian Schlatter, Paris

CASTELLI, CASTELLANI, **1998**
120 x 150
Galerie Daniel Templon, Paris

RAYMONDRIAN, **1998**
120 x 150
Galerie Daniel Templon, Paris

CASTELLI, LES JARDINERIES DU SUD **[Castelli, southern gardening], 1998**
120 x 150
Galerie Daniel Templon, Paris

Untitled, from CAHORS MUNDI/CAHORS, VILLE DU MONDE **[Cahors, city of the world] series, 1999**
digital gelatin silver print
3 photos, 120 x 150 each
Collection National Contemporary Art Fund, Ministry of Culture and Communication, Paris

LES RAYMONDINES, **2000**
chocolate coins from Pâtisserie Périn, Cahors
Collection Christine Macel, Paris

EUROS EN CHOCOLAT **[Chocolate Euros], 2000**
chocolate coins

DISCOBOLE **[Discobolus], 2001**
plaster, IKB blue paint
45 x 26 x 15
Collection the artist

MON ENCYCLOPÉDIE CLARTÉS **[My own "clarity" encyclopedia], 2001**
website MON ENCYCLOPÉDIE CLARTÉS **visible on www.centre.pompidou.fr, designed for Raymond Hains by Opixido, Paris.**

SELECTED EXHIBITION HISTORY

ONE-PERSON EXHIBITIONS, EVENTS, PRIZES

1936 Astra Margarine prize for drawing of liner *Normandie* in sand of L'Écluse beach, Dinard.
1948 "Photographies hypnagogiques," Galerie Colette Allendy, Paris.
1949 "Photographies hypnagogiques," Les Nourritures terrestres bookstore, Rennes.
1950 La Falconnerie de Tytgat, Knokke-le-Zoute, Belgium.
1953 *Hépérile éclaté* presentation in exhibition "Camille Bryen," Galerie Colette Allendy, Paris.
1957 "*Loi du 29 juillet 1881* ou le lyrisme à la sauvette," with Jacques Villeglé, Galerie Colette Allendy, Paris.
1960 *Pénélope* screening, Centre Culturel Français, Milan, Italy.
Signs constitutive statement of Nouveau Réalisme, at home of Yves Klein, rue Campagne-Première, Paris, October 27.
1961 "La France déchirée," with Jacques Villeglé, Galerie J, Paris.
Dissolution of Nouveau Réalisme, at La Coupole, boulevard du Montparnasse, Paris, October 8.
1962 "Affiches lacérées de Hains," Galerie Aujourd'hui, Palais des Beaux-arts, Brussels, Belgium.
Galerie Aenne Abels, with Mimmo Rotella, Cologne, Germany.
Galerie Félix Handschin, Basel, Switzerland.
1963 "Menu-hommage à Raymond Hains l'Abstrait, Sigisbée de la Critique," by Pierre Restany and Daniel Spoerri, restaurant of Galerie J, Paris, March 8.
1964 "SAFFA et SEITA," Galleria del Leone, Venice, Italy.
1965 Galleria Sampietronico, with Mimmo Rotella, Bologna, Italy.
"La Biennale déchirée di Raymond Hains," Galleria Apollinaire, Milan, Italy.
"*SEITA & SAFFA, copyright by Raymond Hains,*" Galerie Iris Clert, Paris.
1966 "La Biennale 1964 déchirée par Raymond Hains," Galleria del Leone, Venice, Italy.
1968 "*La Biennale éclatée,*" Galleria L'Elefante, Mestre, Italy.
1970 "La manna di San Andrea," Studio San Andrea, Milan, Italy.
"*SAFFA,*" Galleria Blu, Milan, Italy. Catalog.
Galleria Ferrari, Verona, Italy. Catalog.
1972 Galleria dei Mille, Bergamo, Italy.
1973 "HAINS-SAFFA-SEITA," Galleria della Trinità, Rome, Italy. Catalog.
1976 "La Biennale éclatée di Raymond Hains," Galleria Graziussi, Venice, Italy.
Galleria Inquadrature, Florence, Italy. Catalog.
"Les Palissades de Beaubourg," Galerie Verbeke, Paris.
"L'art à Vinci," Galerie Lara Vincy, Paris.
"Raymond Hains et la photographie" [aka La chasse au CNAC], CNAC, Rue Berryer, Paris. Catalog.
1983 "*Le monochrome dans le métro,*" Galerie Éric Fabre, Paris.
1986 "Hommage au marquis de Bièvre," Fondation Cartier pour l'Art Contemporain, Jouy-en-Josas. Catalog.
"Jonier Marin à Beaubourg?," Galerie Lara Vincy, Paris.
1987 "Paris-Pâris," Galerie Passages, Troyes, organized by FRAC Champagne-Ardenne, Reims. Catalog.
Grand Prix National de Peinture, Ministère de la Culture et de la Communication, awarded at Centre Georges Pompidou, Paris, December 22.
1988 Galerie Heyram, Paris.
1989 "Du côté de chez Frédé. Hommage à Boronali," Galerie Duval-Dunner, Paris.
"Le coup d'État du 1er avril 1989," Institut Français, Cologne, Germany.
"Photographies de vacances," Editions GDL, Nice.
"Photographies de vacances," Galerie Lara Vincy, Paris. Traveled to:
Musée Sainte-Croix, Poitiers; FRAC Poitou-Charentes, Hôtel Saint-Simon, Angoulême; P.S. 1 Contemporary Art Center, Long Island City, New York. Catalog.
"*Le piédestal du Louis XIV,*" Galerie de Paris, Paris.
1990 "La nouvelle architecture du Grand Louvre," Galerie de Paris, Paris.
Galerie Heyram-Mabel Semmler, Paris.
Galeries Contemporaines, Musée National d'Art Moderne, Centre Georges Pompidou, Paris. Catalog.
"Langue de cheval et facteur temps. Causerie," Centre Georges Pompidou, Paris, June 11.
1992 "La nouvelle architecture du Grand Louvre," stand at the Galerie de Paris, FIAC, Grand Palais, Paris.
1993 With Jacques Villeglé, FRAC Nord/Pas-de-Calais, Espace Lumière, Hénin-Beaumont.
"RaYmOnD HaInS. Coll. avant-poste," Galerie B.A.L., Hérouville-Saint-Clair.

1994 Galerie Daniel Templon, Paris.
"Les 3 Cartier. Du Grand Louvre aux 3 Cartier," Fondation Cartier pour l'Art Contemporain, Paris. Catalog.
1995 "Les cadres du jeu," L'Atelier Soardi, Nice.
"Raymond Hains. Gast auf der Durchreise," Portikus, Frankfurt, Germany. Catalog.
"Raymond Hains: Akzente 1949–1995/Accents 1949–1995," Museum Moderner Kunst Stiftung Ludwig, Vienna, Austria. Catalog.
1996 "Citroën, moi j'aime...," Galerie Daniel Templon, Paris.
"La Langue des oiseaux," talk accompanying exhibition "Comme un oiseau," Fondation Cartier pour l'Art Contemporain, Paris.
1997 Procession of "La Géante *Iris Clert, messagère des Arts*," from Musée de l'Objet to monument Denis Papin, Blois, October 17.
Prix Schwitters, awarded at Sprengel Museum, Hannover, Germany, May 27.
1998 "Brève rencontre avec Raymond Hains. Documenta X quai Voltaire," Galerie de la Caisse des Dépôts et Consignations, 13 quai Voltaire and display windows of quai Voltaire, Paris.
"Du côté de chez Frédé. Hommage à Boronali," Galerie Martine et Thibault de la Châtre, Paris.
Galerie Lara Vincy, Paris.
Procession of "La Géante *Iris Clert, messagère des Arts*," Galerie de Caisse des Dépôts et Consignations, from 13 quai Voltaire to Galerie Nationale du Jeu de Paume, Paris, February 28.
Prix Allais à Thouars, awarded at Honfleur, September 5.
"Lemot passe à travers," FRAC des Pays de la Loire, Nantes.
"Tableaux abstraits," L'Atelier Soardi, Nice.
"Tours et détours de R. Hains," Le Collège, FRAC Champagne-Ardenne, Reims.
"Langue de cheval et facteur temps," conversation with Marc Dachy at the Café du Palais, Reims, during exhibition "Tours et détours de R. Hains," at the FRAC Champagne-Ardenne, April 8.
1999 "Jean Lemaire de Belges. *Macintoshages*," Galerie Clara Rainhorn, Brussels, Belgium.
Kunstraum München e.V., Munich, Germany.
MACBA, Barcelona, Spain.
"*Castelli, les Jardineries du Sud*," Galerie Daniel Templon, Paris.
"La Langue des Martiens. Conversation," during exhibition "1 Monde réel," Fondation Cartier pour l'Art Contemporain, Paris, October 21.
2000 Museu Serralves, Porto, Portugal.
"Les Tuyauteries du centre," Galerie Daniel Templon, Paris. Catalog.
"Oeuvres déposées par l'artiste," Musée d'Art Moderne, Saint-Étienne.
L'Atelier Soardi, Nice
"Oeuvres récentes," MAMAC, Nice. Catalog.
2001 Presentation of new flag of town of Dinard by mayor Marius Mallet, Salle Buren-Matisse of the Musée d'Art Moderne de la Ville de Paris, January 4.
"Raymond Hains, La Tentative," Musée National d'Art Moderne, Centre Georges Pompidou, Paris. Catalog.
2002 "Raymond Hains: Art Speculator," Goldie Paley Gallery, Moore College of Art and Design, Philadelphia. Catalog.

GROUP EXHIBITIONS

1951 Kunstraum, Zurich, Switzerland.
1952 "Exposition mondiale de la photographie," Lucerne, Switzerland.
1953 "Französische Meisterfotografie," Institut Français, Innsbruck, Austria. Catalog.
1959 "Lacéré anonyme," chez Ginette et François Dufrêne, Paris.
"Hains, Dufrêne, Villeglé," Galerie du Pont-Royal, Paris.
"Biennale de Paris," Musée d'Art Moderne de la Ville de Paris. Catalog.
"Salon des Réalités Nouvelles," Musée des Beaux-arts de la Ville de Paris. Catalog.
1960 "Les Nouveaux Réalistes," Galleria Apollinaire, Milan, Italy. Catalog.
"Ungegenstandlische Photographie," Gewerbes Museum, Basel, Switzerland.
"Festival d'art d'avant-garde," Palais des Expositions, Porte de Versailles, Paris. Catalog.
"Salon Comparaisons," Musée d'Art Moderne de la Ville de Paris. Catalog.
"Hommage à Colette Allendy," Galerie Colette Allendy, Paris. Catalog.

1961 "Les Nouveaux Réalistes," Galerie Samlaren, Stockholm, Sweden.

"Der Koffer," Galerie Haro Lauhus, Cologne, Germany.

"Salon Comparaisons," Musée d'Art Moderne de la Ville de Paris. Catalog.

"Biennale de Paris," Musée d'Art Moderne de la Ville de Paris. Catalog.

"The Art of Assemblage," The Museum of Modern Art, New York. Traveled to Museum of Contemporary Art, Dallas, 1962; San Francisco Museum of Modern Art. Catalog.

"Bewogen Beweging," Stedelijk Museum, Amsterdam, Netherlands; Moderna Museet, Stockholm, Sweden; Louisiana Museum of Modern Art, Humlebaeck, Denmark. Catalog.

"À 40° au-dessus de Dada," Galerie J, Paris. Catalog.

"Le Nouveau Réalisme à Paris et à New York," Galerie Rive Droite, Paris. Catalog.

"Festival du Nouveau Réalisme," Galerie Muratore, Abbaye de Roseland, Nice. Catalog.

Sharing of Entremets de La Palissade at Festival du Nouveau Réalisme, Nice, July 13.

1962 "Salon Comparaisons," Musée d'Art Moderne de la Ville de Paris. Catalog.

"Décollagistes," Galleria Apollinaire, Milan, Italy.

"The New Realists," Sidney Janis Gallery, New York. Catalog.

1963 "Salon Comparaisons," Musée d'Art Moderne de la Ville de Paris. Catalog.

"Deuxième Festival du Nouveau Réalisme," Neue Galerie im Künstlerhaus, Munich, Germany; Galerie Forum, Brussels, Belgium. Catalog.

"Dufrêne, Hains, Rotella, Villeglé," Galleria Schwarz, Milan, Italy. Catalog.

"N. R.," Galleria del Leone, Venice, Italy.

1964 "Salon Comparaisons," Musée d'Art Moderne de la Ville de Paris. Catalog.

"L'affiche lacérée," Gres Gallery inc., Chicago. Catalog.

"50 ans de collages," Musée d'Art et d'Industrie, Saint-Étienne; Musée des Arts Décoratifs, Paris. Catalog.

"Neue Realisten & Pop Art," Akademie der Künste, Berlin, Germany. Catalog.

"Pop, etc.," Museum des 20. Jahrhunderts, Vienna, Austria. Catalog.

1965 "Le Nouveau Réalisme et le baptême de l'objet," Galleria del Leone, Venice, Italy. Catalog.

"Pop Art, Nouveau Réalisme, etc.," Palais des Beaux-arts, Brussels, Belgium. Catalog.

"Round Table on Pop Art," Galleria L'Elefante, Mestre, Italy, July 26.

"Pop Por, Pop Corn, Corny," Galerie Rive Droite, Paris. Catalog.

1966 "Mostra di pittura contemporanea Comunità europea. Premio Marzotto," Valdagno, Italy. Catalog.

Paolo Marzotto awarded the Barrette du Mérite artistique, by Gérard Deschamps, July 18.

1968 "Documenta 4," Kassel, Germany. Catalog.

1970 "Xe anniversaire du Nouveau Réalisme," Rotonda della Besana, Milan, Italy. Catalog.

Shares Tarte de Milan for L'Ultima Cena, at tenth anniversary of founding of Nouveau Réalisme, Ristorante Biffi, Galleria Vittorio Emanuele III, Rome, Italy, November 29.

"Nouveau Réalisme. 1960–1970," Galerie Mathias Fels, Paris. Catalog.

1971 Auction of sugar matchboxes and award of the Prix du Découragement Artistique by Otto Hahn, at Daniel Spoerri's Eat Art Gallery, Düsseldorf, Germany.

1972 "Douze ans d'art contemporain en France," Galeries Nationales du Grand Palais, Paris. Catalog.

1976 French Pavilon, 37th Venice Biennale.

"Beautés volées," Musée d'Art et d'Industrie, Saint-Etienne. Catalog.

1977 "Paris-New York," Musée National d'Art Moderne, Centre Georges Pompidou, Paris. Catalog.

1981 "Bryen éclaté," Musée des Beaux-arts, Nantes. Catalog.

"Commémoration de la loi du 29 juillet 1881," Galerie Mathias Fels, Paris. Catalog.

"Paris-Paris," Musée National d'Art Moderne, Centre Georges Pompidou, Paris. Catalog.

1982 "Les Nouveaux Réalistes," Galerie des Ponchettes and Galerie d'Art Contemporain des Musées de Nice. Catalog.

1984 "Écritures dans la peinture," Villa Arson, Nice. Catalog.

1985 "Le Centre artistique aéré," Musée Ephémère et Ubiquiste, École Nationale d'Art, Cergy-Pontoise.

1986 "1960. Les Nouveaux Réalistes," Musée d'Art Moderne de la Ville de Paris; Kunsthalle, Mannheim, Germany; Kunstmuseum, Winterthur, Switzerland, 1987. Catalog.

1987 "Lettre(s). Verbes d'État," MAMAC, Nice. Catalog.

"Un artiste/Un musée," Villa Médicis, Musée de Saint-Maur, La Varenne-Saint-Hilaire. Catalog.

1988 "Les années 50," Musée National d'Art Moderne, Centre Georges Pompidou, Paris. Catalog.

1990 "Décollage: Les Affichistes," Zabriskie Gallery, New York.
"Art et pub," Musée National d'Art Moderne, Centre Georges Pompidou, Paris; Sezon Museum of Art, Tokyo, Japan, 1991; Hyogo Prefectural Museum of Modern Art, Kobe, Japan. Catalog.
"High and Low," The Museum of Modern Art, New York; Art Institute of Chicago, 1991; Museum of Contemporary Art, Los Angeles. Catalog.
"La France à Venise. Le pavillon français de 1978 à 1988," Peggy Guggenheim Foundation, 44th Venice Biennale. Catalog.
1991 "L'objet de la sculpture," Rotonda della Besana, Milan, Italy. Catalog.
"L'amour de l'art," Halle Tony Garnier, First Biennale d'Art Contemporain de Lyon. Catalog.
1993 "Poésure et Peintrie. D'un art, l'autre," Centre de la Vieille-Charité, Musées de Marseille. Catalog.
"Atelier de la rue, poésie des Alltags," Ludwig Museum im Deutschherrenhaus, Koblenz, Germany. Catalog.
"Chambre 763," Hôtel Carlton Palace, Paris. Catalog.
1994 "Logo non logo," Thread Waxing Space, New York.
"Hors limites. L'art et la vie. 1952–1994," Musée National d'Art Moderne, Centre Georges Pompidou, Paris. Catalog.
"La ville. Art et architecture en Europe. 1870–1993," Musée National d'Art Moderne, Centre Georges Pompidou, Paris. Catalog.
"Murmures des rues," Galerie Art et Essai, Université Rennes 2; Galerie du TNB et Musée des Beaux-arts, Rennes. Catalog.
1995 "Fragments d'un paysage amoureux," Association de Prévention du Site de la Villette, Parc de la Villette, Paris. Catalog.
1996 "Face à l'histoire. 1933–1996," Musée National d'Art Moderne, Centre Georges Pompidou, Paris. Catalog.
1997 "Skulptur. Projekte in Münster," Münster, Germany. Catalog.
"Ici et maintenant," Association de Prévention du Site de la Villette, Parc de la Villette, Paris. Catalog.
"From one point to another," L'Atelier Soardi, Nice. Catalog.
"De Klein à Warhol," MAMAC, Nice. Catalog.
"ZERO et Paris 1960. Et aujourd'hui," Galerie der Stadt Esslingen, Villa Merkel, Esslingen, Germany; MAMAC, Nice, 1998. Catalog.
"L'Autre," Halle Tony Garnier, 4th Biennale d'Art Contemporain de Lyon. Catalog.
"Made in France 1947–1997: 50 ans de création en France," Musée National d'Art Moderne, Centre Georges Pompidou, Paris. Catalog.
"Documenta X," Kassel, Germany. Catalog.
Procession of "La Géante *Iris Clert, messagère des Arts*," along the Strepenstrasse, opening of "Documenta X," Kassel, Germany, June 21.
1998 "Ici et maintenant (encore)," Galerie de la Caisse des Dépôts et Consignations, 13 quai Voltaire, Paris.
"Rendez-vous: Masterpieces from the Centre Georges Pompidou and the Guggenheim Museums," Guggenheim Museum, New York. Catalog.
"Premises: Invested Spaces in Visual Arts, Architecture, and Design from France: 1958–1998," Guggenheim Museum SoHo, New York. Catalog.
1999 "Georges Pompidou et la modernité," Galerie Nationale du Jeu de Paume, Paris. Catalog.
"La peinture et l'abstraction. 1955–1975," Musée d'Art Moderne de la Ville de Paris. Catalog.
Les champs de la sculpture, Direction des Affaires Culturelles de la Ville de Paris, avenue des Champs-Élysées, Paris
"Extraetordinaire," Le Printemps de Cahors, Cahors. Catalog.
2000 "Sensitive," Le Printemps de Cahors, Cahors. Catalog.
"Voilà. Le monde dans la tête," Musée d'Art Moderne de la Ville de Paris. Catalog.
"Voyager à la verticale," Association de Prévention du Site de la Villette, Parc de la Villette, Paris. Catalog.
Distribution of matchboxes produced by NSMD, ABN-AMRO, and Serge Aboukrat, Salon Paris Photo 2000.
2001 "Le BHV inspire les artistes," Bazar de l'Hôtel de Ville, Paris.
"Les années Pop," Musée National d'Art Moderne, Centre Georges Pompidou, Paris. Catalog.
2002 "Paris: Capital of the Arts 1900–1968," Royal Academy of Arts, London, England. Catalog.

BIBLIOGRAPHY

Writing, ephemera, and other deformations by the artist

1952 "Graphisme en Photographie: Quand la photographie devient l'objet [Graphic art in photography: When photography becomes an object]," *Photo Almanach Prisma*, no. 5.

1953 With Jacques Villeglé, *Hépérile éclaté. L'intrusion du verre cannelé dans la poésie*, leaflet announcing the publication of *Hépérile éclaté*, Librairie Lutétia, Paris.

With Jacques Villeglé, *Hépérile éclaté*, Paris, Librairie Lutétia.

1955 "Flagrant-Dali," *Combat*, no. 3385 (May 20).

1960 Cover of catalog *Les Nouveaux Réalistes*, Galleria Apollinaire, Milan, Italy.

Name of Tinguely distorted for invitation to exhibition "L'Art fonctionnel de Tinguely," Galerie des Quatre Saisons, Paris.

1963 Title distorted on the cover of review *KWY*, no. 11, spring.

1964 *Petit Larousse déformé*, given to François Dufrêne, author of the *TPL* (Tombeau pour Pierre Larousse), reproduced in *Écritures dans la peinture*, Centre National des Arts Plastiques/Villa Arson, Nice, 1984, and in *François Dufrêne. Cahiers de l'Abbaye Sainte-Croix* (Les Sables-d'Olonne), no. 60, June 1988.

"Le Nouveau Réalisme et le baptême de l'objet," text by Pierre Restany deformed, *Dix ans d'art actuel*, catalog of "Salon Comparaisons," Musée d'Art Moderne de la Ville de Paris.

1966 "Valdagno, cité mamertine," *Mostra di pittura contemporanea communità europea 66–67*. Premio Marzotto [Marzotto Prize], Valdagno, Italy.

1970 *Disque bleu pour SAFFA*, 45 rpm record, Galleria Blu, Milan; reproduced in single format in *Raymond Hains*, Paris, Centre National d'Art Contemporain, 1976.

1979 "Visions hallucinées ou visions scientifiques," *Salvador Dalí*, Éditions du Centre Georges Pompidou, Paris.

1987 "Raymond Hains l'Abstrait, Sigisbée de la critique," *Remo Bianco, Drapeaux-Bandiere*, Galerie Lara Vincy, Paris.

1990 *Cour Saleya*, greeting card, published by La Villa Arson, Nice.

1997 Parker felt-point pen with blue ink put out by NSMD, ABN–AMRO and Serge Aboukrat.

1998 Pack of ten postcard editions for exhibition "Lemot passe à travers," Nantes, FRAC des Pays de la Loire.

Pack of nine postcard editions for exhibition "Tours et détours de R. Hains," Reims, FRAC Champagne-Ardenne.

2000 *Raymondines*, chocolate coins minted by Pâtisserie Périn, Printemps de Cahors.

Matchbox with detail from a hypnagogic photograph, edition by Fondation NSMVie, ABN-AMRO and Serge Aboukrat for Paris Photo 2000.

2001 *Point d'ironie*, no. 21, Paris, agnès b.

Vedettes, Galerie du jour, Paris, agnès b.

Matchbox featuring *L'âne vêtu de la peau de lion*, published by the Fondation NSMVie, ABN-AMRO, and Serge Aboukrat for opening reception of Raymond Hains exhibition at Centre Georges Pompidou, June.

Watch reproducing one of the *Échelles optométriques*, edition for the Fondation NSMVie, ABN-AMRO and Serge Aboukrat, December.

FILMS BY RAYMOND HAINS

Le Pardon de Saint-Anne-la-Palu, 16 mm, black and white, silent, 1946.

Saint-Germain-des-Prés-colombiens, 16 mm, black and white, silent, 1949.

With Jacques Villeglé, *Loi du 29 juillet 1881*, 16 mm, color, silent, 1949.

Short film around a billboard, Porte de Clichy, 1950.

With Jacques Villeglé, *Pénélope*, shot 1950–54, editor Jean-Michel Bouhours 1981, 16 mm, color, silent, 14'.

With Jacques Villeglé, title sequence for UNESCO, commissioned by Jacques Brunet, head of UNESCO film department, 1952.

Études aux allures, 16 mm, color, sound, 4'29", original music by Pierre Schaeffer, production Service de Recherche de l'ORTF, 1960.

CATALOGS OF ONE-PERSON EXHIBITIONS, ARTWORKS, AND DOCUMENTS

Hépérile éclaté. L'intrusion du verre cannelé dans la poésie, leaflet, written by Camille Bryen on occasion of publication of *Hépérile éclaté*. Paris: Librairie Lutétia, 1953.

Manuscript text drafted by Jean-Philippe Talbo on the occasion of exhibition "*Loi du 29 juillet 1881* ou le lyrisme à la sauvette." Paris: Galerie Colette Allendy, 1957. Reproduced in catalog *Raymond Hains*. Paris: CNAC, 1976.

Text by Pierre Restany, invitation card for exhibition "La France déchirée." Paris: Galerie J, 1961.

Iris.time. SEITA & SAFFA, copyright Raymond Hains, no. 21, October 12, 1965; text by René Brô and Iris Clert.

Raymond Hains. Verona: Galleria Ferrari, 1970.

Hains: SAFFA SEITA. Rome: Galleria della Trinità, 1973.

Raymond Hains. Florence: Galleria Inquadrature, 1976. Text by Paolo Castellucci and Pierre Restany.

Raymond Hains et la photographie. Paris: CNAC, 1976; Daniel Abadie (ed.), witnessed by Camille Bryen, Iris Clert, François Dufrêne, Otto Hahn, Jeanine Restany, Pierre Restany, and Jacques Villeglé.

Sur les murs. L'art fun ou l'enfance de l'art. Ateliers en liberté. Raymond Hains. Jouy-en-Josas: Fondation Cartier, 1986. Text by Marie-Claude Beaud and Aude Bodet.

Paris-Pâris. Troyes: FRAC Champagne-Ardenne, 1987. Text by Catherine Bompuis.

Raymond Hains. Poitiers: Éditions Musée de la Ville de Poitiers et de la Société des antiquaires de l'Ouest, 1989. Text by Aude Bodet, Blandine Chavanne, Michel Frizot, Jacques Ohayon, and Guy Tortosa.

Hains & la pansémiotique. Paris: AFP Éditeur, 1989. Text by Guy Bodson, Daniel Daligand, Joël Ducorroy, Bruno Duval, Richard Sünder, and Jean-Louis Vincendeau.

Raymond Hains. Guide des collections permanentes ou mises en plis. Paris: Éditions du Centre Georges Pompidou, 1990. Text by Jean-Hubert Martin, Catherine David, and Catherine Bompuis.

Les Trois Cartier, du Grand Louvre aux trois Cartier. Paris: Fondation Cartier pour l'Art Contemporain, 1994. Text by Nicolas Bourriaud, Hervé Chandès, Hélène Kelmachter, and Allen Weiss.

Gast auf der Durchreise. Stuttgart: Oktagon, 1995. Text by Hervé Chandès, Robert Fleck, and Kasper König.

Raymond Hains: Akzente 1949–1995/Accents 1949–1995. Vienna: Museum Moderner Kunst Stiftung Ludwig, 1995. Text by Nicolas Bourriaud, Robert Fleck, Lorand Hegyi, Michel Nuridsany, and Roberto Ohrt.

Langue de cheval et facteur temps. Conversation with Marc Dachy, FRAC Champagne-Ardenne/Actes Sud, Arles, 1998.

Raymond Hains. Oeuvres récentes. Nice: Mamac, 2000. Texts by Gilbert Perlein, Robert Fleck, and Caroline Cros.

Les Tuyauteries du centre. Paris: Galerie Daniel Templon, 2000. Text by Nathalie Ergino.

Raymond Hains. J'ai la mémoire qui planche. Paris: Éditions du Centre Georges Pompidou, 2001. Text by Jean-Jacques Aillagon, Alfred Pacquement, Christine Macel, Maria Candéa, Mary-Annick Morel, Pierre Leguillon, and Matthieu Orléan.

Raymond Hains. La tentative. Paris: Éditions du Centre Georges Pompidou, 2001. Text by Christine Macel and Christian Schlatter.

Raymond Hains. Barcelona: Actar/Macba, 2001.

SELECTED ARTICLES

"Le vernissage de l'exposition de photographies hypnagogiques de Hains à la Librairie des Nourritures terrestres." *Ouest-France* (20 May 1949): 5.

"À la galerie aujourd'hui. Les affiches lacérées de Robert sic Hains." *Les Beaux-Arts* [Brussels], no. 968 (9 March 1962): 5.

"Raymond Hains: la chasse au Cnac." *Affiches parisiennes* (29 May 1976).

"Vernissage de l'expo Raymond Hains." *Villages-Val de Marne*, no. 45 (4 November 1987): 9.

"Nîmes sur les cimaises de Beaubourg." *Nîmes-Matin* (16 June 1990).

"Raymond Hains." *L'Express Paris* (29 June 1990).

Abadie, Daniel. "Raymond Hains. La déchirure initiale." *Art Press*, no. 123 (March 1988): 30–33.

Abrioux, Yves. "Raymond Hains. Troyes." *Kanal Magazine*, no. 35–36 (spring 1988): 46–47.

Albert-Lévin, Marc. "Raymond l'abstrait, grand découvreur de la palissade." *Cimaise*, no. 71 (November 1964–January 1965): 30–39.

Allain, Patrice. "Le mot qui passe à travers ... Hains y soit-il." *Talent*, no. 44 (May 1998).

Baron, Jeanine. "Hains, pourfendeur de mensonges." *Le Quotidien de Paris* (31 May 1989).

Bellet, Harry. "Raymond Hains." *Le Monde* (13 January 1994).

Bergez, Wladimir. "Raymond Hains/Toulouse-Pau, été 2001." *Art Présence* (January 2002).

Blase, Christoph. "Der Gastauf der Durchreise gewinnt immer." *Frankfurter Allgemeine Zeitung* (3 April 1995).

Bodet, Aude. "Je préférerais ne pas (exposer). Raymond Hains et la critique." *Les Cahiers du Musée National d'Art Moderne*, no. 78 (winter 2001–2): 92–107.

———. "Raymond Hains." *Beaux-Arts Magazine*, no. 69 (June 1989): 131.

———. "Raymond Hains l'inclassable." *Beaux-Arts Magazine*, no. 54 (February 1988): 14.
———. "Raymond Hains lu et approuvé." *Public*, no. 3 (September 1985–February 1986): 22–23.
———. "La saga des petits-beurre LU." *303, La Revue des Pays de la Loire* (spring 1986).
Bordaz, Jean-Pierre. "Hains." *Flash Art*, no. 114 (November 1983): 75–76.
———. "Hains: Anti-rétrospective." *Beaux-Arts Magazine*, no. 51 (November 1987): 111.
Boudaille, Georges. "40° au-dessus de Dada." *Les Lettres françaises*, no. 878 (1–7 June 1961).
Boudaille, Georges, Michel Ragon, Pierre Restany, and Herta Wescher. "Après la première Biennale de Paris." *Cimaise*, no. 47 (January–March 1960): 38–64.
Bouisset, Maïten. "Hains: l'art de saisir au vol." *Beaux-Arts Magazine* (July 1990).
Braxton, John. "Jonier Marin à Beaubourg?" *Kanal Magazine*, no. 27–28 (mid-January 1987): 78.
Breerette, Geneviève. "Hains le piéton." *Le Monde* (9 June 1976): 23.
———. "Raymond Hains, grand désordinateur des signes et de la rue." *Le Monde* (4 July 2001).
Breuvart, Valérie. "Raymond Hains in Barcelona." *Artforum*, vol. 38, no. 1 (September 1999).
Buchloh, Benjamin H. D. "From Detail to Fragment: Décollage Affichiste." *October*, no. 56 (spring 1991): 98–110.
Cassagnau, Pascale. "Raymond Hains. Galerie Templon, Paris." *Artforum*, vol. 37, no. 9 (May 1999).
Cenni, René. "Hains, itinéraires d'un prédateur." *Nice-Matin* (9 July 1995).
Colard, Jean-Max. "L'aide-mémoire." *Les Inrockuptibles*, supplement to *Le Printemps de Cahors*, no. 203 (16 June 1999).
———. "Raymond la Science." *Les Inrockuptibles* (7 April 1998).
———. "Raymond Hains." *Artforum* (December 2001).
Courtois, Michel. "Raymond Hains and Jacques de la Villeglé." *Arts*, no. 622 (5 June 1957): 12.
Cuvelier, Pascaline. "Glose de styles." *Libération* (2 July 1990).
Dagbert, Anne. "Raymond Hains: Fondation Cartier." *Artforum*, vol. 33 (April 1995): 98–99.
Dagen, Philippe. "Les méandres d'une conversation à l'art libre." *Le Monde* (4 July 2001).
———. "Raymond Hains, jardinier des illusions mortes." *Le Monde* (23 January 1999).
Daive, Jean. Interview. "Les sisyphes & le tournant décisif ou l'art à Raymond." *Fin*, no.11 (January 2002): 60–72.
Dard, Bertrand. "Décollages en délire." *Info arTitudes*, no. 9 (June 1976): 8.
Debailleux, Henri-François. "Raymond Hains. L'art chocolat." *Libération*, supplément *Cahors 2000* (16 June 2000).
Descargues, Pierre. "Photographies surréalistes et abstraites de Hains." *Arts*, no. 177 (6 August 1948): 5.
Deschamps, Pierre-Olivier. "La fête à Hains." *Connaissance des arts*, no. 409 (March 1986): 94.
Dobbels, Daniel. "Hains l'ultra de la rue." *Libération* (4 July 1990): 37.
Dufrêne, François. "Cantate pour un prognathe léger. À Raymond Hains." *Ex*, no. 3 (1954).
Estienne, Charles. "Tour d'exposition." *Combat* (7 July 1948).
Faveton, Pierre. "Raymond Hains." *Connaissance des arts*, no. 292 (June 1976): 23.
Firmin-Didot, Catherine. "Raymond Hains. Collages et décollages." *Télérama*, no. 2, 688 (18 July 2001).
Fleck, Robert. "Ausstellung Raymond Hains." *77* (*Revue de l'Institut Français de Cologne*) (March–April 1995): 7.
———. "Raymond Hains." *Connaissance des arts* (July–August 2001).
Francblin, Catherine. "Documenta X, Cassel." *Art Press*, no. 227 (September 1997): 82.
Frisach, Montse. "Raymond Hains confon art i vida al Macba." *Avui* [Barcelona] (30 September 1999).
Gallot, Jacques. "Les décollages d'un piéton nocturne." *Ouest-France* (15 April 1988).
Gauville, Hervé. "M'Hains alors!." *Libération* (30 June 1994): 40.
Giroud, Michel. "Débordements de limites. Kurt Schwitters. Raymond Hains. Hors limites." *Art Présence*, no. 13 (winter 1995): cover, 35–45.
Hahn, Otto. "Hains: les mots et les couleurs." *L'Express* (31 May 1976).
———. "Lettre de Paris et d'Amsterdam." *Opus international* (December 1965): 51–52.
———. "Lettre de Paris et de Bruxelles." *Opus international* (April 1965): 67–69.
———. "Raymond Hains." *Beaux-Arts Magazine*, no. 34 (April 1986) 60–63.
Humeau, Edmond. "Le lyrisme des murs." *Combat* (5 June 1957): 3.
Jarton, Cyril. "Hains glisse sur les calembours." *Beaux-Arts Magazine*, no. 129 (December 1994): 127.
Jouffroy, Alain. "À 40° au-dessus de Dada." *Art et architecture d'aujourd'hui*, no. 32 (July 1961).
———. "L'aventure extraordinaire de Raymond Hains et de ses compagnons Jacques de la Villeglé and François Dufrêne. *Opus international*, no. 18 (June 1970): 36–41.
———. "La Biennale de Paris." *Arts*, no. 743 (7 October 1959): 9.
———. "Une révolution du regard." *Combat* (26 December 1960): 5.
Kerner, Anne. "Raymond Hains. La moëlle pépinière." *Beaux-Arts Magazine* (July 2001).
Lascault, Gilbert. "Raymond Hains: portrait de l'auteur en araignée." *XXe Siècle*, no. 47 (December 1976): 152–53.
Lavier, Bertrand. "Raymond Hains. Si André Gide s'était appelé Mauriac." *Art Press*, no. 103 (May 1986): 18–19.
Leguillon, Pierre. "Raymond Hains récupère Cartier." *Le Journal des arts*, no. 9 (December 1994): 13.
Lemborelle, Guy. "La Biennale de Paris." *Genèse* (15 October 1959): 32.

Lemée, Jean-Philippe. "Raymond Hains, Jacques Villeglé. De Rennes à Milan." ***Arts de l'Ouest. Études et documents (Centre de recherches sur les arts anciens et modernes de l'Ouest de la France,*** **Université de Haute-Bretagne) (1st trimester 1984).**

Lepage, Jacques. "Le Nouveau Réalisme à Nice." ***Les Lettres françaises,*** **no. 886 (27 July 1961): 10.**

Lévêque, Jean-Jacques. "Raymond Hains, un vagabond." ***Le Quotidien de Paris*** **(31 May 1989).**

Lindgaard, Jade. "Raymond Hains, du coq et jusqu'à l'âne." ***Aden*** **(25 February 1998).**

Marcadé, Bernard. "Raymond Hains et le cheval de Troyes." ***Art Press,*** **no. 120 (December 1987): 70.**

Martins, Celso. "Geografias mentais." ***Expresso Cartaz*** **[Lisbon] (29 January 2000): 21.**

Maugis, M.-T. "Confrontation sans passion. Comparaisons au Musée d'Art Moderne." ***Les Lettres françaises,*** **no. 816 (17 March 1960): 12.**

Morucchio, Berto. "Hains." ***Il Cerchio,*** **no. 1 (1966): 74.**

Mosset, Olivier. "SEITA & SAFFA et Raymond Hains." ***Le Petit Colosse de Simi,*** **no. 1 (1966): 24–25.**

Moulin, Raoul-Jean. "La France déchirée." ***Les Lettres françaises,*** **no. 881 (22–28 June 1961).**

Nuridsany, Michel. "Hains: d'un Castelli l'autre." ***Le Figaro*** **(26 January 1999): 15.**

———. "La libre ballade de Raymond Hains." ***Le Figaro*** **(June 29, 2001).**

———. "Raymond Hains et ses calembours visuels." ***Le Figaro*** **(25 January 1994).**

———. "Raymond Hains, l'homme qui s'affiche." ***Le Figaro*** **(4 October 1994).**

Onfray, Michel. "Raymond Hains, éleveur du coq à l'âne." ***Beaux-Arts Magazine,*** **no. 167 (April 1998): 42–49.**

Petiteau, Jean-Yves. "Itinéraire de Raymond Hains." ***02,*** **no. 5 (April–June 1998): 7–9.**

Piguet, Philippe. "Raymond Hains." ***L'Oeil,*** **no. 387 (October 1987): 79.**

———. "Raymond Hains, éloge du rebond." ***L'Oeil,*** **no. 467 (December 1994): 81.**

Prodhon, Françoise-Claire. "Raymond Hains." ***Flash Art,*** **no. 154 (October 1990): 163–64.**

Ragon, Michel. "Lyrisme et abstraction: à 40° au-dessus de Dada." ***Cimaise,*** **no. 54 (July–August 1961): 89.**

———. "Plus vrai que nature." ***Arts,*** **no. 827 (21 June 1961): 7.**

Régnier, Philippe. Interview. "L'actualité vue par Raymond Hains." ***Le Journal des arts*** **(31 August 2001).**

———. "R. Hains à Reims." ***Le Journal des arts*** **(24 April 1998).**

Restany, Pierre. "Hains, un primitif fractalisé de la condition post-moderne." ***Opus international,*** **no. 118 (March–April 1990): 58–60.**

Richard, Anne. "Hains et la morale de l'affiche déchirée." ***Opus international,*** **no. 112 (February–March 1989): 18–23.**

———. "Raymond Hains. Guide des collections permanentes ou mise en plis." ***Opus international,*** **no. 121 (September–October 1990).**

Rivière, Claude. "Art-mouvement au musée d'Amsterdam." ***Combat*** **(12 April 1961).**

———. "Du monde pictural à la palissade." ***Combat*** **(5 October 1959): 9.**

———. "La fausse querelle du figuratif et de l'art abstrait." ***Combat*** **(26 December 1960): 5.**

———. "Malraux est-il trahi par ses clercs?" ***Combat*** **(12 October 1959): 9.**

———. "Proposition d'avant-garde." ***Combat*** **(16 July 1959): 5.**

———. "Rien n'altère notre regard." ***Combat*** **(3 October 1961): 9.**

Rivière, Claude. "Salon Comparaisons." ***Combat*** **(14 March 1960): 9.**

Smith, Roberta. "Three French Artists Brought to Light." ***The New York Times*** **(24 November 1989).**

Soutif, Daniel. "Hains, le dada de Troyes." ***Libération*** **(19 November 1987).**

———. "Pélerins, bâtons et coquille." ***Libération*** **(15 November 1989): 40–41.**

———. "Raymond Hains." ***Artforum,*** **vol. 26 (January 1988): 128–29.**

Tortosa, Guy. "Raymond Hains: quand la photographie devient attitude." ***Art Press,*** **no. 170 (June 1992): 57–59.**

———. "Raymond Hains. Thaumaturgie, fatrasie, glossolalie, et abstraction." ***Galeries Magazine,*** **no. 33 (October–November 1989): 124–29.**

Tronche, Anne. "Les promeneurs des deux rives." ***Opus international,*** **no. 112 (February–March 1989): 11–12.**

Vetrocq, Marcia E. "Mixed Messages." ***Art in America*** **(May 1995): 41–47.**

Vidal, Jaume. "Raymond Hains exhibe en el Macba su obra y su propuesta vital." ***El País*** **(30 September 1999).**

Violet, Alexis. Interview. "Rétrospective des Nouveaux Réalistes." ***Rouge,*** **no. 1220 (28 August–3 September 1986): 18.**

Warnod, Janine. "Mots de la faim. Calembours et victuailles pour l'enterrement provisoire du Cnac." ***Le Figaro*** **(8 June 1976): 32.**

PHOTO CREDITS

cover. Archives Éric Fabre, Brussels.

page 1. Courtesy Musée National d'art Moderne, Centre Pompidou, Paris. Photo: Jean-Claude Planchet.

4. Courtesy Galerie Jousse-Seguin, Paris.

6. Photo: George Dupin, Paris.

9. Photo: George Dupin, Paris.

11. Photos: Christine Macel, Paris.

12. Courtesy Musée National d'art Moderne, Centre Pompidou, Paris. Photo: Jean-Claude Planchet.

13. left: Courtesy Musée National d'art Moderne, Centre Pompidou, Paris; right: Archives Jean-Louis Milin, Paris.

15. Archives Raymond Hains, Paris.

16. Courtesy Galerie Jousse-Seguin, Paris.

19. left: Photo: Harry Shunk, New York; right: Courtesy Galerie Lara Vincy, Paris.

21. left: Courtesy Musée National d'art Moderne, Centre Pompidou, Paris. Photo: Jean-Claude Planchet; right: Photo: Harry Shunk, New York.

22. Courtesy Musée National d'art Moderne, Centre Pompidou, Paris. Photo: Jean-Claude Planchet.

27. Archives Éric Fabre, Brussels.

28. Courtesy Musée National d'art Moderne, Centre Pompidou, Paris. Photo: Jean-Claude Planchet.

30. left: Courtesy Musée National d'art Moderne, Centre Pompidou, Paris; right: Courtesy Musée National d'art Moderne, Centre Pompidou, Paris. Photo: Jean-Claude Planchet.

31. Courtesy Musée National d'art Moderne, Centre Pompidou, Paris.

32. left: Courtesy Musée National d'art Moderne, Centre Pompidou, Paris. Photo: Jean-Claude Planchet; right: Archives George Dupin, Paris.

33. top: Archives Christine Macel, Paris; bottom: Archives Raymond Hains, Paris.

34. Courtesy Musée National d'art Moderne, Centre Pompidou, Paris.

35. Courtesy Musée National d'art Moderne, Centre Pompidou, Paris. Photo: Jean-Claude Planchet.

36 and 37. Courtesy Musée National d'art Moderne, Centre Pompidou, Paris. Photo: Jean-Claude Planchet.

38 and 39. Courtesy Musée National d'art Moderne, Centre Pompidou, Paris. Photo: Jean-Claude Planchet.

40. Courtesy Musée National d'art Moderne, Centre Pompidou, Paris. Photo: Jean-Claude Planchet.

41. top: Courtesy Musée National d'art Moderne, Centre Pompidou, Paris. Photo: Jean-Claude Planchet; right, and next page: Courtesy Musée National d'art Moderne, Centre Pompidou, Paris.

42 and 43. Archives Raymond Hains, Paris.

44. Archives Raymond Hains, Paris.

45. left: Archives Raymond Hains, Paris. Courtesy Musée National d'art Moderne, Centre Pompidou, Paris; right: Courtesy Musée National d'art Moderne, Centre Pompidou, Paris.

46. Courtesy Musée National d'art Moderne, Centre Pompidou, Paris. Photo: Jean-Claude Planchet.

47. Courtesy Musée National d'art Moderne, Centre Pompidou, Paris.

49. left: Courtesy Musée National d'art Moderne, Centre Pompidou, Paris. Collection Musée de l'Objet, Blois; right: Archives Raymond Hains, Paris.

50. Courtesy FRAC Champagne-Ardenne, Reims.

51. Archives Éric Fabre, Brussels.

56 and 61. Courtesy Galerie Georges-Philippe and Nathalie Vallois, Paris.

57. Courtesy Musée National d'art Moderne, Centre Pompidou, Paris. Photo: Jean-Claude Planchet.

58, 59, and 60. Courtesy Musée National d'art Moderne, Centre Pompidou, Paris. Photo: Jean-Claude Planchet.

61. Courtesy Musée National d'art Moderne, Centre Pompidou, Paris.

62. Courtesy Musée National d'art Moderne, Centre Pompidou, Paris. Photo: Jean-Claude Planchet.

63. Courtesy Musée National d'art Moderne, Centre Pompidou, Paris. Photo: Bertrand Prévôt.

67. Photo: Harry Shunk, New York.

71. Photo: Harry Shunk, New York.

74 and 75. Archives Éric Fabre, Brussels.

76. Courtesy Galerie Daniel Templon, Paris.

78. Courtesy Musée National d'art Moderne, Centre Pompidou, Paris. Photo: Jean-Claude Planchet.

79. top: Courtesy Réunion des Musée Nationaux/Musée National d'art Moderne, Centre Pompidou, Paris. Photo: Jacques Faujour.

80. Courtesy Musée National d'art Moderne, Centre Pompidou, Paris. Photo: Jean-Claude Planchet.

81. Courtesy Musée National d'art Moderne, Centre Pompidou, Paris. Photo: Jean-Claude Planchet.

82. top and bottom: Courtesy Musée National d'art Moderne, Centre Pompidou, Paris. Photo: Jean-Claude Planchet.

82 and 83. Courtesy Musée National d'art Moderne, Centre Pompidou, Paris. Photo: Jean-Claude Planchet.

84. top: Courtesy Musée National d'art Moderne, Centre Pompidou, Paris.

84, 85, and 86. Courtesy Musée National d'art Moderne, Centre Pompidou, Paris. Photo: Jean-Claude Planchet.

88. Archives Raymond Hains, Paris.

89. Courtesy Musée National d'art Moderne, Centre Pompidou, Paris.

90. Courtesy Musée National d'art Moderne, Centre Pompidou, Paris.

91, 92, and 93. Archives Raymond Hains, Paris.

94. Archives George Dupin, Paris.

95. Courtesy Galerie Daniel Templon, Paris.

96. Courtesy Galerie Daniel Templon, Paris.

96 and 97. Archives Raymond Hains, Paris.

112. Photo: George Dupin, Paris.

back cover. Courtesy Musée National d'art Moderne, Centre Pompidou, Paris. Photo: Jean-Claude Planchet.

Raymond Hains at home, Nice, 2000. Photo: George Dupin, Paris.
back cover: Raymond Hains aboard the Lutétia, Borghese room in the Hotel Lutétia, Paris, 2001.

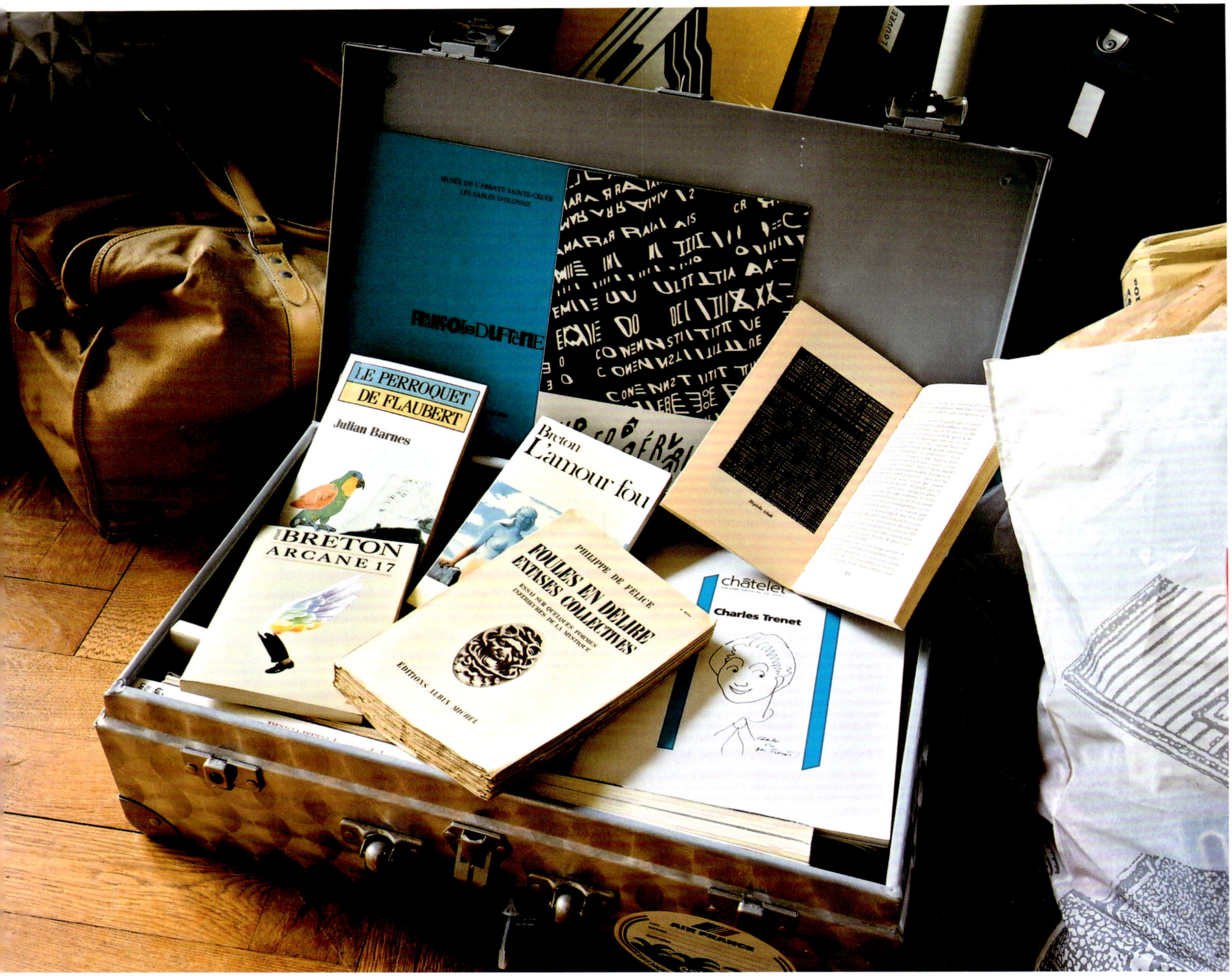